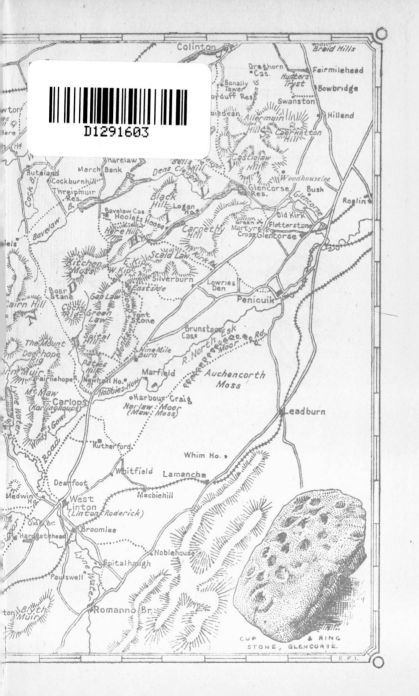

CUP   & RING
STONE, GLENCORSE.

THE CALL OF THE PENTLANDS

THE CALL
OF THE PENTLANDS

A Land of Glamour and Romance

WILL GRANT

OLIVER AND BOYD
EDINBURGH: TWEEDDALE COURT
LONDON: 98 GREAT RUSSELL STREET, W.C.

FIRST PUBLISHED 1927
SECOND EDITION, ENLARGED . 1951

DA
880
·P37
G7
1951

PRINTED IN GREAT BRITAIN BY
A. WALKER & SON, LTD., GALASHIELS
FOR OLIVER AND BOYD, LTD., EDINBURGH

PREFACE TO SECOND EDITION

In this new and enlarged edition, alterations and additions have been made in the book, and the information brought up to date. The Chapter on The Kirk o' Glencorse has been partly re-written, as although erected into a Parish Church in 1647, it had a previous separate existence and had no connection with St Katherine's in the Hopes united to Penicuik in 1635. Chapters 19-21 contain new material of interest to lovers of the hills.

TO
MY FRIENDS
ROUND THE HILLS

CONTENTS

CONTENTS—*continued*

ILLUSTRATIONS

INTRODUCTION

THE Pentland Hills are homely and friendly hills; they lie near the bounds of our city habitation, and frequent visiting begets an intimacy and friendship that is real and lasting. The most outlying parts may be reached in the course of a day's walk, and places of silence, where none will intrude, are easily accessible.

Their drove roads and tracks, their peaks and glens, their sykes and streams, and the winding road that encircles them make a strong appeal to every thoughtful walker. Many stirring events and incidents in history, religion, and literature have taken place in and around the Pentland country; and kings and queens, knights and fair ladies, battles and skirmishes, forays and foraging parties, Covenanters and gipsy clans, Cromwell and Prince Charlie, Druids and monks, rebels and reivers, drovers and shepherds, and men of light and leading, literature and law, are all bound up in their glamour and romance.

Every village has its share. Carlops vies with Colinton in its lawyer lairds and literary lions; Carnwath, Dunsyre, and Dolphinton are delightful centres for the Pentland enthusiast in search of pastures new; Newbigging has its Cross and memories of the old weavers; Ninemileburn has its traditions of monks and "Robin Tamson's Smiddy," while, with the Minstrels, the Esk vies with Bonnie Bonaly, and the stories of Woodhouselee, Woodhall, Newhall, Romanno, and Linton Roderick have more romantic charm than has ever been proclaimed in any single book.

And after we have roamed the hills from end to end, crossed and recrossed them, climbed the peaks, explored the wild places and the water-courses, and feasted our hearts and minds again and again, we come back to the folks who dwell among them. Fortunate are the walkers who can descend from the rolling hills and the breezy hill-tops to the honest hospitality of these happy homes. Ah! these hill folks; are there to be found more generous and genuine hearts anywhere? They carry this glamour and romance in their hearts and lives, and seal our visits to the heights and nature's own domain with the human touch and the stamp of human worth.

The Pentlands with their wealth of colour and variety of shape win us back time after time. One never grows tired of roving amongst them. White of Selborne in one of his letters says, "Though I have travelled the Sussex Downs upwards of thirty years, yet I still investigate that chain of majestic hills with fresh admiration year by year, and I think I see new beauties each time I traverse it." So, many a walker has found a like bountiful field of wonder and delight in our hills of home, from which new beauty and inspiration seem to spring eternally.

The hills are more frequented to-day than ever before by lovers of the open, and the value and benefit of hill-walking and hill-fellowship is being increasingly recognised. A desire has consequently arisen not so much for a guide as for a book about the Pentland Hills, whose historic and literary associations have made the Pentland countryside glow with all the glamour of a great romantic interest. The fruits of research along these lines are here presented in the hope that they may aid towards a fuller knowledge and wider appreciation of the hills that mean so much to those who love them. The exercise of walking means fitness of body, mind, and spirit to many whose interest in the hills is real and practical. But there are others to whom the exercise may not always be possible, but who delight to read about it, to think of the great walks they are going to take, and the hills they hope to climb, whose interest it may be is but sentimental. And there are those now far over-seas, whose love for the Pentland Hills is wrapped round their fondest thoughts of home. May all such, as they read this book, be able to catch something of the magic atmosphere they know and love, and feel the tang of the dewy moorland and the purple heather, and be revived by the fresh and bracing winds that blow from off these Hills of Happy Memories.

To some it may renew thoughts of days when they were more supple of body and lithe of limb. To my young friends, eager for adventure, I hope it may inspire a love for the hills, and a desire to know them better, that in the experience of the fuller revelation that nature has to give, there may be brought to them the wider vision to fit them for the service of their fellows.

It is not always possible or easy for city folk to get away to the breezy heights and the sunny moorlands and the sweet-smelling countryside. But how we like to read about it all, how we like to lose ourselves in thought among the hills and moors, and smell the odour that the hill wind brings, and experience the sunlit memories and the old remembrances of places we have known, and friendships that have stood the test of time.

The western half of the Pentlands will in future claim more attention from the experienced walkers, now that a new generation has discovered the delights of the more easily accessible parts, and to these lesser known regions special consideration is given. For the naturalist, botanist, geologist, antiquarian, and angler there is something to gladden the heart and delight the mind in this " farther out " section of the range, and many a quiet sequestered spot where intimate acquaintance may be made with the sights and sounds of nature. And for the simple wayfarer with a hunger in his heart which only the hills can satisfy, there is the wide heaven above and the open road before him that leads to his Arcadia, where amidst the glorious hills he enjoys the pleasures he counts the best; for he knows the fragrant perfume that the spring wind carries, he enjoys the smile of wayside flowers, and the cheery song and echoing cry of birds, and through the senses his heart is touched. He it is who at the day's end will say that life is good, that he is satisfied, for that he has found a new song wherewith to sing the praises of a new land in the Pentland Hills.

The book does not pretend to be a complete guide; that could not be adequately contained within a single volume of comfortable dimensions. Bartholomew's Map, and a real desire, and will to fulfil the desire, to venture forth among the quiet delectable places with the mind and heart open to impression—these are the best prerequisites. There is a description of a series of walks, an estimate of the charm of the Lang Whang and the spell of the old road to Linton, and some of the experiences that have come in the course of thirty years of tramping, and in it all, an endeavour to comprehend in part the glamour and romance of the hills.

The more we tramp these breezy uplands, the more friendly they become; and the more we love them, the more they give to us: their call is unmistakable, and their appeal is as varied as the sky of an April day. Upon such in the hills is real and practical. But there are others to whom the exercise may not always be possible, but who delight to read about it, to think of the great walks they are going to take, and the hills they hope to climb, whose interest it may be is but sentimental. And there are those now far over-seas, whose love for the Pentland Hills is wrapped round their fondest thoughts of home. May all such, as they read this book, be able to catch something of the magic atmosphere they know and love, and feel the tang of the dewy moorland and the purple heather, and be revived by the fresh and bracing winds that blow from off these Hills of Happy Memories.

To some it may renew thoughts of days when they were more supple of body and lithe of limb. To my young friends, eager for adventure, I hope it may inspire a love for the hills, and a desire to know them better, that in the experience of the fuller revelation that nature has to give, there may be brought to them the wider vision to fit them for the service of their fellows.

It is not always possible or easy for city folk to get away to the breezy heights and the sunny moorlands and the sweet-smelling countryside. But how we like to read about it all, how we like to lose ourselves in thought among the hills and moors, and smell the odour that the hill wind brings, and experience the sunlit memories and the old remembrances of places we have known, and friendships that have stood the test of time.

The western half of the Pentlands will in future claim more attention from the experienced walkers, now that a new generation has discovered the delights of the more easily accessible parts, and to these lesser known regions special consideration is given. For the naturalist, botanist, geologist, antiquarian, and angler there is something to gladden the heart and delight the mind in this "farther out" section of the range, and many a quiet sequestered spot where intimate acquaintance may be made with the sights and sounds of nature. And for the simple wayfarer with a hunger in his heart which only the hills can satisfy, there is the wide heaven above and the open road before him that leads to his Arcadia, where amidst the glorious hills he enjoys the pleasures he counts the best; for he knows the fragrant perfume that the spring wind carries, he enjoys the smile of wayside flowers, and the cheery song and echoing cry of birds, and through the senses his heart is touched. He it is who at the day's end will say that life is good, that he is satisfied, for that he has found a new song wherewith to sing the praises of a new land in the Pentland Hills.

The book does not pretend to be a complete guide; that could not be adequately contained within a single volume of comfortable dimensions. Bartholomew's Map, and a real desire, and will to fulfil the desire, to venture forth among the quiet delectable places with the mind and heart open to impression—these are the best prerequisites. There is a description of a series of walks, an estimate of the charm of the Lang Whang and the spell of the old road to Linton, and some of the experiences that have come in the course of thirty years of tramping, and in it all, an endeavour to comprehend in part the glamour and romance of the hills.

The more we tramp these breezy uplands, the more friendly they become; and the more we love them, the more they give to us: their call is unmistakable, and their appeal is as varied as the sky of an April day. Upon such a subject we can all rejoice in our own opinions, cherish our own interpretations of experience, and claim no infallibility in matters of historical, traditional, and literary lore; and the more we differ in our experiences and opinions the greater shall become our interest and longing to discover for ourselves the real secret of the hills.

I am grateful to the following gentlemen for their generous permission to quote from the works referred to: Mr C. E. S. Chambers (Woodhouselee MS.), Dr W. B. Blaikie ("Edinburgh at the Time of the Occupation of Prince Charles"), the Rev. W. B. Strong of Glencorse and the Presbytery of Dalkeith (Records of Glencorse Kirk), to Messrs Macmillan & Co. (Sir Archibald Geikie's "Scenery of Scotland"), and to Mr Lloyd Osbourne for quotations from the works of R. L. Stevenson.

WILL GRANT

CHAPTER I

THE ROAD ROUND THE HILLS

1. EDINBURGH TO CARNWATH

By Colinton, Currie, and the Lang Whang

THE road round the hills is also the road to the hills, and herein lies its double fascination. It is as we approach them, with high hopes and full of expectation, dreaming of the silent spaces of nature's wonderland which we are to explore, or returning full of peace and contentment, that unsuspectingly the old travelling road will make its appeal to us. But apart from whether it be in our going out or in our coming in, the road has a story of its own that appeals to all lovers of the old highways; and happy are they who have found its fascination.

It is no ordinary road, this one round the hills. In some parts it is the old road of centuries modernised, in other parts the centuries-old road has grown green again, and its atmosphere is undisguised; it has all the charm and personality of old age grown beautiful and wise, to whose companionship wayfaring men now come as to a mother for counsel and consolation.

But whichever stretch we take we find it full of the glamour and romance of the history of bygone days. Ghosts of long ago make their appearance, then disappear, thrilling us with a sense of wonderment and mystery. Druids in their long robe, with white surplice, amulet necklace, and white magic wand, Cistercian monks in white robe, cassock, and black scapulary, barefooted friars making for St Katherine's-in-the-Hopes, Knights Templars in white mantle with red cross, and Knights of St John with black mantle and white cross, were all at one time walkers on the Pentland Hills; and upon this ancient road

1

bands of armed men with banners gleam through the mists, then fade away, giving place to the men of the Covenant, lonely shepherds, horsemen and wayfarers, yea, kings and queens and their retinues, travellers in state, huntsmen, smugglers, robbers—all will play for us their part as we take our journey of adventure upon this old road.

Let us try to catch, if we may, something of its spirit or personality and try to feel in some fashion its atmosphere so strangely mingled with the days of old romance and the modern age of speed. Yet this is not an easy thing. We dare not generalise. Like the contemplative man's way of understanding its secrets, we must go slowly, and study it in sections. The spirit of the old road is an elusive thing, its appeal may be clear and manifest to the favoured ones, the kindred spirits who love to muse upon the days of chivalry and deeds of high renown, as well as the tragic epics of the highway and the bold incursions of Border raiders. True, it may be that a few stretches may interest no one except the road-mender, but other parts of it will send us far into the fairy wonderland of imagination, beauty, and romance, where, who shall say which spirit shall be our guest?

Roughly, it covers a distance of fifty miles. Much depends upon whether we can feel the spell that nature and romance have laid upon it. The road like a child of the hills has grown up round about them, and the pageant of the centuries is there for our reconstruction. In its keeping is the wisdom of the years. It smiles its welcome to us in the spring and summer sunshine and beaks in the noonday's heat; while in the days and nights of frost it is leal to all travelling friends, who love it as a brother.

The picturesqueness of the road appeals to us at once. After it leaves the city it runs westward to COLINTON and thereafter accompanies the river by the villages of Juniper Green, Currie, and Balerno, where it becomes the Old Lanark Road—the Old Road to Air, as the Carnwath

Cross indicates. Nor does it ever leave the company of the hills, the moors, and the woods.

The neighbourhood of Colinton, situated under the shadow of the hills and set upon the banks of the Water of Leith, abounds in old castles and mansion houses—Colinton, Spylaw, Woodhall, Hailes, Dreghorn, Redhall; and, as we pass on our way to Colinton by Craiglockhart Hill and its ruined tower, we recall the history of the strong Castle of Redhall that gallantly withstood a week's siege at the hands of Oliver Cromwell and his army in 1650. In Nicol's *Diary* (Bannatyne Club) there is an account of this siege, with which we open our story of the brave and noble men who played their part in the history of the road.

" Cromwell pushed from Berwick to Collingtoune, without opposition until he came to the house of Reidhall, within three miles be west Edinburgh. In the whilk house of Reidhall the Laird of Reidhall (Sir James Hamilton) with threescore sodgeris, lay with provisions and keepit and defendit the house aganes the Englishes, and gallit his sodgeris and put them back several times, with loss of sindry sodgeris. The English General taking this very grievously that such a waik house sould hald out aganes him and be an impediment in his way, he and his airmy lying so neir unto it, thairfor he causit draw his cannon to the house, and thair, from four hours in the morning till ten in the foirnoun that day, he causit the cannon to play on this house, encampit a great number of his sodgeris about it with pike and musket, but all to lytel purpose; for the Laird and the pepil in the house defendit it voliantly ever till thair powder failed; and efter it failed, they did not giver over, ever lucking for help from our awin army, wha was then lying at Crosstorfyn (General Leslie's) within $\frac{3}{4}$ of ane myle to the house: of whas help thai was disappointed. General Cromwell percaiving their powder to be gone and that no assistance was given thame, he causit Pittardis to be brocht to the house, quhairwith

3

he blew up the dures, entered the dures and windowes, and efter slaughter on both sides (but much moir to the Englishes than to the Scottis) tuik all that were in the house prisoners, tirred them naked, seased on all the money and guides that were thairin, quhilk was much, be reason that sindry gentlemen about haid put their guides thair for saiftie. So this house and pepil thairin were taken in the sicht and face of our airmie, quha thocht it dangerous to hazard thameselves in such ane expedition, the enemy haiffing the advantage of the ground and hills about him for defence." "Efter the enemie had taken the Laird of Reidhall prisoner, he thaireftir put him to liberty, commending much his valour and activitie for halding out so stoutlie aganes him that house of Reidhall."

Redhall was owned in 1672 by the notorious John Chiesley, the Laird of Kersewell near Carnwath, and of Dalry House, Edinburgh, who shot Sir George Lockhart of Carnwath, then President of the Court of Session, in the Old Bank Close, in 1689, in revenge for a Court decision in a family litigation.

In many of these old residences we read to-day the story of our transition age. The seventeenth-century Castle of Dreghorn belongs to the War Department. Colinton House and Policies, with cedar-trees and holly hedges dating from 1680, has been purchased by Merchiston Castle School. Woodhall House, of the ancient family of Foulis, that once housed the famous " Bannatyne Collection " of Scottish poetry, presented to the Advocates' Library in 1770, is a private residence. It was George Bannatyne who preserved the poetry of Scotland during the great plague that ravaged the land in 1568, and obtained a grateful commemoration by the institution of the Bannatyne Club, and the compilation of his Memoirs by its first President, Sir Walter Scott.

Much of the history of Colinton is epitomised in the words " Romans," " Cromwell, 1650," " Covenanters, 1666," " Charles, 1745," inscribed on the capital of the

4

tall monument erected by the late R. A. Macfie of Dreghorn, close to the roadside above the castellated lodge at Dreghorn Bridge. Evidences of archæological and historical interest abound in the district—the old Roman road from York to Carriden near Abercorn is said to have passed through what is now Comiston Farm, and the high road between Fairmilehead Toll and Bow Bridge is almost on the line which it followed; there is a British Fort at the west end of Clubbiedean Pond; Hailes House, where the original Parish Church of Hailes[1] stood, has provided sculptured stones of great antiquity, and other relics of a bygone age. Several stone coffins were found in the course of widening the road at Hailes in 1925. The strongly built Castle of Colinton is now scheduled as an " Ancient Monument "; and the ruins of the ancient manor house of the Foulises form the setting of Mrs Oliphant's ghost story, *The Open Door*.

The Church of St Cuthbert at Hailes, with right to the teinds and lands, was gifted to the monks at Dunfermline by Ethelred, Earl of Fife, son of Malcolm Canmore, early in the twelfth century, and later transferred to the canons of Holyrood, because, according to the legend, there was a deficiency of wine after supper for the Bishop of St Andrews on the occasion of a certain visit. It was explained that the Bishop's own attendants had helped themselves to what had been reserved for their master. Doubtless it would be regarded by the monks as poor recompense for the loss of the revenues that they were declared to be free from blame in the matter! From the monks of Holyrood it passed to the Hospital of the Knight Templars of St Anthony in Leith in 1445, with whom it continued until the Reformation.

The present church in the Dell was built in 1907-8. Near the door lies an iron mort safe which was placed

[1] Till 1697 Colinton was called Hailes, and thence till 1747 Hailes or Collingtoune.

across the newly made grave to prevent its depredation, in the times of Burke and Hare; and passing the house at the gate, where the watch was kept for the grave robbers, we cross the old Colinton Bridge, built in 1686, which was for many a day Colinton's only bridge over the Water of Leith.

It was the gentle and courteous minister—Lewis Balfour, Robert Louis Stevenson's maternal grandfather, interested in all antiquities, and quietly humorous despite his apparent sternness and " Spartan ways," who tells us that —for brewing and selling " aile " in the school-house " so near to ye Kirk and hard by the minister's yate," John Craw the schoolmaster was deposed in 1655; and that a few years later the Kirk Session had to enact that the Communion tables were not to be lent for penny weddings. He lamented the passing of old customs and employments, and thus concludes the writing of the Statistical Account of his parish in 1839—" Considerable changes have taken place in the various manufactures. The distillery has disappeared; the skinnery! its very name is lost, having given place to the more poetical designation of Laverock Dale; the magnesia factory is in ruins; the noise of the waulk mill no longer reminds the passenger of its existence; and the mill for beating flax is, comparatively speaking, in little use. Still the parish flourishes; the population has increased; the rental has improved; and could a little more of that right-hearted prudence which inclines, and, through God's blessing, enables man to value and steadily comply with the counsels of heavenly truth, be infused into the bosom of the generality of the people, they would be blessed indeed."

Colinton was in a transition stage even in those days.

The quiet and peace with which Colinton was synonymous is being disturbed, so that even the rooks and the crows, the wind among the tree-tops, and the sound of running water, can scarcely now be heard. The electric tram has arrived in the village, and with its coming there came the widening of roads and bridges, and well-loved paths, hedges, and trees have in turn disappeared.

Many old landmarks and customs have gone, and even their remembrance is in the possession of but a few of the older natives. The tram terminus adjoins the site of the village " smiddy," dairy, and " sweetie-shop "; the place of the village pump is now occupied by the Episcopal Church, while the old school is now the Registrar's Office. Happy villagers on summer evenings danced around " The Sixpenny Tree," whose successor spreads its leafy branches at the corner of Redford Road. Some will tell you that a sixpence was paid for dancing, others that a coin was planted along with the sapling, others again, that once upon a time the old tree was sold for that sum, and they will tell you where the deal took place: but all these stories must be surmise if the following be true. The tree originally called " The Sixpence Tree " stood in the high road opposite Old Farm, and seats were arranged around it. Here the employees of the paper-mills not only of the Water of Leith Valley, but also of the Esk Valley at Penicuik, and elsewhere, came to make payment of six-pence, their contribution to the Paper-makers' Union, whose business was conducted there, hence the name of the tree. It was cut down some years ago, but as evidence of its local interest, the stump remains within the grounds of Colinton House.

The modern country village is no longer a separate com-munity, and the old customs will soon be forgotten. One of these, the " Colinton Play," which was discontinued forty-six years ago, was held on the second Friday of July, and was the event of the year in all the surrounding districts.

Old inhabitants, who recall " the Play " with enthusiasm, tell us of the village as they knew it with its two thatched inns, its few houses, post-office, and three shops; of the bridge over the railway that was built simultaneously with the line to Balerno in 1874, and of the time when the road through the village went by way of the inns across the old brig and up the Kirk Brae to Curriemuirend.

Continuing along the wooded highway we come to JUNIPER GREEN, which has changed considerably since the days when Carlyle spent part of his early married life there; and Dr John Brown and his father would not now, as in 1840, have the road to themselves as they galloped out to Juniper Green. The old gentleman "flashing through the arch under the Canal at Slateford, his white hair flying," got far ahead of the young doctor who inquired of a stone-breaker if he had seen a gentleman on a chestnut horse—"Has he white hair?" "Yes!" "And een like a gled's?" "Yes!" "Weel, then, he's fleein' up the road like the wund; he'll be at Little Vantage [a toll-house nine miles away] in nae time, if he haud on."

It was at Baberton House, near Juniper Green, that Charles X. of France, the last of the Bourbon kings, resided for a time during his stay at Holyrood, in the days of the French Revolution, and again in 1830, after he had abdicated the French throne.

CURRIE with her Auld Brig and Auld Kirk, the Toll-house and the Inn, still breathes an old-world atmosphere, although it is gradually fading away. The "ferm-folk" still come in to Currie, if not to get supplies and the current news of the countryside as in the olden days, then to get the 'bus " tae the toun "; and the anglers " frae the toun " often take a step up to the Brig-end in the course of their journey up the water, just as their forefathers did. Currie Brig is said to have stood for nearly six hundred years. The water is deep beneath it, and this gave rise to the proverb " as deep as Currie Brig," indicating selfish cunning as well as shrewdness. It was across the old bridge that Dalziel of Binns and the Royalist Army marched to Rullion Green by the Maidenscleuch—formerly Cleuchmaidstone —to meet the Covenanters.

Currie has an ancient and interesting history both civil and ecclesiastical. The district, like that of Colinton, has been noted as the place of residence of many eminent lawyers, among whom were Sir John Skene of Curriehill, Lord Register, his son Sir James Skene, Lord President in the reign of James XV., the Scotts of Malleny, both father and son, the latter being elevated to a seat on the Bench, and Sir Thomas Craig of Riccarton, Lord Advocate. It has been recorded that Currie was one of the first rural places in Scotland to enjoy the services of a Presbyterian minister, as Calder House was the scene of one of the earliest open administrations of the Holy Sacrament by John Knox in 1556. It is this incident in the Great Hall at Calder that forms the subject of Sir David Wilkie's last great historical painting, showing the group of armed warriors reverently waiting upon Knox, and it is from this portrait showing the well-known features of the Reformer, with the long flowing beard and Geneva cap and gown, that most of the published portraits have been engraved.

Adjoining the fine old Scots Kirk at Currie is a remnant of the older Kirk, which is now a family vault. Two Knights Templar stones stand in the vestibule, and one in the churchyard with incised cross and sword of the thirteenth century. There is a local tradition that the stone came from the river side, where there once stood a Templar establishment at Killeith—the chapel by the Leith. A monument to Pastor Lichton, uncle to Archbishop Leighton, and son of Currie's first Protestant minister, stands behind the church; while one of the many works of Currie's "old parochial" schoolmaster, a genius of real worth, as were most of that order, one Robert Palmer, who with Sir William Gibson-Craig founded the Caledonian Curling Club, is seen in the sundial near the old school.

The whole district, like that of Carlops on the other side of the hills, is connected with ancient religious observances. The name Currie may be derived from the Celtic Corrie, signifying a hollow or glen; or it may be a corruption of the Latin Coria, the name given to the place by the

9

Romans, and the Roman Station or Exploratory Camp on Ravelrig Hill beyond Balerno, once named Castlebank, and a neighbouring station called the " General's Watch " (both marked on an old plan of Ravelrig estate) give additional weight to the latter suggestion.

When digging for the foundation of the present church on the site of the old one five centuries ago, part of a crucifix or altar candlestick was found having thereon a spiral scroll with the inscription in Saxon letters—" Jesu Fili Dei miserere mei."

Nor can we leave the Currie Old Brig without noticing the five hundred years old Ale-house at the north end— " the wee shop that the brig has closed up the door o'," as George Kirkhope used to say even in the days of living memory, and then point to the closed-up window as the place " whaur the auld wife handed oot the ' gabbens ' (nips of whisky), cakes, baps, and ale." The brig has been considerably heightened since it was first built. Beside the thatched cottage of two storeys are the ruins of the meal mill, and the kiln opposite, often mistaken for a ruined tower. The old Inn is now a ruin.

James Grant, in *Harry Ogilvie, or The Black Dragoons*, tells of how the Laird of Linn and Carlourie came forth from the desolate Lennox Tower, closed the ponderous iron gate, " composed of welded yetlan bars," and rode down to the change-house at Currie brig-end with the grotesque face carved on each of its lower crowsteps, and bearing " the usual sign of a village shop:—

" Dundee threid—Edinburgh breid and new-laid eggs
By me Lucky Legget Ail-browstar."

From the old and wrinkled proprietrix the laird learns that Sir Henry Lennox and his daughter are dead and buried in Currie kirkyaird, whereupon, leaving Carlourie to his ale, Linn goes to " the burial place of the Lennoxes," and here he found the graves " marked by a stone carved with a sword and the old French Cross of Mount Carmel, on the south side of Currie Kirk."

The place well repays a visit, if only to obtain a new view-point of an interesting countryside.

Lennox Castle or Tower, an ivy-covered ruin a little farther up the Water, must at one time have been a place of considerable strength, with walls seven and a half feet thick, surrounded by a moat, and having a rampart that goes round the brow of the hill, extending to 1212 feet, and a traditional subterranean passage. It is said to have belonged to the Lennox family, and to have been the occasional residence of the youthful Mary Queen of Scots —" when love was young and Darnley kind." Darnley was son of the Earl of Lennox, but no account of the history of the tower and its original name has so far been found; and the real name may have a closer connection with the adjoining lands of Lymphoy, of which it was probably the tower, than with Lennox. Montrose rested at Lymphoy on his way to Philiphaugh.

From her earliest years Mary was fond of riding and hunting; she hunted the stag through the ancestral forests of France, and did all her travelling in Scotland on horseback. She was devoted to the then fashionable and healthful amusement of hawking, like her father and grandfather. James V., her father, kept a Master-falconer, with seven others under him, and Mary, in 1562, when twenty years of age, had special hawks brought from Orkney. Her riding habits were of serge of Florence, stiffened in the neck and body with buckram and trimmed with lace and ribands. No doubt it was for hunting and hawking on the Pentland Hills and neighbouring moors that she came to Lennox Tower, which, along with Malleny and Baberton Houses, was also a hunting-seat of James VI.

All the villages along this picturesque valley are starting-off points for the hill-walker and to each he may be brought by either car or 'bus. It is as he travels to his starting-place that for a little he bears with the chronicler telling the story of the road. But a little of this is enough for the walker eager for the far-spreading hills and the

11

exhilaration that comes with exercise in the snell Pentland air.

At Colinton we may make for Bonaly Hill and the Glencorse right-of-way; or by way of Dreghorn Loan proceed through Howden Glen and over the hills to either Allermuir and Caerketton, or Castlelaw. Attempts have been made from time to time to close this road, and a former proprietor of the estate put gates across it, but this was met by the inhabitants commissioning a horseman to ride over the path through the Howden Glen annually, to preserve the right-of-way. By way of Torduff and Clubbiedean we may join the road to Malleny and Glencorse. There is no difficulty in finding these paths, which are marked upon the map.

Currie is also a favourite starting-point, but probably Balerno is the most popular, as the crossings from here, while being farther to the westward and consequently leading through wild and less frequented paths, are also more numerous and diversified. At Balerno we take the Old Lanark Road on our travel round the hills. To Carnwath it is eighteen miles—a road full of picturesque and beautiful stretches, compensating the walker for the miles of hard highway as he makes for the hill tracks leading to the Boar Stane, the Cauldstaneslap, the Garval Syke, the Crane Loch near the Twin Laws, the Covenanter's Grave, and the purple moors around Dunsyre.

On the right we pass Ravelrig Hill, Dalmahoy Craigs, and Kaimes Hill, now being quarried and rapidly changing in shape. The first road to the left after passing "Boll of Bere" Farm takes the walker by Haugh-head and the foot-bridge over the Water of Leith to the Boar Stane right-of-way to Carlops. Part of the old inn of "Boll of Bere" still survives in the shape of a farm "bothy." Dalmahoy forms part of the estate of the Earl of Morton. The Dalmahoys obtained a grant of the lands in the time of Alexander III.

On the Boar Stane road, between Buteland Farm and

Buteland House, with red tiled roof and yellow-coloured walls, stands " Temple House," now known as " the herd's hoose," and before we come to the spreading loch at Harper-rig we pass the Temple Hill. Yes, there were Templars here in the days of old, and in a deed of 1602 the Temple Lands at Harper-rig are described as bounded on the north by the Water of Leith, on the east by the Dean Burn, on the west by Temple Dyke, which extends from the south to the Water of Leith. The Priory of Torphichen, twelve miles to the west, was founded in 1124, when David I. was king, and succeeding Scottish kings bestowed grants and privileges upon this Order of the Knights Hospitallers or Knights of St John of Jerusalem, also called Friars Hospitallers.

There was also the military Order of the Knights Templars, whose history is that of the Crusades, but this Order was suppressed in 1312, and their vast and rich domains became the property of their rivals and their enemies, the Knights of St John. Sir James Sandilands of Torphichen, who became Preceptor of the Order in Scotland, resigned his Lordship into the hands of Queen Mary on his joining the Reformers, but the Queen allowed him to purchase the possessions of both Orders for 10,000 crowns of the Sun, a large sum in those days, being equal to £1100 sterling, and 500 merks of annual feu-duty. Queen Mary's Charter of 1564 confirmed the estate and dignity to Sir James, and Lord St John of Torphichen " became a territorial honour inherent in the possession of certain acres of land adjacent to the ancient Preceptory of Torphichen." Little land now remains around the Priory, but what we may perhaps note with most interest is that the Order became extinct at the time of the Reformation in Scotland, and that prior to that time the robed figures of Templars and Knights of St John must often have been seen upon this ancient highway—the " Lang Whang."

It is the section of the Old Lanark Road from the Toll-house at "Little Vantage," through the open breezy moorland to Carnwath, that is known as the "Lang Whang." How many centuries ago it got this name I cannot say, but doubtless it earned it well, as many a straggling body or weary coach-traveller looking up to the hills, which may have been to many of them synonymous with home, thought they were never going to get within sight of the Metropolis. So they travelled the road, up hill and down dale—"up-along, down-along, out-along," but aye there was another "lang whang" in front. Walkers know what it all means. The Lang Whang is not a level road: it rises and falls, it turns and twists, it runs through a wood here and there, over streams and past farms, within sight of the lochs of Harper-rig, Crosswood, and Cobbinshaw, with the heights of far Craigengar, with its shepherds' cairns, and Colzium guarding the nearer hills of Torweaving and Mealowther, and the boulders known as the "Ewe and Lamb," by many a syke and rig and knowe, cleuch and hope, tumble-down cottage, milestone and signpost.

At one time much of the moorland across which the Lang Whang passes, especially about Crosswood, must have been covered with forest and woodlands.

The local rhyme stays:—

> "Calder wood was fair to see
> When it came to Camilty;
> Calder wood was fairer still
> When it came to Crosswoodhill."

It was a hunting ground favoured by the Scottish kings. There are few stretches of the road to-day without some feature of interest. It isn't all so dreary, as many writers would have us believe, and even the most picturesque road would be described as "dreary" or any undulating stretch a "lang whang" by tired walkers or weary folk. Our enjoyment of any road is dependent upon whether we can fit in with the spirit of the road, and our capacity to assimilate with its surroundings. Should we grow weary of the road, get on to the heathery hillocks above, and obtain a new view-point, and rest awhile, and let the silence of the wide spaces sink into the soul. Ah! how the walker loves the silences! " That I might obtain some of that within me," he muses to himself. " In quietness and in confidence shall be your strength," comes the reply. And those who have eyes to see will discover wondrous colours everywhere, and colour is an antidote to weariness. The moor birds also have their varied cries, and the air is fresh and scented with the breath of the heather and the moorland. The Lang Whang seldom dips below the 1000 feet contour line, and in the hollows of the moorland all the eerie fancies seem to centre, among the bogs and mosses—the Hagieræ Moss, the Crow Moss, and the Middlemuir, and the peat-hags showing dark against the ground colour of the hills, with their ghosts and warlocks and spunkies in winter time, and fairies and the wee folk from the Pentland sykes up-bye in summer time. And it is from the Lang Whang with the far-stretching moorland before us, with the rolling hills for background, that we see the wonderful effects in the varied seasons of the year, of nature's handiwork in the glistening snow in the winter's sunshine, and all the artistry of the frost in filigree and lacework, the light and shade of sun-streaked cloud, the filmy autumn mists, and clear shining after rain.

If there were many a whang or slice of road to be covered in the course of the journey from Edinburgh to Lanark, there were also many places of refreshment on the way, many a wayside tavern and change-house at which the stage-coach stopped. In the beginning of last century three coaches a week started from the Grassmarket and Princes Street for Lanark by the Lang Whang; and Currie Inn, " Jenny's Toll " (nine miles from Edinburgh), " Boll of Bere," " House on the Muir," " Little Vantage," " Cairns Castle Inn," " Half-way House "—half-way between Edinburgh and Lanark—situated between Wester Causey-end and Crosswood Burn, and " South Toun Toll-bar " (Tarbrax), where the first change of horses was made, were all places of bustle and good cheer.

There were also romantic and exciting incidents upon the turnpike. Drivers and guards were personalities in whom the travelling public were intensely interested, and as the rubicund driver of the Lanark stage drove his galloping team down the steep slopes on the Lang Whang, one may be sure that he did not scare his passengers as he skilfully manipulated his team and coach in taking the angular, narrow bridges that carry the road at intervals. The no less daring, but less skilful driver of the modern motor-car, who clears the bridges by inches with his car on two wheels, cannot expect to earn the respect of his no less interested passengers, who, out of sympathy, let us say, blame the builders of the bridges.

The guard with his horn would awaken many a fox in its lair along the hills, and no doubt he looked to his blunderbus as the clamorous coach rolled along in sight of the Drove Roads by Currie and the Boar Stane, and the " Thieves' Road " through the Cauldstaneslap; lonely places with lots of cover for gipsy robber-men waiting for the stage, or that " Gentleman Gipsy," Captain Baillie of Biggar, mounted on his horse, with his sword by his side, and his greyhounds behind him, who could act the gallant or the robber at will.

The traveller along the Lang Whang to-day, as he looks across to the Cauldstaneslap between the Cairn Hills, recalls that this pass was once a main drove road. Those were lawless days, and many a convoy was surprised in the pass by freebooters and moss-troopers, the road coming to be known as the " Thieves' Road." It was a lonely place, and far from human habitation. And so it came about that the owner of the lands, and of the Castle at East Cairns by the lochside, Sir George Crichton, who was High Admiral of Scotland, Earl of Caithness, and builder of Blackness Castle, appointed himself warden of this gateway through the hills. The Castle has stood the storms

16

and tempests that rage along the Pentland hillsides for nearly 500 winters. It originally consisted of two square towers, forty feet high, with a turret stair giving access to the upper flats of both wings; the basement was vaulted, with two massive cylindrical arches supporting the main floor of the Castle. Beneath the arches were dungeons or cellars approached from outside by a circular headed doorway, and having an arrow slit in the wall. Some seventy years ago the two towers were intact, one has since disappeared, and the other is held together by an iron tie-rod. The house adjoining was erected in 1872 by the father of the present proprietor, Mr W. H. Hamilton, Writer to the Signet, who loves the hills and the Lang Whang, and counts the varied winter days among the best in all the year.

Mr H. C. Lawlor, in *A History of the Family of Cairns,* suggests that the basement of the Castle may be part of an older building of the thirteenth or fourteenth century. He is of opinion that 1060-1100 may be about the time when the owners of this estate derived their surname from the lands of Cairns, and he finds that in 1349 it was in possession of " William de Carnys."

The strong Castle at Cairns did not prevent the depredations of the cattle-thieves from the other side of the Slap. At the time when James V. was travelling frequently down the Lang Whang to Cowthally Castle, Carnwath, the owner of Cairns was one of the King's " familiar servants," one John Tennant, a man at arms in Edinburgh Castle. That the Cauldstaneslap required a keeper, the lairds of Cairns were well aware. They held the lands of Harehope on the other side of the pass, and there were frequent raids from the Tweeddale side upon the drovers and shepherds crossing the hill, as well as upon the farm-steadings bordering on the Lang Whang.

The Armstrongs and Liddells, the Earl of Morton's men, carried out a midnight raid one Hallow-e'en, and stole the stock of ewes and wedders from Harehope, and the laird complained to the Council against the Earl in 1582.

Another band of raiders claiming protection of the laird of Branxholm, and described as "disobedient and unansuerable thevis and lymnaris haveing schaikin of all fear of God, reverence of the law and regaird of honestie," came over the pass to the haughs at Harper-rig one day in August 1600, and carried off fourscore oxen and several horses, but only after they had slain and wounded divers of His Majesty's good subjects who rose to the fray in defence of their master's property.

A short distance westward from the old Castle of Cairns there once stood another Tower and Fortalice which is mentioned in connection with the lands of Easter Colzium in 1609, and the present house, it is thought, now occupies the site of the former place of defence.

The wild glens, recesses, and caves around the Cairn Hills and the Garval Syke, as around Dunsyre, were sheltering places for the persecuted Presbyterians in the Covenant times, and many meetings took place on the banks of the West Water and the Polintarf, along the rocky ravines of the Medwin, and around the jagged peaks of the Wolf Craigs under Craigengar.

Often does the walker on the Lang Whang and on the hills around pause to think of their historic associations. And as he falls a-dreaming he sees a Roman Legion on the Lang Whang, for despite what all sceptical modern antiquarians say about the presence of the Romans round the hills, pottery and coins of Vespasian, Hadrian and Marcus Aurelius, have been dug up two miles from Causewayend—the end of the Causeway or Roman road —and they had camps and stations at Ravelrig and Kaimes.

The Pentland walker bound for the hills does not require to do much tramping upon the Lang Whang. He merely crosses it as he passes from Auchengray, making across the hills for Dunsyre or West Linton by the right-of-way paths, or from Harburn to Dolphinton, while in his course from Mid-Calder by the Cauldstaneslap he travels the high road for less than a mile. It is possible if he is tramping westward along the hills, making for Carnwath, he will soon give up the idea of following the paths, for the heather has covered them over long ago, but with a right sense of direction he will strike the road without much difficulty. This was my experience one autumn day. I missed the track soon after crossing the Medwin, and found the heather tracks knee-deep for miles. It would be better, one thought, to strike the Lang Whang, where the going would be better, now that it was past sunset and dusk would soon be gathering, but no sign of a road could be discerned. I rested and listened; there was silence everywhere on this evening of an Indian summer day. Then a faint sound of a farm cart on a rough road, but that cart seemed a long way off. I continued the heather step, determined to find the road if possible. In a short time I came upon the Lang Whang, which I welcomed as a friend. The tall heather had hidden it completely from view. Soon I met two country folks, and on inquiring how far it was to Carnwath was told it was five miles. Five miles more after so many did not matter much, and I felt relieved. After tramping about two more miles I again made inquiry of two fishers on a stream near by. But fishers have no idea of distance, they were intent on getting trout before darkness came down, and again I was informed it was five miles. Well, well, I thought, I am at least holding my own. Then the September moon rose, and cheerily I swung down into Carnwath. Two things were needful, food and a railway time-table. While greedily satisfying a ravenous appetite in the inn, I inquired if there was a train that night to Edinburgh. Yes, there was a train. " And when does it start?" " In ten minutes." " And how far was it to the station?" " About a mile." " But I can't walk a mile in ten minutes," I expostulated. " Oh," replied the innkeeper, " but there's a short cut through the wood." " Is it a dark wood?" " Aye, it's gey dark, gey dark, but there's a mune the nicht."

I left the inn hurriedly, caught hold of a boy at the door, and pressed him into my service to show me the road through the wood. We arrived at the station, where faint lights glimmered from the oily lamps, but no sound was heard. "Are you sure there is another train, my lad?" I asked eagerly. "Oh, aye," he replied, "but it's sometimes late, an' it doesna' maitter much, there's naebody traivillin'." So I waited in the silent frosty night, and the train came, a special: at least it stopped specially, or only for me. I was glad, for it had been a long day, but a glorious one, and I did it all alone, and that's why I remember every step of it, although it happened a quarter of a century ago. The heather tracks across the hills has been followed on countless occasions since that day, and the experiences and impressions on the first crossing have been a continual feast for the memory during many a tramp.

2. CARNWATH, NEWBIGGING, DUNSYRE, AND DOLPHINTON

CARNWATH is situated at the west end of the hills, on the Lang Whang, eight hundred feet above sea-level.

The main street of this clean little village, that lies open to the bracing Pentland winds, is about three-quarters of a mile long, and grouped round the centre of it were the ancient Jail, with crow-stepped gable, the Court House, and the village Cross, while opposite the old Church stands Carnwath House, a famous place in the history of the Lockharts, and in which Prince Charlie is reported to have stayed. The Jail and Court-House have been removed.

Hugh, the fifth Lord Somerville, built the Cross in 1516, upon which was emblazoned the family coat-of-arms, and the names of Lord and Lady Somerville. But the Cross, like that of the neighbouring village of Newbigging, has had its vicissitudes. The coat-of-arms and names have disappeared, and the shaft bears in old lettering a list of

ST. MARY'S AISLE, CARNWATH

the stages and distances between Edinburgh and Ayr, and Peebles and Glasgow. This example of a Scottish market cross consists of a pedestal with base and cornice, standing on four ascending steps—a shaft unusually square and large, crowned with a deep cornice and pear-shaped finial. Fourteen years later the noble lord built the Jail and Court House.

As Lord Somerville was zealous in assisting King James V. to establish law and order and to bring the notorious Border robbers to justice—of whom John Armstrong, Cockburn of Henderland, and Scott of Tushielaw were the most famous—it is not unlikely that the erection of the Court House with its two cells below—which may still be seen—for outlaws, freebooters, and criminals, was a token of his desire that Carnwath, in keeping with its tradition, should give the lead to other towns in the erection of a local Court of Justice. The market-place adjoined the Court House, and old inhabitants still remember when the local smith collected the dues from the farmers as they brought in their sheep and cattle.

As becomes a village on the old highway between Edinburgh and Lanark and Ayr, and still upholding its importance, Carnwath has several ancient hostelries, one of which bears the old Scots maxim printed on the gable end—" Better a wee buss than nae bield."

This inn was built several centuries ago, and its situation was then at the " toun-heid," where the Lang Whang entered Carnwath. Even in the matter of inn names Carnwath was not lacking in originality, for this one was known as " The Hens' Balks." No doubt the hens roosted on the cross beams forming a loft in the roof of the common room of the inn.

The history of Carnwath is largely bound up in the story of its chief families—the Somervilles, the Dalziels, and the Lockharts, many of whom are buried in St Mary's Aisle, now used as a mausoleum, adjacent to the present Parish Church, and the only remaining part of the ancient

21

Church of Carnwath. The large window of the aisle, facing the public road, is one of the finest specimens of Gothic architecture in Scotland, and the arched stone roof is of rare design. The door is kept locked, but the visitor may see the coat-of-arms of the following families upon the outside walls: St Clairs of Roslin (next the Church); Somerville; Edmonston—the carving upon this shield is much decayed; and Campbell. The second wife of Thomas, first Lord Somerville, was Lady Marie St Clair, one of the nine daughters of Henry, first Earl of Orkney, and of Roslin Castle, whom he married in 1407. In 1424 Carnwath Church was in a ruinous condition, and Lady Marie persuaded her husband to rebuild it, with the aisle thereof, and to dedicate it to St Mary. 1446 is the date when Roslin Chapel was founded by Sir William St Clair, third Earl of Orkney, so that St Mary's Aisle is older than Roslin Chapel, and the family of the St Clairs of Roslin were interested in the building of both. A carved stone figure of a Crusader, supposed to be that of the founder of the Church, stands against the western wall of the churchyard.

The name of the village first appears in connection with the gift to the See of Glasgow of the Church of Carnwath, Karne-wid, or Carnewith—built and founded in 1185-7 by William de Sumervilla. Carnwath denotes a cairn or mound in the wood: the cairn may have reference to the ancient mound to the west of the village now known as The Moat, a name probably derived from *mote,* signifying a fortified place. Many place-names bear witness to the fact that the district was richly wooded—Woodhead, Westsidewood, Crosswood; and Cowthally, the Somerville residence, signifies a sheltered spot, the traditional belief being that there was an avenue of full-grown oaks from the Castle to the village.

The Somervilles were of Norman extraction, Sir Gaulter de Somerville coming to England with William the Conqueror. In Scotland John Somerville is said have received from William the Lion, in 1174, the lands of Linton in Roxburghshire, along with a knighthood, as a reward for having killed a great serpent, boar, or wolf that devastated the neighbourhood. Like his successors he was fond of hunting, and was Chief Falconer to the King in Scotland. Sir Walter Somerville of Newbigging was one of the few barons who supported Wallace, and commanded the third Brigade of Horse at the Battle of Biggar. Sir David, his son, was also present, along with Sir John Tinto of Crimp-Cramp; while Sir Walter's cousin, Sir Rodger, commanded a regiment of the English army. The Cadger's Brig at Biggar, it is locally believed, gets its name from the tradition that Wallace crossed it disguised as a cadger to reconnoitre the English camp, and accomplished his purpose unrecognised, except by one whose suspicions were aroused and who remarked:—

> " He's crippled of a foot, and he's blin' of an e'e,
> But he's as like Willie Wallace as ever I did see!"

Sir John Somervill, Baron of Linton and Carnwath, second son of Walter, was a supporter of Bruce, and was taken prisoner at the age of twenty-four, after Bruce's defeat at Methven, and later obtaining his freedom, had part in the victory of Bannockburn. He married the eldest daughter of Sir James Douglas of Loudoune Hill, to whom the lands of Carnwath belonged in 1300, and they remained in the Somerville family for more than three hundred years. In 1317 the lands were erected into a barony by King Robert the Bruce, and in 1602 they were purchased by the Earl of Mar, who sold them in 1634 to Robert, Lord Dalziel, created Earl of Carnwath in 1639.

The history of the Somervilles is contained in a quaint old chronicle entitled *The Memorie of the Somervilles,* written in the reign of Charles II. Sir Walter Scott continued the family narrative, and also edited the whole work, which was published in two volumes in 1815. These volumes are now somewhat rare, but in *The Baronial House of Somerville,* by James Somerville, Carnwath (1920), there is a valuable record, in clear and concise form, of this ancient family, that played so large a part in Scottish life and history.

The Pentland moors around Carnwath were hunting-grounds of the Scottish Kings, and James III., IV., and V. were frequent visitors at Cowthally Castle, which was noted for its lavish hospitality, its feasts and entertainments. In connection with these feasts we read in *The Memorie* that it is "uncontravertedly asserted they spent a cow every day in the year, for which cause it is supposed that the house was named cow-dayly," and for centuries the Castle was known by that name.

On the occasion of one of James III.'s visits, when the feast lasted for several days, three cows besides many sheep were consumed daily, when 300 to 400 persons dined every day; while at the Homecoming Feast of Sir John of Quothquan and his bride, at which James IV. was present, in 1489, "there was no fewer beasts killed than 50 kine, 200 sheep, 40 boles of Malt, 16 boles of meal, 20 stones of butter spent at this infare, besides fishes tame, and wild fowl in such abundance that both the King and the Nobility declared they had not seen the like in any house within the Kingdom." James III. said Lord Somerville's kitchen bred more cooks and better than any other nobleman's house he knew. In this he was corroborated by James IV., while James V., between the age of eighteen and thirty-two, frequented no nobleman's house so much as Cowthally, and regarded Lady Somerville as his mother, nicknaming her May Maitlane. There was of course a reason for the frequent visits of the gallant and amorous king.

It was at a marriage feast at Cowthally in 1532 that James V., the Merry Monarch, fell in love with the sixteen-year-old-daughter of Sir John Carmichael, Captain of Crawford, but the young lady was so carefully chaperoned by the alert hostess, Lady Somerville, who was a Maitland of Lethington, "virtuous and wise," that James could not converse with her alone. Weeks and months passed, but the love sickness departed not from the King, so off His Majesty set again from Edinburgh, down the Lang Whang to Carnwath and Cowthally Castle, with a large suite in attendance. It is narrated that the kitchen at Cowthally was always equal to any such emergency. His Majesty sought an interview with Lady Somerville, with what object may be surmised, who referred His Royal Highness to " her father's house as being a much fitter place where your Majesty would be welcomed in honouring the family with your Royal presence "; to which His Majesty, discomfited, but merry still, was heard to remark to a lady standing near: " Your neighbour here, the Lady Somerville, is the most scrupulous person under heaven for another's concern; but I will have my revenge in being often her guest to eat up all the beef and the pudding too."

Next morning the King, after hearing Mass, rode off with his retinue to Crawford Castle, having been preceded by a courier, who carried the news of his coming. Poor little Katherine, however, was much affrighted when she heard the King was at hand. " In great trouble of spirit she remained in a careless dress until His Majesty's arrival." But her father and mother were much elated with their apparent good fortune. Persuasion and blandishments were of no avail; she resisted the King's advances for the space of twelve months, but eventually surrendered, and together they lived happily in the house which the King built at Crawfordjohn, where two children were born. But by the time Katherine was twenty-two the fancy of the fickle, self-indulgent King changed, and several proposals of marriage were offered to Katherine by him on behalf of some of his noble wards, but she would have none of them.

At another feast in Cowthally Castle, some years later, on the occasion of the marriage of Lord Somerville's second daughter, Katherine met Lord Somerville's nephew, John Somerville of Cambusnethan, and she entered on a

25

new career, when with the King's assistance she married Cambusnethan, a union which was entirely happy.

Jean Stuart, one of the two children born to Katherine Carmichael and King James, became wife of the fifth Earl of Argyle, and was a favourite with her half-sister, Mary Queen of Scots, with whom she was present on the night of the murder of Rizzio at Holyrood, and later held the infant James VI. at his baptism by commission from Queen Elizabeth. She lies buried in Holyrood Abbey, in the same vault with James II., James V., and Darnley, while Bishop Adam Bothwell, who crowned Mary's son at Stirling, is buried near the High Altar in the Chapel. Katherine's son became Earl of Bothwell, and resided at Crichton Castle, Midlothian.

Illegible handwriting is often responsible for strange mistakes. On one occasion in 1474, when John, third Lord Somerville, was to return to Cowthally Castle by the Lang Whang from Edinburgh, accompanied by King James III., who was to enjoy hunting on Carnwath Moors, he advised Lady Somerville to prepare the usual royal feast, adding a postscript—" Speates and Raxes," that is, Spits and Ranges, meaning that the feast was to be of a sumptuous nature, and that the spits and ranges, or framework on which the food was prepared, should be put into employment. A newly appointed Steward, unacquainted with his lordship's writing, interpreted the postscript to be " Spears and Jacks," jacks—doublets of leather, quilted with iron plates—being the armour of irregular cavalry of the period. Assuming therefore that an armed force was required, Lady Somerville ordered the raising of all the vassals and retainers in the baronies of Carnwath and Cambusnethan and the bailiery of Carstairs, to meet early next morning and proceed to Edinburgh. Imagine, therefore, the consternation of Lord Somerville, the King, and his hunting companions when they met this force of two hundred armed men on the Lang Whang, a mile west of Crosswoodhill, where the road crosses a stream. The King demanded an explanation from Lord Somerville and asked his lordship if this was " another hunting trick," and added that if it was treason, his head would pay for it; but Lord Somerville protested his ignorance of the reason for such a state of matters, and advanced to make inquiries. The letter, the Steward, and the explanation were soon forthcoming. Asked to read the letter again, the Steward read out " Spears and Jacks "; here was the mistake, but Lord Somerville " knew not whether to laugh or be angry at the fellow," and returned to the King, who, on hearing the story and reading the letter, laughed heartily, and remarked that he would have made the same mistake himself. Lady Somerville's fears of having incurred the King's displeasure were quickly banished by His Majesty's tactful congratulations upon the arms which she had so quickly provided for her husband's defence, adding that should the occasion arise he hoped that she would have an equally brave force to place at the service of the King.

Sir Walter Scott has retold this episode in the *Tales of a Grandfather*.

Carnwath was a centre of Jacobitism both in the 'Fifteen and the 'Forty-five, the Lockharts being ardent supporters of both the Old and the Young Chevaliers.

Not the least interesting event in the lives of the inhabitants of this quiet country village is the foot-race held in August each year for the prize of a pair of " redhose—made of one ell of English cloth." This race, which came into existence as a condition of the Charter granted by King James IV., in 1500, of the barony of Carnwath, has been run for centuries, and up to the end of the eighteenth century it is reported that the laird had a messenger in attendance ready to convey the result of the race to the Lord Advocate in Edinburgh. It is the oldest foot-race in Scotland. Another condition of the tenure was " ane new fair and weekly Market upon the Sabbath "; but in 1590 Lord Somerville was cited to appear before the General Assembly for holding such a fair on that day, and after having pled that this authority was given to him and to his predecessors by James IV. and confirmed by James V., he was threatened with the censure of the Church, and agreed to abolish it.

In Nimmo's *Songs and Ballads of Clydesdale* there is a story of a native of Carnwath that would seem to illustrate the resourcefulness of the lads of this Pentland parish. His name was Rob Whiteley, an apprentice to the stocking-making trade at Carnwath, and also a poacher. At length the wily Rob was caught poaching, and sentenced to a month's imprisonment in Lanark Jail, but he so gained the confidence of his jailer that he was allowed to go out upon his parole, and visit his friends. On a certain night he tarried late over the toddy and the song-singing, for he was a great lover of the Auld Scotch Sangs, and it was far past the appointed hour for his return when he came to the gate, and the jailer remonstrated—" Rob, whatna' wark's this wi' ye; I'll just tell ye plainly, sir, if ye dinna keep mair reg'lar 'oors, I'll bar ye oot a' thegither." " Freend," replied Bob, " I'll just tell *you,* if ye dinna keep a mair ceevil tongue in yer heid, I'll change ma ludgin's; dae ye really think I'm tae be bothered an' insulted by a body like *you*; but just keep quiet, man—it's nae use for you an' me tae cast oot; just hae patience, man—if aince ma time was oot, if I dinna send ye in twa o' the fattest hares that Libberton Muir can turn oot, ma name's no Bob Whiteley." And the Carnwath men are men of their word, " men with opinions and a will," ready to uphold the honour of Carnwath toun.

The favourite " howffs " in the old village of long ago, where the weavers and local worthies foregathered in the evenings, were John Copland's shop and Morris's Smiddy. Here were held debates and discussions on every conceivable topic—

> " For a' that has been in this world they ken,
> A' that has been prentit, or written wi' pen;
> Frae the heaven aboon to earth's centre they're ready
> To explain every mystery in Morris's Smiddy."

The Hills of Home

Continuing our circle round the hills, we leave Carn-wath, and in the next two and a half miles to NEWBIGGING pass the hamlet of Kaimend, and the slow-moving Medwin making for the Clyde. On the one hand are views of the grassy slopes of towering Tinto and Upper Clydesdale, and on the other the sloping moorlands leading up to the out-lying spurs of the Pentlands, a district steeped in historical and traditionary lore of the Scottish Covenanters.

NEWBIGGING—pronounced locally " Neebicken "—has a fine specimen of a Scottish Market Cross, which is the subject of much good-natured disputation in the country-side, seeing that it is claimed not only by the Neebicken folk but also by the inhabitants of Dolphinton, Dunsyre, and Skirling. At one of these discussions among some of the local farming community I was informed that this was the original Market Cross of Dolphinton, and that when the markets were removed to Dunsyre the Cross followed, and was placed on the market ground at Burn-grange, now moorland, north of Weston Farm, where there was once a village of considerable size. In course of time the market or fairs at Skirling, which were instituted in 1592 and continued to be held for two hundred years—the Skirling September Fair being revived in 1925—came to be more important than those of Dunsyre, and it was deemed fitting that the Cross should follow the markets and be taken to Skirling. All went well with the convoy carrying the Cross till they came to Newbigging, when a violent snowstorm came on, farther progress was impossible, and the Cross was left there for a time until the roads were opened again. On returning to Newbigging the Skirling men found the weavers turned out in force to dispute pos-session, and the Skirling valiants " feught " the Newbigging weavers for it; but the weavers prevailed, and there it remains until this day, still a subject of banter and con-troversy. No doubt the natives of Dolphinton, Dunsyre, and Skirling now all agree that the ancient Cross standing upon a knoll in the centre of the village green still serves a good purpose in adorning this little clachan, which, although it now holds but a handful of folks, was once a hive of industry, inhabited solely by handloom weavers to the number of nearly five hundred. At one time this Cross must have been an ornate piece of workmanship. Six ascending steps and a large square stone form an appropriate base. The shaft and the head are of one stone. The shaft is square and the head is flattened out into eight foliated projections, a mediæval form of the true Cross, bearing in the centre a lozenge-shaped panel containing a Latin cross, while in each of its spandrils is carved a circular ornament. But time's effacing fingers have robbed it of much of its beauty. The whole story of the Cross has not yet, however, been told. The evidence of Carnwath must still be heard. On the back of the Cross is cut the date 1693 and the initials G. L.—presumably George Lockhart; and the Carnwath folks will tell you that this is the original Newbigging Cross erected by Sir Gaulter (Somerville) of Newbigging in the thirteenth century, and referred to by Lord Somerville, the author of *The Memorie,* in 1679, as having " neither letters nor other armes " upon it, and differing from the original Carnwath Cross in this respect. They admit that the Cross was lost for a time, and was afterwards found near Dolphinton, and restored to Newbigging, when the date and initials were inscribed upon it. If the date 1693 is the authentic date of the Cross, the Cross must have been copied from an older model, as the design is of earlier date than the seventeenth century. Whatever wanderings it may have had, it is not improbable that this is the original Cross of Newbigging of the thirteenth century.

Our next village, DUNSYRE, is one of the most delectable places around the hills. The motorist may elect to go to Dolphinton by Elsrickle, and in so doing will join the Biggar Road at Melbourne, where there was once a toll-house and inn, but Dunsyre should not be missed. Set upon the hillside with its ancient church overlooking the valley, the village is not only beautiful for situation, but in its picturesque surroundings and bracing Pentland air, the visitor and the walker may here enjoy many a pleasant ramble over the moorlands or by the banks of the Medwin and West Water. Here too the eager lover of the hills may climb the heathery heights and tramp along the tops to Edinburgh five and twenty miles away, and enjoy the solitude of the lonely hills to his heart's content, or if that be too far, then with the aid of a map he will lay his course for West Linton or Carlops, where lone enthusiasts and seekers after the romantic life of the countryside are wont to descend to take their ease at the inn. A long summer day in June may be spent very delightfully by taking the morning train to Carnwath, and walking from there to Dunsyre, and by the course of the West Water, the Covenanter's Grave, Craigengar, the Cairns, and the Kips, traverse the hills from end to end.

Dunsyre, as its name " Dun seer "—the hill of the prophet—would seem to signify, was for centuries a religious centre. The present Church is supposed to stand upon the site of a Druidical Temple, and between 1180 and 1199 the living and Church were gifted to the Abbot and Convent of Kelso. In 1601 began the Protestant succession of Ministers of Dunsyre under Robert Somervaille, and the gravestone of William Somervell, the third in succession, who died in 1646, is in the churchyard. In 1750 the Church was a thatched building, and six years later the manse was built. The district was a meeting-place of the Covenanters, and many conventicles were held in the cleuchs among the Pentlands above Dunsyre. Major Learmonth, who led the Covenanters' horsemen at Rullion Green, died at Newholm near-by in 1693, at the age of eighty-eight, and was buried in Dolphinton church-yard, of which Church he was an elder. There was a secret passage to his house from the banks of the Medwin, through which persecuted preachers might escape to a room sunk underground outside Newholm House. Four times

31

was Learmonth's servant led out blindfolded to be shot, but refused to tell the secret of how his master eluded his pursuers by lifting a flagstone guarding the entrance to this passage under the overhanging banks of the river, and escaping to the concealed room. The chimney of the fireplace in this secret room was connected with the fireplace in the hall of Newholm House.

The Rev. Donald Cargill preached his last sermon on the common of Dunsyre, and was afterwards apprehended at Covington Mill by Irving of Bonshaw, being led through the streets of Lanark on horseback, his back to the horse's head, and his feet tied below its belly, then taken to Edinburgh, and hanged in the Grassmarket in 1681.

William Veitch, another noted Covenanter, who afterwards became a Parish Minister in Peebles and Dumfries, was tenant in Westhills, and when efforts were being made to capture him he found refuge in the hills, and along with Colonel Wallace sought shelter in a barn in Dunsyre, within a mile of his own dwelling. Veitch was so disguised that when the Dragoons were searching Anston House for him, he was actually holding the reins of their horses. He assisted the Earl of Argyle to escape. The Earl was dressed as a servant to Veitch, and when they were travelling in England Veitch read an advertisement and said, " Here's a fine prize for us, man, if we could get a haud o' Argyle; there's £500 offered to anyone who will give information where he is to be found." Veitch was eventually captured, and was ably defended in court against the Scottish Government in the last days of the persecution, by Sir Gilbert Elliot, afterwards Lord Minto, and obtained his freedom. The story is told of how Veitch and Lord Minto met in Dumfries many years after the latter had obtained recognition of his able advocacy on behalf of the former, and the subject was playfully recalled —" Had it no been for me, my Lord," said Veitch, " ye'd been writing papers yet at a plack a page "; " And had it no been for *me,* Willie," retorted Lord Minto, " the pyets wad hae pyked your pow on the Netherbow Port."

Even the wells in the district have their religious nomenclature, one on Anston Farm being consecrated to St Bride, while another on the Glebe is called the Curate's Well, said to have got its name from the before-mentioned William Somervell, who in defence of his life took to the hills, and lived near this spring. Another flows out of the rock face of Dunsyre Hill.

There are also records of the thumbkins and the boots for torture which were kept in the Tower of the Castle, which stood in the green haugh below the railway station, while the " Jougs "—the iron collar by which offenders were tied up outside the Church—may be inspected in the case affixed to the Church wall facing the road. This is one of the few complete specimens now remaining.

No place within the circuit of the hills would be complete without traces of the Romans, and besides Roman relics, which have been found, there is the way by which it is said Agricola's army marched through the Garvald Valley to Cleghorn Camp. And so on through the years pass the generations. A pageant of Dunsyre, presented in its varied settings of scenic beauty, would be of rare historical and educational interest. At one time Dunsyre with the numerous fortalices with which it was guarded, its Castle, Kirk, and Market, must have been a populous place; now there are comparatively few inhabitants: even the blacksmith and the tailor have gone, and while no one remembers an inn, the older natives will tell you of the Smugglers' Cave and Well at Craigengar, and many a " still " that was worked up in the wild fastnesses and cleuchs of the heathery moorland at this end of the Pentland Hills.

But after you have heard all these things, you will find, if you tarry here and visit the silent hills around this little hamlet, that there are other things more real, and more potent in influence, stimulating the imagination, uplifting and purifying the soul—the gradual fading of the summer night along the hills, and the subduing influence of the gloaming to quiet thought and suggestion as the earthly symbols grow shadowy and fade away; the weather-gleam or " wuther-glum "—the clear belt of light that runs along the hill-tops with the dark heaven above and dim heights below—" the highway of the spirit-land that encompasses the solitudes of earth "; the grey dawn struggling up over the hill-tops—" the greyking of the day," as the old Scottish poets had it—with its strange and wondrous beauty, bepraised in a living chorus of a thousand moorland voices—a fleeting vision of the glory of life, spread high in the heavens, pure and unstained by human striving and endeavour—all these things have a strange fascination for him who loves the solitudes of the high places where the spirit yearns for the wisdom that lies beyond in the Great Unknown. And whether it be through the calm of eventide, or the magic gateway of the spirit-land, or the glory of the sunrise that the experience may come, he feels through the silence the high call to adventure " beyond the utmost bounds of human thought." It is for such moments of fleeting vision and imaginative thought, and all that they mean to him, that the walker loves his wanderings among the solitary places of the hills, because they minister to the homing instinct of his spirit.

The way from Dunsyre to DOLPHINTON is by a winding leafy road through Newholm Estate, and, ascending to the farm of Croft-an-righ—the King's Croft—from which one of the finest views of this side of the Pentland Hills is obtained, we thereafter descend to meet the Biggar Road, at the Parish Church and School of Dolphinton. At the corner of the road stands an old plane-tree that was brought as a sapling from Craigmillar, and planted there in the year of the 'Forty-five.

The walker who prefers to keep far from the highway will take the farm track from Dunsyre by the Medwin Water to Garvald and Fernyhaugh, where he finds direc-

34

tion by the fir woods and the valley to North Slipperfield and West Linton. This countryside, where the Pentland Hills and moors and waters are still unspoiled and little known, is a walker's paradise.

There was a great desire to get the railway through the parish of Dolphinton once upon a time, and the local worthy after attending a meeting rejoiced that he had " done what the Romans found very hard to do, he had beaten the Caledonians!" This had reference to the seventeen years' controversy in the course of which there were discussions for railways from Carnwath to West Linton; Leadburn to West Linton; Leadburn to Carstairs by Linton, Dolphinton, Dunsyre, and Newbigging, the last to cost seventy thousand pounds. Finally it was agreed that a new Company with a capital of forty thousand pounds should construct a line from Leadburn to Dolphinton by Linton, to be known as " The Leadburn, Linton, and Dolphinton Railway Company." This was in 1862. But all did not go smoothly—the " Caledonians " threatened objection, then withdrew their opposition, and later built their own line of eleven miles from Carstairs, so that to-day there are two terminal stations that sit glowering at each other in this rural countryside, while motors with a seeming note of triumph over both the Caledonians and the North Britons salute the stations with a hoot of the horn, as they turn the leafy bend of the road, and cross the bridge, on each side of which the stations lie beaking in the summer sunshine and the still air.

Sir Archibald Geikie, the famous geologist, in *Scottish Reminiscences,* tells the story that after spending a day upon the Pentlands he made his way to the station, which was solitary as a churchyard, and sitting down in one of the carriages, overheard the engine-driver shout to the guard: " Weel, Jock, hae ye got your passenger in?"

Dolphinton village, with her gardens gaily decked in summer flowers, greets the visitor with a smile. There is a mellowed sweetness in the air, and a sense of comfort and

35

of well-being in this quiet pastoral countryside. Farm names such as Townhead and Townfoot, about three-quarters of a mile from the present village, in the Biggar direction, mark the site of the ancient village, where once there were corn, lint, and waulk mills, although no trace of these is now to be found. The parish also boasted two inns, but these have also disappeared, only the Smiddy remains, situated " ayont the burn "—the Garvald or Garrel, that marks the boundary between Lanarkshire and Peeblesshire.

Long before and after the 'Forty-five the houses in Dolphinton were built of mud and covered with turf, and tenants paid their rent mainly by driving lead to Leith, and purchasing south-country meal at Peebles, and carting it to Carnwath. Later, natives were granted permission to quarry stone and cut timber, free of charge, to build their own houses, which were occupied free of rent, on condition that on the death of the owner the house reverted to the Superior. The estate has been in the possession of the Mackenzie family since 1755. Dolphine, a brother of Coss Patrick, first Earl of Dunbar, acquired the property early in the twelfth century and a dolphine fish is represented in the Arms of the principal heritor.

Dolphinton men have been famed for their strength of arm and length of days, and it needed a robust manhood to cope with the Border raiders and Annandale lifters that scoured the countryside. There was not a revolution in Scottish history but what Dolphinton had its quota engaged in it; and the historian records that " in early times, but a small proportion of our parishioners died in their bed."

The quaint old Parish Kirk is one of the smallest buildings of its kind in Scotland, and as we view it, set upon a green hill and surrounded by grey, lichen-covered tombstones, recumbent and upstanding and set at every kind of angle, we are reminded of the antiquity of this religious house. Early recorded history tells us that in 1253 John de St Andrews was Rector, that in 1296 John Silvester swore allegiance to Edward I., that James Donaldson was ejected for nonconformity to Prelacy in 1663 but was reinstated twenty-five years later, while Alexander Somerville, a man of great influence and power in the parish and Church at large, refused to use the Liturgy, though threatened with imprisonment and ejection. "You have had stirring times in the parish," I remarked to a local antiquarian, as I read the list of ministers who had striven to uphold the Faith; "you have even had a minister who was deposed for profane swearing in 1684." At first he gave signs of great astonishment, then with a twinkle in his honest eyes and a smile on his rosy cheeks, the old man remarked: "Oh, aye, nae doubt, nae doubt, ye see in 1684 sweirin' wad be quite a common thing. An' deed, it's no sae very uncommon yet: I sometimes hear it on the curlin' pownd."

Then he showed me the long flat slab near the Kirk door that marks the grave of Major Learmonth, and a stone of apparently similar antiquity alongside, but no words of the inscription are legible. "I suppose that centuries of wind and weather have worn away the stone and the lettering," I ventured, because one must be very precise and circumspect when making any remark to an antiquarian! "Weel, no' a'thegither: the schoolboys used to jump frae yin stane to the other, and their tackety boots soon made short wark o' a' the inscription."

We then turned to the "Jougs," of which only a few rusty links remain, affixed to the ivy-covered Kirk wall. The Jougs were in frequent use in the district at one time. Session Records make frequent reference to the men and women who were punished in this manner, in consequence of sentence pronounced upon them by the Session in some matter of law and order as then interpreted by the Kirk.

The monument surmounting the conical turf-covered hill —called "Kippit Hill"—near the village post-office is to the memory of Captain Kenneth Mackenzie of Dolphinton, who fell in the Great War. When digging for the foundations of the monument in 1920 a Cist was found, built of four slabs of red sandstone, containing human remains, among which were found fragments of iron, indicating perhaps that the burial belonged to the early Iron Age. Upon examination of the skull a deep gash was found upon one of the cheek-bones, suggesting that the body may have been that of a warrior who had met his death in battle.

As the topmost part of the hill is of a different colour and appearance from the lower part, it is possible that when the warrior was buried the Cist was placed upon the flat top of the hill and the sand heaped up over it, and so completed the cone-shaped top.

How the hill got its name is uncertain, but Sir Archibald Geikie, in the *Scenery of Scotland,* in referring to such sand and gravel mounds or long rampart-like ridges, or " Kames," comments upon the legendary lore to which they have given birth. He writes: " It was a quaint and beautiful superstition that peopled such verdurous hillocks or ' tomans ' with shadowy forms, like diminutive mortals, clad in green silk, or in russet grey, whose unearthly music came faintly sounding from underneath the sod. The mounds rose so conspicuously from the ground, and whether in summer heat or winter frost, wore ever an aspect so smooth and green, that they seem to have been raised by no natural power, but to be in very truth the work of elfin hands, designed at once to mark and guard the entrance to the fairy world below. The hapless wight who, lured by their soft verdure, stretched himself to sleep on their slopes, sank gently into their depths, and after a seven years' servitude in fairyland awoke again on the self-samespot." Like Young Tamlane:

> " The Queen of Faeries keppit him
> In yon green hill to dwell.

The lands surrounding the Kippit or " Keppit " Hill were anciently called the " Kippit lands."

Names such as " Sandy Hill Nick " and " Nick's Plantation " occur around the " nick " or valley through the sandy ridge not far from the Kippit Hill, at the Dolphinton end of the old road to Linton, and Michael Scott—" Auld Michael," the famous warlock—is said to have dug the trench there, and piled up the Kippit Hill in a single night. Another local tradition is that Old Nick, standing on the site of the hill, riddled the sand and rocks which were thrown into his " sieve " from the sandy knolls on Ingraston Hill opposite, and threw the rocks into Biggar Moss, seven miles away, while the sand that fell through the sieve formed the Kippit Hill, or, as it is termed locally, " The De'il's Riddlin's."

" The ' Kames ' are connected in some way with the action of ice," says Sir Archibald, " and seem to point to abundant streams of running water from the rapid melting of snow and ice."

Among the many ancient relics that have been found in the countryside are stone and flint implements, a stone axe, arrow-heads, dagger blades, knives and saws, a brass sword or poniard, and a torc or collar, with forty star-marked gold pellets, believed to have been used as money by the early Scots, while in one of the three cairns on the west side of Mendick Hill an earthen urn with human remains was found.

3. THE HIGH ROAD TO LINTON AND THE CARLOPS

West Linton or Linton Roderick, and the Brig'us Inn

There is always a singular joy in reading the words " Old Road " on a map. Let all walkers and lovers of the hills look up their " Bartholomew " for the section of the OLD BIGGAR ROAD from Dolphinton to the Carlops, because to all Pentland enthusiasts there is awaiting a discovery that will bring to them, if not the finest walk in the Pentlands, the finest bit of " Old Road " round the hills. Moreover it is a road reserved for them alone. There is no dust there, neither fumes nor petrol smell.

It begins at a point west of the railway stations. Here we will find a cart track that crosses the railway lines and winds up past a cottage and some sandy knolls, through " Sandy Hill Nick " and " Nick's Plantation," and continues along the hillside overlooking Slipperfield Loch.

This " Old Road " forms the *via media* between the " hard " road and the hill track. It passes by springs and scented pine woods, Mendick Hill keeps guard over it, and it seldom dips below the thousand-feet contour line. There are five-barred gates to be opened and shut, but for the most part it is open and unfenced. How carefully the true hill-walker opens and shuts these gates. It somehow begets in him a sense of possession, although in reality it is his care for other folk's property in return for the privileges he enjoys out of their good pleasure and goodness of heart that moves him.

Moreover this road is the original " High Road to Linton," the road of the tune that every fiddler knows. In the days when there was more fiddle-playing among the country folks than now, all this district along the hill foots was famous not only for experts in playing, but experts in making fiddles and composing tunes, and the well-known air, " The High Road to Linton," was composed by Dickson of Medwinbank, of which family of millwrights and joiners several generations have lived in the house adjoining Fernyhaugh. Medwinbank at one time was an industrious clachan of spinners and weavers, dyers, dressers, joiners, and wheelwrights. Many a farmhouse and cottage in the district has furniture made at Medwinbank, and cart wheels made there sixty years ago are still in daily use. The test of a well-fashioned chair was to throw it out of the window of the upper storey of the workshop, and if it stood the test, it was passed as fit for use. These were days when a workman was proud of his work, and was satisfied with nothing but the best, whether in making chairs or making fiddles.

I shall never forget the first time I explored this road,

one afternoon in early spring. It seemed as if I had found a new friend, or an old friend in a new place, and the beauty and softness of the surrounding landscape, the hills, woods, and fields, were fitting company for the wanderer upon the unknown road. There was no mystery about this attractive, grass-grown road, no doubting as to whether it would forsake one like many a hill road that starts so bravely. The Turnpike Act of 1753 specially referred to this highway as " the road from Ingraston through Carlops, where it entered Midlothian "; and I grudged every mile I put behind me, there were then so many less to travel. Even upon one's first acquaintance with it, the interest of the Old Road brought immediately a feeling of companionship, more than any other of the old roads in the hills; and one did not wish to hurry, but rather to saunter and enjoy its company, for it has a fascinating history as well as personality and charm. This was the old coach road to Biggar and the South, a relic of the travelling days of centuries ago, and into its life Nature and Romance have woven their spell.

The March wind was blowing in from the ocean, pure and cold and clean, and every cloud was swept from the sky, leaving the sapphire blue clear and translucent. It was a day for brisk movement, however much one wished to linger. Winter alternated with spring. Half an hour ago the wind blew up a hail shower that whitened the ground for half a minute. Then the sun struck out with sudden warmth and genial splendour, and all the neighbouring hills and fields were sparkling as they do in sunny spring-time after rain. How glad it made one feel.

Two pairs of horses are working in the field below. I can hear the ploughman's conversation with his team, and the horses like his company and understand all he says, for I hear them hinny their reply. The fields are full of life and movement. The starling flock keep much by themselves; the gregarious rooks are there; and Jim Crow strutting so pompously, looks admiringly at his two black feet, expands his breast, nods his head, and shows how he loves his independence. But the best sight of all is the smart little wagtails, tripping so excitedly, and yet seeming at times to remind themselves that they must maintain a proper dignity among the other birds. The curlews too are calling as they swoop and wheel back and forward between the field and hillsides, and high up in the sunshine a sky-lark pours forth his silvery notes, brilliant as the sunlight upon the snow.

When the air is clear and vibrant in the spring-time, the hillsides and the heavens above seem to echo back to earth the calling and the singing of the birds. So joyously insistent are they, so spontaneous, as they company with the ploughman and his team, that they form a unity that puts love at the heart-strings, like the calling of spring itself.

The hill road that takes one to the open door at the back of an old farm-house, far from other habitations, is one of the joys of walking; but when in passing the farm there comes the fragrant odour of the blue peat-reek, ah! there is no hurrying past. I retraced my steps so that I might catch it again, for it is sweeter and more subtle than any other scent to those who know it well. It is powerful to awaken memories, and there arose before me visions of sea-girt Islands in the West in the still glow of evening sunshine, and grey sequestered homesteads in the North, bielded by the purple hills and waving pines and the warm hearts of Highland folk. There was no resisting the open door after that, and the good woman gave me just such a welcome as one would expect. Yes, they burned peat, and she showed me where they cut it " before the May term," and where they stacked it, and understanding my silent appreciation of the view from where we stood, she completed the picture by telling me, " Aye, it's a bonnie place, a bonnie place on a simmer mornin'; it's ca'd ' Hargitheid,' has been ca'd that since the days o' Queen Elizabeth; it will be on your map," and so it was—" Hardgatehead."

I mean to see it on a summer morning! Then the significance of the farm name dawned upon me—Hardgitheid—the heid o' a hard gait, marking the top of a stiff road, from Dolphinton on the one side and Slipperfield on the other.

And so continuing my journey, thinking of Queen Elizabeth, I had not gone far when I came to a stone bridge crossing the West Water that came tumbling down foam-flecked from the hills, and lo! the date upon it was 1620! Here was something for the lover of old romance! "Since the days o' Queen Elizabeth," I kept repeating to myself. "In such matters," said a voice, "tradition is seldom altogether groundless."

That this old road was in existence long before 1620 there is ample evidence. In the twelfth century the lands of Slipperfield were bestowed upon the Augustinian monks of Holyrood, and part of the boundary of the lands was marked by a Cross that stood beside the West Water—then called the Pollentarf—at the very point of the highroad where the bridge crosses the stream. The ford over the Lyne was then called "Biggeresford," and Mendick Hill was "Menedict" and "Mynidicht."

There are lands to-day in Linton called Chapelhill, and it was probably to the Chapel of St Mary, dedicated to the Virgin, that the lands of Ingolistun were given between the years 1233 and 1249 to maintain three chaplains to say Mass daily.

The road was also known to Warriors of old, and to none better than to William of Douglas, son of Sir James Douglas of Lothian, the valiant "Knight of Liddesdale," who with his galloping horsemen engaged in many a skirmish around these foothills in the days of the English invasions. He was the owner of lands in West Linton, named in the Charter confirmed by King David II.—"Lintonrothirrikis," for which he paid a rent of a silver penny in the Parish Kirk at the Feast of the Nativity, and for his "faithful service and help rendered" he obtained from the Lord of Dalkeith a grant of the neighbouring lands of Newlands and the Barony of Kilbucho.

There is no mention of Hardgatehead in these far-off days, but it is not improbable that the farm existed " in the days o' Queen Elizabeth," who began to reign in 1558 and died in 1603. In 1585, however, after the Raid of Ruthven, this district was the headquarters of the Rebel Lords, and in West Linton they vowed that never would they separate until the King (James VI) should receive them into favour, declaring their enterprise to be " The defence of the truth, the deliverance of the King from corrupt counsellors, and the preserving of amity with England." With an army of several thousands of horse-men they advanced across the hills by the Cauldstaneslap to Falkirk, and ordering themselves in battle array at the Church of St Ninians, they entered Stirling with little resistance, where, as narrated in Spottiswoode's *History of the Church of Scotland,* book vi., " the borderers according to their custom, fell upon the stables and made prey of all the gentlemen's horses, whereof they found good store." The King received the banished lords, acceded to their requests, granted to them his pardon, and thus was the Linton plot entirely successful.

The commotion caused by the gathering of the Rebel Lords, and the mustering of their forces for the national issues which were at stake in these troublous times, may account for the tradition at Hardgatehead of its connection with " the days o' Queen Elizabeth."

Mary Queen of Scots and Darnley her husband, with an army, passed along this road on 8th October, 1565.

On the first of that month she issued a Summons, which is preserved in the British Museum, with the signatures " Mari R " and " Henry R," addressed to certain noble-men, to attend a General Assembly of the Scottish army at Lamington, where they were to join the army marching from Biggar to the South, to engage the Rebel Lords of her day, styled the Lords of the Congregation, who on the occasion of the Queen's marriage with Darnley viewed with special dislike her husband's adherence to the Roman faith, and broke out in rebellion against her.

Queen Mary and her husband travelled from Edinburgh to Biggar, where she had summoned her faithful subjects to assemble.

Two days later, at the head of her army, whose main body was commanded by Lord Darnley, supported by the Earls of Bothwell, Morton, and Mar, she entered Dumfries by way of Coulter and Lamington; but the rebels had fled, so the army was disbanded, and she returned to Edinburgh by Moffat, Tweedsmuir and Peebles.

The Chronicler of the *Diurnal of Remarkable Occurrents,* referring to the 8th of October, says: " Upon the samen day our souranis with thair army depairtit of Edinburgh towart Biggar," and the appearance of the Queen as she passed along this ancient highway by Hardgatehead, we are told, was decidedly warlike. She rode a stately charger, and had a pair of pistols stuck in the holsters at her saddle bows; and it is said her scarlet and embroidered riding-dress covered a suit of defensive armour, and that under her hood and veil she wore a steel casque, while Darnley wore a suit of gilt armour.

A gay and stately pageant it must have been, with all the glamour and romance of newly wedded love and chivalry. Amidst the artistic setting of the Pentland Hills we see the Royal cavalcade decked in the shining accoutrements of war, accompanied by their escort of horsemen with bright pennons flying, following the undulations of the highway winding round the hillside. They cross the Lyne at Biggeresford, pass the Cross on the banks of the Pollentarf at Slipperfield, and move on to the farm of Hardgatehead. Did they pause to look across the strath, one wonders, with the rolling landscape stretching away to the farther hills and down to the vale of Biggar, and did the October sunshine fill the land that was mellowed in the hues of autumn? Or as they passed under the shadow of the Hill of Menedict were the royal hearts filled with fear? It is hardly likely: love then was young, and a loyal welcome awaited them at Biggar, such as they had never before experienced, from the most gallant array of Scottish chivalry ever witnessed there, an army of 18,000, including nobles, barons, knights and retainers from every part of the Kingdom, ready to fight for their Queen and her cause.

After crossing the ancient bridge, which was restored in 1892, we continue along the Old Road and come in sight of the West Linton Golf Course. Near the right-of-way post directing the wayfarer " To Auchengray and Dunsyre " are the ruins of stables of the old stage-coach days that adjoined the famous Bridgehouse (Brig'us) Inn, part of which is now incorporated in Medwin House.

It was toward evening as I crossed the valley of the Lyne and climbed the hilly road in view of Stoneypath on the way to Carlops. The sun had gone down behind the hills; Mendick and King's Seat and the lesser heights were suffused in the faint pink afterglow, purple mists were filling up the distant valleys, and heaven's fairest star suddenly twinkled and rose, sending a throb of life and action into the very heart of the silence. The evening hush lay over all the changing landscape. In the foreground the Lyne appeared as a silver streak coming down from the hills in a gorge that is wide and deep. On the left a line of wind-swept scraggy pines stretched across the moorland, and the nearer plough-lands, edged with grass and laced with silver, glowed richly brown and velvety, while the silence was made musical in the tiny note of a falling rill singing in the treble clef to the deeper notes of the Lyne in the distance. The voice of the waters in tone and undertone rose as an evening thanksgiving.

In the wood between Stoneypath and Linton above the old Inn there is a place called " The Siller Holes," because it is the traditional site of silver-mines, but nature has changed the aspect and covered the remaining vestiges of the old-time workings; the hollows always remind me of

" Dingle Dell," and I fancy I see the ashes of the camp fires of gipsy occupants.

As I pursued my way towards the summit of the road that rises to a thousand feet above sea-level, the silence grew intense, the cadence of the river grew fainter the farther one left it behind, then the long panorama of the Pentland peaks came into view—the Scald Hill, the Black Hill, Monks Rig, and Paties Hill looking strangely high and dark against the deep blue evening sky; but the landscape was continually changing its hue with the approach of dusk. All the birds had gone to rest: no! there goes a bloodthirsty " hoodie "—this bird has few friends, he is the grouse's worst enemy, and has betrayed at some time most of the other birds; no one speaks well of " the hoodie crow."

But after all the other birds have gone to rest the peewits are calling eerily across the fields, and the musical whirr of their wings comes from the solitude of the Windy Gowl.

Now we are at Fairslacks, another reminder of the stage-coach days. Here stood a blacksmith's shop at the road-side, which was a regular stopping-place of the stage, and as the driver got down from his seat and made inquiry of the smith as to how things were going he invariably got the same reply— " Things are fair slack, fair slack," and the blacksmith's nickname became the name of the farm. The neighbouring cottages of Waterloo and Trafalgar were named after these historical events; the croft of Waterloo, of which no trace now remains, was owned by James Knox, a Waterloo veteran, while a son-in-law of an adjoining crofter took part in the Battle of Trafalgar.

The name of the last cottage on the Old Road before it joins the present highway and enters Carlops has remained unchanged since it was built in 1808. The first tenant, who was a shepherd employed by the Carlops laird, was named Hart, and as the cottage stood on Hart's side of the road, the dwellings came to be known as " Hartside." It is a picturesque, red-tiled cottage, embowered in roses and honeysuckle, forming a striking note of colour against the dark background of fir-trees, and catching the eye of every traveller approaching the Carlops from Linton. It has a local interest in that it was the residence of the last Carlops weaver, while beside the weaver's cottage stood the Carlops Smiddy; but from this village, as from almost every other village around the hills, the weavers and the blacksmiths have all passed away, leaving but a memory of picturesque callings enshrined in a halo of honest work that redounded to the credit of the countryside.

WEST LINTON has attractions that appeal to the nature lover and the walker, and all in search of an interesting rural countryside with a fresh and bracing atmosphere.

Sheltered from the north by woodlands and the sloping foot-hills of the Pentland range, with the Lyne tumbling through a picturesque ravine, and flowing through the village, it forms a centre with a varied choice of old highways and by-ways leading over hills and moors and valleys, and after the day has been spent in the open uplands there is always the hospitable little village to return to in the evening, with peace and quiet brooding over it, undisturbed by train and little traffic.

One does not require to walk far to experience either the far view or the sylvan beauty of wood and stream. The Golf Course is reached by an avenue of pine, beech, maple, and lime, and the road to Baddinsgill continues into the open heathery moorland up among the Pentland heights.

As we approach Baddinsgill Farm a post directs the way " To Carlops by Stoneypath," and the route may be varied by going through the Windy Gowl. The track takes us over the Lyne by a wooden bridge, and along the opposite hillside, from which extensive views of the hills are obtained, till we come to Stoneypath Farm, near which we join the old turnpike road, and return to West Linton (5¾ miles). A long summer's day will appear all too short in which to enjoy the full delight of this interesting ramble.

The Old Biggar Road and Mendick

Many lovers of woodland scenery love to wander along the banks of the Lyne by the winding pathway known as " The Cat's Walk," and to linger around the old picturesque bridge over the river where it comes rushing through the wooded ravine at Lynedale. Here we are upon the romantic coach road, and imagine we hear the notes of the horn echoing among the hills and woods as the coach rolls down the incline, over the bridge, and swings round the corner and up the hill to the old " Brig'us."

Fine views of the Pentland peaks are to be obtained from Harlaw Muir, and there is a pleasant five-and-a-half-miles walk from Linton by the Deanfoot Road leading into the moorland, in the course of which we traverse the lands of Whitfield. In a Charter of these lands, granted by King Robert I. on 23rd September 1313, the name is spelt " Quyfeld," and in 1378 it is referred to as " Quhite-feilde in the Barony of Lyntonrothrike."

Passing by South Mains Farm and Rutherford we reach the Carlops-Linton road, and return to our village by the most picturesque approach. Just as Linton village comes into view there is one of the finest prospects in the district. We look across the most level farm lands in Peeblesshire, to Linton in the foreground outlined against the trees and hills, and to the farther hills beyond Romanno and the Moorfoots and the higher peaks beyond the Tweed; and whether it be in spring or summer, or on a still afternoon in autumn as daylight merges into twilight and the rim of the distant hills is lit by the sunset glow, or when the hills have a mantle of snow, the view of the village from this point and the colour harmonies of the landscape seldom fail to appeal to all lovers of natural scenery.

Romanno Bridge may be visited by the road leaving West Linton, crossing the Lyne near the toll-house, and after a walk of three miles we join the road to Romanno. Returning by Stoneyknowe—a pleasant wooded way—our round extends to six and a half miles.

Within this circle there are the Temple lands, on the Lyne, half a mile below the village, where stone coffins have been found, Spitalhaugh, Chapelhill, and Paul's Well, grouping together memories of the Templars, an ancient Hospitium or hospital, a Chapel, and a Holy Well under Apostolic invocation.

Romanno took its name from a family of that name which became extinct in the sixteenth century. The ancient family of Pennecuik, on the other hand, took its name from the estate.

There are many other picturesque and shaded walks among the woods and by the streams, and all the joys of the Old Drove Road over the hills, and the old stage-coach turnpike to Dolphinton, while light motor-buses afford facilities for reaching Carlops, " Habbies Howe," and the scenes of *The Gentle Shepherd;* Ninemileburn and the site of " Robin Tamson's Smiddy "; Peebles and Biggar, Lanark and the Falls of Clyde.

There may often be much virtue in a name, and grace might be added to virtue, and to the many charms and attractions of this village, if the prosaic postal nomenclature of " West Linton " were dropped, and the village called by its ancient name of LINTON RODERICK.

Moreover it is meet that the inhabitants be proud of of Roderick, for he was a Christian King of Strathclyde—Rydderich Hael (Roderick the Liberal), a leal supporter of Kentigern, commonly called St Mungo, the first Bishop of Glasgow. He first appears in history in 573, when he defeated the forces of paganism on the plains of Liddesdale, and established Christianity in the Borderland. He identified himself with the town on the Lyne, which became known as Linton Roderick, and the lands of the principality are so described in the earliest Registers and Chartularies.

In a field near Yarrow Kirk stands one of the oldest Christian monuments in Scotland—that to two young Princes, Cetilous and Nennus—the sons of King Roderick, slain in battle between the Angles and the Britons.

Roderick died in 603, the same year as St Mungo and Merlin; regarding the latter's fate the simple tradition of Tweedside is " that he lies with Arthur and his Knights in the enchanted halls under the purple Eildons, in a sleep that shall never be broken until the mythic sword be drawn and the mysterious bugle sounded."

The Church of Lyntunruderic—the name is spelt in a variety of ways—was conveyed in 1160 (557 years after the death of King Roderick) to the Church of St Marie of Kelso and the monks serving there, and the benefice remained with the Monastery until the Reformation in 1560. In a Charter of the land granted by King Robert the Bruce on 8th March 1315 the name of the town is Lyntounrothryk.

In view of the associations attaching to the name of Roderick, and of the services rendered to the religious faith of our land by him, this historic Pentland village, which has had an intimate connection with nearly every phase of our age-long religious struggle, would do honour to itself, and render a service to posterity, by taking steps to return to its ancient heritage, and claim once again the name of LINTON RODERICK.

Loyalty to religious conviction has been a noted characteristic of the natives of this hillside parish from early times. Riotous scenes were witnessed here in 1731, when a company of military were held in readiness to protect the Presbytery, on the occasion of the enforced settlement of the Reverend Thomas Findlater. The result was a secession from the Parish Kirk of a body of its members. West Linton was one of the first places in the South of Scotland where a congregation of Seceders was publicly recognised by the Secession Fathers. For long the local body had no sure abiding-place, and met on the slopes of the hills, by the banks of the Lyne and the Pollentarf, in deserted shielings, and in weavers' cottages.

The Lairds of Linton, presided over by a Bailie, managed the local affairs such as boundaries, herding of cattle and geese, and hiring of horses. An old manuscript (1678-81) in Peebles Museum, entitled, " Acts of Neighbourhood of the Town of Lintoun," refers to this governing body, among which it is ordained " That for avoiding of confusion, no man shall speak in the Court, without he be required, under pain of being fined as the Bailie shall think fit," and " That every man that curses and swears in tyme of Court is lyabell to pay sixpens."

Much of the life and merriment of the countryside is reflected in the poems of Alexander Pennecuik (1652-1722), a celebrated local doctor, who resided at Romanno House. In the notes to his *Description of Tweeddale* (1715) we learn that the pride and poverty of the Linton Lairds of the time was a standing joke in the countryside, and fifteen of the forty-five were " on the box "—got assistance from the Poor's Fund. One of the Lairds is mentioned oftener by name than any of the others—this is Gifford, the spelling of whose name takes diverse forms, even when written by himself. He was a mason and stone-carver in the old village, the houses of which were built in the Danish fashion, with their gables to the street and having narrow closes or lanes between them. He is frequently referred to by R. D. C. Brown, the Laird of Newhall, in the Notes to his edition of Ramsay's *The Gentle Shepherd,* as well as in Dr Pennecuik's Works. In Captain Armstrong's *Companion to the Map of Tweeddale,* published in 1775, sixty years after Pennecuik's Works, we learn that " The Cross " of West Linton, " now decayed, is a lively specimen of natural genius, without the assistance of art, being the entire labour of one Giffard, a small feu-proprietor in Linton, which he erected in 1666, at his sole expence, to perpetuate the memory of his beloved wife and five children. She is represented in a devout posture, on a pedestal, supported with four infants, and a fifth on her head."

There is a tradition that the Linton Laird erected the monument with its effigy of Mrs Giffard and a child at each of the four corners, in the belief that his family group was complete, but a fifth child was subsequenutly born. What was to be done! All the available space was already occupied, his rejoicing was tempered with inward distress: surely the belated infant had right to a place, and so, " after much profound deliberation, and research for a proper stand, every difficulty was at length happily reconciled, and brought to an amicable settlement," continues the Newhall Laird. " by placing the sculptured figure of this new production on its mother's head! from whence, with perfect and sublime regularity, it rose from the centre, towering over, and crowning .the ' lively ' fabric, in evidence of its father's ingenuity, as if, like a little Minerva, it had just sprung from her brain."

One by one the figures fell and disappeared, and in Chambers's *History of Peeblesshire* there is an illustration of " the Lady Gifford Well, erected 1666, renewed 1861," surmounted by the lone figure of " Lady Gifford."

And even now she may be seen, for the effigy has been placed in a niche in the Clock Tower that has been built upon the old village well. There she stands—Laird Giffard's " beloved wife "—between two lamps fixed to the tower, with her arms raised from the elbow, and her hands joined before her breast, " decked out in all the finery of a duchess of the seventeenth century."

One of the figures of the children finds a resting-place in Spitalhaugh House, where there is also a carved and decorated stone fireplace by Gifford. Other specimens of his work are built into the wall of a modern cottage, almost adjoining the village post-office, occupying the site of his thatched cottage that stood until 1864.

Here we can see busts of " James Gifferd and Ewpham Veatch," and other sculptured figures and symbolic decorations, with the inscription, now becoming much defaced, " The first man is I. G. Brother of Shirefhall 1445 " (he was brother to the Laird of Sheriffhall, near Dalkeith, and West Linton was at one time a pendicle of that town),

53

" Six Progenetors of James Geferd w(ith) His awne Portract and Eldest Sone." " Wrought by me James Geferd, Architector, ye 7th May 1660." A sundial supported by four carved figures, in the gardens of Newhall House, is also attributed to him.

This interesting laird, who has left so many memorials of himself in and around the countryside, was a prominent member of " The Jovial Smith of Linton's Club," an elder in the Parish Church, and a member of the kirk-session that summoned the Earl of Queensberry and Lord Linton before them for remaining in the Brig'us Inn and being absent from the Kirk on the Lord's Day. The former pleaded that he had been " under physic " for eight days before in Edinburgh, and that after riding out to West Linton on the Saturday, he was unable to rise out of bed before twelve o'clock next day, and at the afternoon sermon which he attended he was unable to remain above a quarter of an hour; while the latter said he was taken ill after the morning service, and that he had thereafter drunk three chopins of wine, which he did not consider scandalous, " considering the number of persons who were in company at the time." They were both visited by the minister, and admonished by the session, being told to " beware of giving scandal, and to study to walk close with God."

Shortly thereafter, the Earl of Traquair, an elder of the session, was summoned for " scandalous drinking " in the Brig'us Inn and Carlippes, but Purdie, the innkeeper of the Brig'us, declared otherwise, and the matter dropped. Three months afterwards the Earl brings a similar charge against William Douglas, Spittalhaugh, and another elder and the session-clerk are forthwith despatched to visit the accused, but they found him a sober man, only he had " ane high totek."

The tide of history both in national and urban affairs touched the town of Linton at many points, and stirring events took place within the barony.

As was natural, the old Brig'us Inn played a not in-consequent part in these matters. Scenes of much bustle and activity were frequently witnessed at the Inn, situated on the stage-coach turnpike between Edinburgh and the South. Writers of those days tell us it was much frequented by travellers. It was on the Cauldstaneslap Road over the hills, and near the famous Markets. In 1660 it belonged to Robert Purdie, " but antiently to the name of Douglass." Early in the nineteenth century it had "lately been repaired," when the adjacent corn-mill was rebuilt, and the Lint-mill for bruising and switching flax was erected—1804. The stone bridge was repaired at the same time as the Linton Kirk and Steeple in 1710. When the new road and the new Inn were built in 1833, the Brig'us Inn became a dwelling-house.

Along this old highway from Edinbrugh, King James IV. rode to Lynton on 21st October, 1490—"efter supper," when the Lord High Treasurer supplied him with funds amounting to twenty unicorns (gold coins of the value of 18s each). We do not know whether he squandered it all at the Brig'us Inn, but on the 30th of the same month a similar sum was sent him at Bygar (Biggar). In conse-quence of his love of music, he had a liking for distributing considerable sums to pipers, fiddlers, and luters, and also to tellers of tales, priests, and poor men; and the tell-tale Treasurer's accounts note that when in Biggar, on 24th February, 1503, 4s was paid " to ane piper and ane fiddler, be the King's command," and on 13th November, 1507, the priests in West Linton were presented with a donation of 20s from His Majesty. Thereafter he rode to Edinburgh by Fairmilehead and the Old Braid Road to St Roque's Chapel, Grange Loan, then part of the Burgh Muir, where he made a further gift of 14s. His Majesty also rode over the Cauldstaneslap on 25th November, 1490, " before day," having " boycht a horss " in Lythgow, for which the Lord High Treasurer's Accounts tell us there was paid the sum of £5 6s 8d. It was the same young and active King who thought nothing of riding out the Linton Road on an October night after supper to make a stay at West Linton, or riding over the Cauldstaneslap from Linlithgow before it was daylight on a November morning, who, the previous year, rode by the Lang Whang from Edinburgh to Carnwath to honour with his presence the " infare " or reception given at Cowthally Castle when Sir John Somerville of Quothquan brought home his bride, Elizabeth Carmichael, and the extraordinary feast was prepared, of which the King declared that he had " never seen the like in any house within the Kingdom." He also originated the " Red-hose race."

In 1745, when vagrant parties from Prince Charlie's army were wandering about the Pentland Hills, the Whig laird of Woodhouselee narrates in his Diary that from his house he saw passing along the highway, Murray of Broughton, the Prince's Secretary, on his way to Linton, along with a companion mounted on the dragoon horse of Colonel Gardiner, who was killed at Prestonpans. The laird knows the purpose of the journey. Broughton's lady, who, he informs us, was a daughter of Colonel Ferguson— " one of the flamingest Williamit Whiges "—was coming into Edinburgh, and, being so imbued with the spirit of the roving Jacobite gangs in the neighbourhood, she does a little plundering on her own account. She learns that the servant of Charles Hope of Craigiehall is at the Brig'us Inn, at West Linton, and forthwith she orders Hope's two horses to be secured in the stable, and the servant searched. Valuable jewels, and £1000 in money and notes, are found upon him, and are seized, and Secretary Murray had come to convoy the treasure from the Brig'us Inn to the city.

The Markets, which were held between the town and the Inn, were the prinicpal sheep markets in Scotland for the Linton breed of " short-bodied, black-faced and legged, horned and coarse-woolled sheep," of which 30,000 were frequently sold at two markets, and thence driven over the Cauldstaneslap to the Highlands and the Ochil Hills.

Originally there were five markets held on succeeding Wednesdays, and a description of these is contained in a poem entitled " Lintoun Green, or the third Market Day of June, 1685," in which the storemasters are referred to as being " as rugged as their rams," and coming " frae heathery hills baith far and near, wi' tups, ewes, hogs and lambs."

There are still a few old inhabitants in the district who have memories of the stage and mail-coach days, when coaches-and-four came rolling along into Linton. Tolls followed one another at West Linton, Carlops, Easter Howgate, Fairmilehead, and Morningside, the toll-money for each machine being fourpence in Mid-Lothian and sixpence in Peeblesshire. Many a stirring tale of heroism and loyalty has been told of those in charge of the mail coach. Would that Dr John Brown had given us more of the stories he used to hear of what the driver could do, and what the guard had done. " Next to preachin' the Everlastin' Gospel I would like to drive the Mail," said the English clergyman as he stood spellbound watching the Carlisle mail thundering down " the Bridges " in Edinburgh. There was some excitement and romance upon the road in those days, as Dickens and Sir Walter have told us; and was it not Mrs Macleuchar in *The Antiquary* who described the " Hawes Fly " or " Queensferry Diligence," as " green picked oot wi' red—three yellow wheels an' a black ane "?

With the coming of the motor, and the disappearance of horses and horse-drawn vehicles from the roads, interesting personalities have also disappeared from our villages and countryside.

This Old Road from Dolphinton to Carlops did not give up its existence as a main highway without a struggle. After much discussion and delay an Act of Parliament authorised the making of the new road, six Linton heritors undertaking to have it constructed at their own risk, on getting an assignation of the four tolls. Begun in 1831, which is the date upon the Bridge over the Lyne, the six

57

miles of road, with a rise of not more than one foot in thirty-seven, was completed two years later, when new inns were opened at Linton and at Rutherford, midway between Linton and Carlops. The latter Inn was much patronised by those who took the waters of the " Heavenly Aqua " Well in the vicinity, to which scientific analysis ascribed the qualities of Tunbridge. How the name of this well originated is unknown, but the waters were celebrated as useful " in restoring relaxed constitutions, in lowness of spirits, and nervous complaints," and were probably administered as such by the Cistercian monks of Newhall. Rutherford House has superseded the Inn—Rutherford Castle Inn, as it is named in the Coach Time-table for 1854.

The Toll system was often inconvenient and troublesome, and sometimes led to cases in Court.

Droves of Highland cattle coming over the Cauldstaneslap, making for the English markets, paid their first toll at Romanno toll-bar, which derived more than half its revenue from this source, but a Toll-bar was erected near West Linton about the time when the new road was in course of construction, to catch these cattle coming over the drove road which from Baddinsgill to West Linton was then being made into a turnpike road. On paying the West Linton Toll the drove was passed free through the Romanno Toll, as double tolls could not be exacted within six miles. The Romanno District felt aggrieved at this loss of revenue, and raised an action to have the West Linton Toll-bar declared illegal, but the action failed on technical grounds.

Another case decided that the tacksmen of Linton Toll-bar charging a toll upon carts carrying oats to be mealed at the mill could not exact a second toll upon their return with the meal.

The idea of a road over the hills in continuation of that to Baddinsgill through the Cauldstaneslap is not a new one. It was advocated by the Rev. Charles Findlater of Newlands in 1802; and the Rev. Alexander Forrester of West Linton.

in the Statistical Account of 1834, writes: " It is obvious that such a measure appears to be equally beneficial to the other side of the Slap, the County of Mid and West Lothian, opening up to them a more ready and direct communication to the south: and as nearly three miles of this road from Linton have already been made it remains with the gentlemen to the north of the Slap to show an equally favourable disposition to the undertaking, and they may be assured that they would be readily met by the heritors of Linton from the south."

It would appear that " the gentlemen to the north of the Slap " were favourably disposed. A tall bridge across the Linhouse Water at Camilty (Midcalder parish) was built about 1830, and there was a design to continue the crossroad at that point over the Cauldstaneslap, but the project was defeated by the Earl of Morton, who objected to such a highway passing through his property, and the road therefore ends at the bridge, which leads out only on to Camilty Moss.

4. THE CARLOPS TO EDINBURGH BY FLOTTERSTANE BRIDGE, GLENCORSE AND SWANSTON

Passing through the village of Carlops, whose story, along with that of Ninemileburn, is treated in another chapter, we continue our journey round the hills. After crossing the Carlops Brig the Old Road is regained by a path through a whinny brake on the left from which we obtain fine views over the Esk Valley to the Girth Hills and Habbies Howe, and up to the towern' taps o' Pentland.

Patie's-hill Farm, Wanton Wa's, Amazondean, and Honeybrae are passed in quick succession, but of the quaint old clachan of Friarstown not a stone remains, and St Robert's Croft by the Monks Burn is the last point of interest before we come to the Inn at Ninemileburn, another haunt of the hungry hillmen. Yet this smiling countryside is full of charm to those who know its history, and with increasing knowledge more closely weaves its spell. Intertwined with the simple pastoral life enshrined in song and story, and the melodious lilt of Scottish reels and festive " kirn," are the glamourous tales of bygone days—of the Carlines' Glen at Carlops, the Fairies' Den at Newhall, and the Mermaid-haunted Loch at Marfield, the romance of the Bower of Mary Crichtoune, and the Castle in the Glen. And away from the coach roads and the highways, and up among the hills and glens are the old roads of drovers and shepherds, monks, moss-troopers, and thieves; and we sense the old-world atmosphere as we pass along the Monks' Way, and hear " the lively knell from 'Spittal of its cheerful Matin bell," or climbing the hill behind the ancient hospice, view the splendours of the Pentland range, and the height that " parleys with the setting sun."

At Walstone Farm there is the choice of two roads to Edinburgh, one by Penicuik, on which we pass the Spear Gate or main entrance to Penicuik House, and note upon the gable wall of the Lodge the arms of the Clerks of Penicuik, showing a huntsman winding a horn and the motto, " Free for a Blast "; while the other, known as the Hill Road, goes by Flotterstane and Hillend, and is the road we travel in completing our circle round the hills.

All lovers of the hills welcome the Scottish Rights of Way Society's guide-posts. They speak of those who have preserved for us, and are still preserving, the old roads and paths across the Scottish hills, a work in which all hill-walkers should be interested. One of these posts stands by the dykeside a short distance from Eightmileburn and Braidwood Farm, pointing the way to Bavelaw and Balerno by Eastside Farm and the Kips. Near this path stood the cottage of Saltersyke, the syke or rill near which the salter or seller of salt lived. He traded through the countryside in this commodity, which was probably purchased at Prestonpans, and upon which, prior to 1823, there was a duty of 15s per bushel, the salt itself being valued at 6d and selling at 4d to 6d per pound. The duty was abolished in 1825. The last inhabitant of Saltersyke was " Ritchie the Carrier," a local worthy.

The next right-of-way post is beyond Silverburn, also directing to Balerno, but this time over the Old Kirk Road by the Grain Burn, the haugh above Loganlee and the Green-cleuch. The hamlet of Silverburn is one of the few places around the hills where the buildings of the red-tiled Smiddy still exist. There is no record of silver having been found here, but up among the hills there once lived in a shack at Fa'laws an old fellow named " Luke Boyle," an Irish drainer and local character, who searched for buried treasure in the shape of a barrel or keg of gold supposed to be buried in the Black Hill!

Between Lawhead and Marchwell Farms there is an interesting by-road to Penicuik through sylvan glades of overarching trees. It crosses the Cuicken Burn and the Loan Burn, and about midway between these streams passes the ruins of Lowrie's Den, and brings us to the Tympany Lodge entrance to the grounds of Penicuik House.

There are several delightful cross-roads and winding country lanes between Flotterstane, Glencorse, and Fisher's Tryst, with wealth of story and tradition surrounding them, which are attractive to all who love the leafy by-ways.

On the west side of Flotterstane Brae there was standing on an eminence in the early part of the nineteenth century the remains of a circle of large stones forty feet in diameter, but the ancient relic was thoughtlessly destroyed and used to build the wall that now runs through the site.

In a wood above a lonely cottage in a field to the westward is the Rullion Green Memorial. The monument was erected mainly through the efforts of a local family named Gill, descendants of a Covenanter, whose son was the first to plough the field after the battle; and Lord President Inglis protected it by having it suitably enclosed.

Sir Walter Scott knew the Biggar Road, Rullion Green,

and the Martyrs' Tomb, and in *Guy Mannering* (chap. xxxvi.) he tells us how the Dominie, having got out of the post-chariot for an instant, saw the Battlefield of Rullion Green, " dear to his Presbyterian predilections," and proceeded to climb the hill to the monument, but on being reminded that the Colonel was waiting for him, exclaimed: " Prodigious! I was oblivious," and retraced his steps. House of Muir Farm adjoining is mentioned in *Old Mortality*.

The House of Muir was noted for the markets held in this district. We read that in 1661 Charles II. confirmed to the town of Edinburgh the privilege of a market at " the House of the Moore within the paroch of Glencorce." The last of these was held about 1871.

The house named " Martyrs' Cross," at the corner of the Bellwood Road, was the old Parish School of Glencorse. In 1859 it was purchased for a dwelling-house, when the name " Martyrs' Cross " was given to it by the proprietor, on account of its proximity to the district associated with the " martyrs " of the Covenanting times, and the fact that there was a cross on the building. The name is therefore a modern one. The endeavour to explain the cross on the building probably led to the idea that the site had some connection with a convent, but no foundation of fact can be traced in this tradition. The cross is an old stone that was found on the ground, and placed in its present prominent position as a means of preserving it.

Behind " Martyrs' Cross " stand the mansion-houses of Bellwood and Mauricewood. The latter was the country house of the late Dr Joseph Bell, Sir A. Conan Doyle's prototype of " Sherlock Holmes." On the road to the Fisher's Tryst by old Glencorse, known to all readers of Stevenson, we pass Glencorse House, built in 1812, and Loganbank, erected two years earlier by the Rev. Dr Inglis (1763-1834), Minister of Old Greyfriars, Edinburgh, and father of the late President Inglis, in whose family the estate of Glencorse has remained since 1854. Mauricewood Colliery was the scene of a pit disaster in 1889, and Mr S. R. Crockett, who was then Free Church Minister at Penicuik, has written that R. L. S. "made him more than once the channel of his practical charity to certain poor miner folk whom disaster had rendered homeless and penniless on the outskirts of his beloved Glencorse."

As we take our way from Flotterstane to the rising ground at Glencorse Manse, we shall turn to survey the surrounding countryside, and if the mood be upon us we shall catch something of the wistful charm that pervades this picturesque hollow with its guardian hills and sentinel hill-tops, waving woodlands, meadows and winding streams, all grouped round the old bridge over which the stage-coach came jangling down from the Inn at Marchwell to the toll-house at Flotterstane village.

But it is when the literary and historical incidents are linked with the scenic grandeur of the district that there comes the spell of the romantic days of long ago. Within a short radius armies have marched to battle. Riding overnight from Biggar, sixteen miles away, Sir Simon Fraser and Sir John Comyn, with an army of eight thousand horsemen, defeated near Roslin in 1302, in three successive encounters, thirty thousand English troops in three divisions, which by the order of Edward I. were laying waste the country—" a happy and gladsome victory " for Scottish Independence, wrought, as the historian has said, " by the power, not of man but of God." The army of Covenanters in 1666, marching from Colinton by Dreghorn and the Linton Road, passed round the back of Lawhead Hill, and fought the Battle of Rullion Green on the eastward slopes of Turnhouse Hill. To the westward of the memorial stone is the site of an ancient British Fort, facing a similar Fort above Castlelaw Farm; but although for centuries these places have been designated " Forts " there is a possibility that these and other " Forts " around the hills were really " hill villages," situated above the marshy ground in the valleys, and defended by ditch and rampart, not necessarily against any organised armed force, but for protection against roving bands or tribes, or even wild animals, which we know roamed the Pentland Hills in early times; and it was among such hill villages in East Lothian that St Cuthbert preached in the seventh century.

Part of Prince Charlie's army passed by Auchendinny, journeying south, in the year of the 'Forty-five.

Kings and nobles have hunted here; knights and fair ladies held tournaments, and formed the themes for historical romance. Holy men have had a habitation in this place. Legend speaks of a Cross in the Glen, of a band of 500 Knights of St John who passed this way from Torphichen to the Carlops, of the miraculous appearance of a cross upon the height of Carnethy, and of a house to which the cross was taken for inspection by pious pilgrims. To-day an annual commemorative Covenanters' Service is held by the river side. Carriers' carts have trundled along the road for centuries, and memories still survive of the stage-coaches, inns, and toll-houses for which the road was famous.

The history of the past tells us of momentous events that happened here and helped to win the heritage we enjoy of civil and religious liberty, and influenced Scottish character. To-day there is still an uplifting influence of poetry and music in the atmosphere that pervades the pastoral and the mountain scene, as the morning and the evening splendours of the day fill the happy vale in turn.

Many famous men appear in the literary and historical associations of the road and the district—the St Clairs of Roslin, Clerks of Penicuik, Trotters of Castlelaw and the Bush, Tytlers of Woodhouselee, Forbes of Newhall, Allan Ramsay, "Christopher North," Carlyle, Scott, and Stevenson. Dr John Brown travelled the road constantly, and tells us that Dr Chalmers found infinite delight in taking a band of children to the nearest hill-top, and making each carry the biggest stone he could find, the Doctor carrying one of enormous size, and then looking upon them with

THE OLD TOWER, WOODHOUSELEE

his broad benignant smile, " like the unnumbered laughter of the sea," set off his own stone rolling down the hillside to come to rest among the bracken, and was followed by the others in like manner, each stone being given a pleasing philosophy of its owner's life-story, much to the wonder and glee of the youngsters.

" The King of the Pentlands " was the title bestowed upon John Wood, shepherd at Castlelaw Farm for forty-nine years, a noted personality and leader among his fellows. At the age of ninety he walked to Penicuik to hear an address by Mr Gladstone, to whom he was introduced by Sir John Cowan of Beeslack. He was ninety-six when he died in 1901.

After passing the hamlet of Easter Howgate we come to WOODHOUSELEE, famous as the residence of the Tytlers from 1748 until 1923, when it was purchased by Mr David J. W. Dundas. In 1936 it became Government property.

The original Castle of Woodhouselee stood on the banks of the Esk, three miles away, and is now in ruins. Part of the building of the present Mansion House consists of a portion of the old Tower or Fortalice of Fulford. The exact date of this Tower is uncertain. There were many such buildings in olden times between here and the city— at Braid, Craiglockhart, Liberton, Redhall, Merchiston, and Wrighthouses—and the date of Fulford may be about the fourteenth century. Before Woodhouselee came into possession of the St Clairs of Roslin, Robert II., in 1379, gave it to Sir John Lyon; in 1501 James IV. granted " Muirhouse, Castlelaw, Estraw, and Wodehouselye " to Patrick Hume of Polwarth and the Lady of Dirleton, while the properties are mentioned in 1545 along with " the Tower of the same," which probably refers to old Woodhouselee Tower, in a deed by Patrick Sinclare to his son.

From the " Book of Woodhouselee," we find that in 1657 Sir William Purves, Bart., obtained a Charter from Oliver Cromwell, erecting the lands of Fulford into a barony. Another Charter by Charles II. incorporated the

F
65

lands of Woodhouselee on the Esk, Castlelaw, and the barony of Fulford into one free barony called the lands of Woodhouselee, and at this time Sir William removed from the Castle on the Esk to the present house on the wooded lee-side of the hills, charmingly situated, and one of the most delightful in all the countryside, rebuilding part of the Tower and making additions with stones and timber brought from the old Castle.

The old vaulted kitchen with walls eight feet thick, and the base of the spiral staircase that communicated with rooms in the Tower, form an interesting part of the present building, which has been added to and improved by the various members of the Tytler family, the additions carried out by James Tytler in 1843 being the work of Kemp, the architect of the Scott Monument.

Three generations of the Tytlers enriched the literature of Scotland. It is, however, during the tenure of Alexander Fraser-Tytler, Lord Woodhouselee, who built the existing Tower in 1795, that interest chiefly centres. He was the eldest son of William Tytler, the Edinburgh Writer to the Signet, who purchased the property in 1748, Professor of Universal History in Edinburgh University, and afterwards a Lord of Justiciary, a voluminous writer on literary, legal, and historical subjects, and held in high regard for his taste, talent, and personal worth. He died in 1813. His fourth son—Patrick Fraser-Tytler, became the author, on Sir Walter Scott's suggestion, of a History of Scotland, which took twenty years to write.

Lord Woodhouselee was one of Edinburgh's famous literary coterie, and many happy gatherings took place at his country-house on the Pentland Hills. Among frequent visitors were Lord Jeffrey, Henry Mackenzie, John Leyden, and Dugald Stewart. Mrs Elizabeth Hamilton, the authoress, was also a visitor, and the happy rural scene at Easter Howgate gave to her the first idea for " The Cottagers of Glenburnie."

One stormy night, when Sydney Smith was staying with

Lord Woodhouselee, the assembled party were much annoyed by the rattling of the window. Sydney Smith asked for a small piece of wood, out of which he fashioned the figure 8 and fixed it with a nail to the centre window in the dining-room, and stopped the rattling. The device is still in position, and is known as " Sydney's Button."

Leyden occupied what is known as " The Shepherd's Room "—named after Allan Ramsay, immediately before his departure for India, and wrote a Sonnet which he left lying upon the table, and which Lord Woodhouselee afterwards transcribed upon the glass of the window, descriptive of the sylvan surroundings of " this classic haunt."

Verses were also written by his lordship upon the window panes in the Tower Room and the Laird's Room.

Several sculptured stones containing armorial bearings and initials of successive owners of the ancient Castle or Tower of Wrychtishousis (acquired as a site for Gillespie's Hospital) were purchased by Lord Woodhouselee, when the Napiers' Mansion House was demolished in 1800, and are fixed into an ornamental gateway in the garden. One of these shows the heraldic distinction of the two families of Wrychtishousis and Merchiston, impaled, from which it appears that in the year of the Battle of Flodden the laird of the former married a daughter of the latter.

Among other interesting relics which were brought from this Bruntsfield Mansion were the stone mantelpiece in the front Hall and an ancient Sundial—a specimen of the most elaborate dial of the lectern type, standing 6 feet 3 inches in height, and containing eight upright dial faces, two of which are overshadowed by square projecting horns, similar to those serving the same purpose at Oldhamstocks.

Sir Walter Scott was also a frequent visitor at Woodhouselee. His admiration of the Pentlands is noted in his *Journal*—" I think I never saw anything more beautiful than the ridge of Carnethy against a clear frosty sky, with its peaks and varied slopes. The hills glowed like purple amethysts; the sky glowed topaz and vermilion colours.

I never saw a finer screen than Pentland, considering that it is neither rocky nor highly elevated."

It is said that he told ghost stories and tales of the Covenanters to the young folks at Woodhouselee. The "haunted Woodhouselee," to which he makes reference in "Cadzow Castle" and the "Gray Brother," was of course the Castle on the Esk; but when the stones were brought to the present house, the Ghost of Lady Anna Bothwell—the tragedy of whose life was her desertion by her false lover, Sir Alexander Erskine, a son of the Earl of Mar—travelled along with them, and was frequently seen to pass up the wooden stairs; and mysterious knockings upon doors and strange footfalls were frequently heard by the members of the Fraser-Tytler family and their friends.

One of these occurrences took place on a winter's night. No soughing wind came driving down the wooded glen behind the house to account in any way for the strange noises that were heard; it was calm and still, with a silence deep as the snow that covered the landscape all around. The Mansion House was shut up for the winter, while the family were absent, save the lower part of the house, which was inhabited by Sutherland, the coachman, and his wife and daughter. About six o'clock in the evening Sutherland went to feed the horses, and shortly thereafter his wife and daughter were startled by a loud and reiterated knocking at the Hall side-door. So terrified were they that neither of them would venture to the door; it might be some tramp or evil-disposed person who wished to take advantage of the lonely surroundings while Sutherland was absent, and force an entrance. The mysterious knocking continued at brief intervals for nearly an hour, and the dog barked repeatedly. At length the knocking ceased. The return of Sutherland was anxiously awaited, and when he came in by the back door, lanterns were procured, and all proceeded to the side door, which was the only one having a knocker. But the snow lay even all around, no marks were found upon the step from which only the knocker could be reached, and no footprints, except those of the track of Sutherland's feet, were visible in the avenue. It was a visitation of the Ghost of Woodhouselee.

The former proprietor jocularly remarked that he thought the electric light must have frightened the Ghost away, because there were now no mysterious loud treble knocks to be heard, or ghostly forms in muslin to be seen.

The farm of Boghall is now the property of the College of Agriculture, while the numerous small holdings dotted over the adjoining fields represent a Government's redemption of its pledges to ex-soldiers. But ere we descend to the farm at Hillend and the junction of the Linton Road with the road from Penicuik by Seafield, and that from Old Pentland, once a hunting centre, we shall pause to admire the vast panorama now spread out before us, guarded by the couchant lion of Arthur's Seat. The view over this portion of Mid and East Lothian makes a strong appeal to the mind and the imagination. Great agricultural, industrial, and mining interests are here represented. In the farthest distance rises Berwick Law with the Bass Rock on one side and Traprain Law on the other. On the right sweep the Moorfoot Hills melting into the Lammermoors, and on the left the gleaming waters of the Firth, the winding shores of Fife, and the nearer waters around Portobello and Prestonpans, Gosford and Gullane.

Many of the towns and villages in the prospect are hidden in the valley of the Esk and the rolling folds of the wooded landscape—Dalkeith and Dalhousie, Lasswade and Loanhead, Roslin and Rosewell, Penicuik and Polton, but Gorebridge stands out upon the uplands rising to the Moorfoots.

There are also extensive coalfields; coal was first worked at Prestonpans in the thirteenth century by the monks of Newbattle, while Morison's Haven, built in 1526, was the harbour of export. The Mid-Lothian coalfield is highly developed, and at Niddrie the mines are deep, and modelled by the highest scientific skill.

Nowhere will we find grouped together in a space so limited so many old castles and mansion-houses as in this pleasant landscape, each vying with the other in the antiquity of its historic lore. In the park of Dalkeith Palace is a relic of the ancient Caledonian Forest. Among the trees on the left rises Mortonhall House. The St Clairs of Roslin held this property along with Morton House in the reign of James III., but since 1641 Mortonhall has remained in possession of the Trotter Family. The first proprietor was John Trotter, an Edinburgh merchant, who made considerable donations to the town, but his successor, who was an enthusiastic Loyalist, was fined by Parliament five hundred pounds for assisting Montrose. Cromwell's army of 16,000 camped on the estate before the Battle of Dunbar, and the August of 1650 maintained its reputation as the wettest month of the year, for 2000 men were on the sick-list when the army lay encamped on the exposed and wind-swept ridge. Other historical buildings in the landscape are the fifteenth-century Tower of Liberton—a simple keep like that of Craiglockhart—and the picturesque ruin of Craigmillar Castle.

Many of the Castles of the Lothians, such as Craigmillar and Crichton, were originally keeps, and were extended into Castles by adding buildings round the courtyards.

No village round the hills is visited annually by so many people from all parts of the world as ROSLIN, where the Chapel, the Castle, and "Roslin's rocky glen," made immortal by Scott in the *Lay of the Last Minstrel,* are the chief attractions. In the old inn, which was built in 1660, Dr Johnson and Boswell dined and took tea in 1773, when on the way to Penicuik House; and Burns and the artist Nasmyth left a High Street tavern one summer morning at 3 a.m. to view the Pentlands, and came down from the hills to breakfast at the inn. Returning from their Highland tour, Wordsworth and his sister walked early one morning from Roslin down the Esk Valley to Lasswade, where Walter Scott and his wife were living, and there the two poets met for the first time, and spent a memorable day together; and in the evening Scott accompanied his two friends back to the village. On the College Hill, which slopes steeply down to the wooded dell, stands the Chapel, which is the choir of what was intended to be a large collegiate church. Its chief interest is in the beauty of the carving on pinnacles, columns, and roof, but especially on the famous 'Prentice Pillar.

The Castle was built about the beginning of the fourteenth century, and after the Battle of Dunbar was besieged by Cromwell's troops under General Monk.

The sites of the threefold Battle of Roslin are also in the vicinity. The first contest took place on the Bilston Burn, and the second and third between Dryden and Hawthornden. Local names perpetuate the sites: (1) Shin-bones Field, where bones have been found when ploughing; (2) the " Hewings," where there was great slaughter; and (3) the " Killburn," a small stream that ran red for three days, and " Mount Marl " Farm, named after one of the English leaders named Marl, who being told that all was lost, was advised by one of his retainers to " Mount, Marl, and ride!"

But we must not leave this Hillend vantage-point without commenting on what is the most conspicuous object in the landscape—the great bings of pink-coloured refuse of the shale-mining and oil-refining industry carried on in Straiton from 1877, and later in Pentland. The operations of the Clippens Oil Company terminated in 1897, when litigation began in connection with the Crawley and Moorfoot water-pipes, which passed through the shale-bearing area, the case going to the House of Lords, under whose decision the oil company were awarded £27,000 compensation, since when the works, which at one time employed over a thousand workmen, have remained closed.

Picturesquely situated on the furzy hillside under Caerketton's height is the Hillend Public Park, and the entrance to it is on the boundary line formed by the

Lothian Burn between Edinburgh and Mid-Lothian. On the other side of the burn is a farm, a smithy, and old-fashioned cottages set in gay surroundings of blackthorns, whins, and wild roses, a pleasant nook beside the hills for city folk to visit.

Here we have the choice of two roads. The one is the hard highway by Bowbridge and Fairmilehead, and the broad boulevard of Comiston, but the other is reserved for walkers and wayfaring folk, who cross the stile between the thatched cottage and the Ingle tea-room, and follow the farm road to the famed hamlet of Swanston.

At Bowbridge, part of the old road is seen fording the Swanston Burn. On one side of the road stood a pig farm, on the other a dairy farm. R. L. S. tells the story in his *Edinburgh: Picturesque Notes,* that the dairy farm was once a distillery, and that the distiller was on terms of good fellowship with the Exciseman who paid him occasional visits to measure his stock, and together they made a pact, that when the latter came to Fairmilehead he would play on his flute " Over the hills and far away " to warn his friend of his approach, whereupon the distiller would instantly harness his horse, and sundry barrels of whisky were got upon a cart and driven round Hillend to be temporarily hidden in the mossy glen behind " Kirk Yetton " so that upon this part of his stock no duty would be paid. In due course the gauger arrived, and the mutual well-wishing was celebrated in the back parlour, where the distiller's whitest napery, fat fowl, and choicest liquor paid compliment to the gauger's musical talent, and, in the evening—somewhat mellow—he took his departure, but not before he had again treated his host to " Over the hills and far away," to an accompaniment of knowing glances.

At Fairmilehead, the walker will cast a glance along the road to Morton House, for here lived one whom most walkers would take to their heart—John Hill Burton, the historian. He was a kind of literary tramp—using his pen every day; an inveterate wanderer, fond of space and air, of Bohemian habits, amazing vitality, never happier than when tramping across the countryside or camping among the heather. One can picture him tramping down from Fairmilehead to the city—walking quickly—the spare, gaunt form, with a perpetual stoop, looking at no one, his black, ill-cut, and shabby surtout streaming out behind him, his well-worn hat thrown far back upon his head: some personality dwells in that tabernacle, we surmise, and those who knew him tell us of the many fine qualities which he possessed. He died at Morton House in 1881.

Let us now return to Swanston, and by the cross-road to Hunters' Tryst, and the field-path by Comiston, complete the circle round the hills. Few Edinburgh citizens out of the many who have never visited this " stilly hamlet home that vies with any earthly paradise " imagine that such a place could exist within ten minutes' walk from a public bus route. This old-world village with its thatch-covered dwellings, ancient trees, gardens, rose-embowered cottages, and flowing stream might well belong to another genera-tion. R. L. Stevenson, who lived at Swanston Cottage at various times from 1867 to 1880, has written about it in several of his books. The early years he spent here, when he learned from Tod the shepherd all about " that hillside business," and when he wandered about the hills and the countryside, quick to every impression of nature and of men, and the voices of the stillness and the storm, so moulded his thinking and his outlook and understanding of life, that much of his writing bears the impress of the Pentland influence. To every country sound, as well as to the silence, he was sensitive; and of all that went to the formation of his personality and originality he has told us. " The trees were all in a tempest and roared like a heavy surf," " the trees are crying out in the darkness," " the birds are asleep outside on the tossing branches, the little bright eyes closed, the brave wings folded, the little hearts that beat so hard and thick are all stilled and quieted in

73

deep slumber in the middle of this noise and turmoil." But it was not the playfulness and joy of nature he felt in the wind—the Pentland influence had also the Edinburgh street influence to contend with, and he wrote: " In my Hell, it would always blow a gale."

A copy of Stevenson's poems makes an interesting companion while visiting Swanston village.

As an author he must be tried by his works, and perhaps as we read the inscription on the St Giles' Memorial we shall come near to his spirit:—

> " Give us grace and strength to forbear and to persevere.
> Give us courage and gaiety and the quiet mind,
> spare to us our friends, soften to us our enemies.
> Bless us, if it may be, in all our innocent endeavours;
> if it may not, give us the strength to encounter
> that which is to come, that we may be brave in
> peril, constant in tribulation, temperate in wrath,
> and in all changes of fortune, and down to the
> gates of death, loyal and loving to one another."

Passing from Swanston village by the farm-house—on the site of which was once a grange belonging to the monks of Whitekirk, East Lothian—Swanston Cottage will be seen, " weel happit in your gairden trees," and continuing this road by the farm-steading we join the Fairmilehead road leading to Colinton. The white farm building to the west is Hunters' Tryst, once a famous meeting-place of Edinburgh clubs. Among these was the Six-feet Club, the stalwart members of which formed a Guard of Honour to the Hereditary Lord High Constable of Scotland. Instituted on 1st February 1826, its purpose was the encouragement and practice of Gymnastics—" A Sportive Association of Young Athletes," as Lockhart describes it. Sir Walter Scott was " Umpire of Games," Professor Wilson, Captain, and James Hogg, Poet Laureate. " What a tail of the alphabet I should draw after me," wrote Scott in his *Journal*, " were I to sign with the indications of the different Societies I belong to, beginning with the President of the Royal Society of Edinburgh and ended with umpire of the Six-foot-high Club!" Their exercise ground was at Stockbridge—on the site of Malta Terrace—not far from "The Ettrick Shepherd's" lodgings in Deanhaugh Street, where he wrote "The Queen's Wake." At Hunters' Tryst they held competitions in rifle-shooting, singlestick, and throwing the hammer, and on such occasions these sons of Anak would enjoy to the full the good fare for which the Inn was famous. But it ceased to be an inn about 1862. Since then Pentland walkers have often wished that it were still a quiet old-fashioned hostelry.

Let it be old and quaint, says the wayfarer, and ever so small, only let it be clean, and let the homely evening meal of which the savoury aroma has filled the house be served daintily on spotless linen for the walkers just arrived. But alas! Hunters' Tryst is now in Suburbia. In *St Ives* R. L. S. refers to this wayside inn with the signboard, "The Hunters' Tryst, by Alexander Hendry, Porter, Ales, and British Spirits. Beds," and describes an "all-night sitting" of the Six-feet Club, following upon an "all-day Saturday tramp" of forty miles; while in *Picturesque Notes* he tells us there was a local superstition that the place was haunted by the devil in person! Satan led the inhabitants a pitiful existence. He shook the four corners of the building with lamentable outcries, beat at the doors and windows, overthrew crockery in the dead hours of the morning, and danced unholy dances on the roof. Every kind of spiritual disinfectant was put in requisition; chosen ministers were summoned out of Edinburgh and prayed by the hour; pious neighbours sat up all night making a noise of psalmody; but Satan minded them no more than the wind about the hill-tops; and it was only after years of persecution that he left the Hunters' Tryst in peace to occupy himself with the remainder of mankind. When German Zeppelins flew over Hunters' Tryst and dropped a bomb upon it at midnight on the first Sunday of April in 1916, the raiders probably knew of the story and intended the bomb as a friendly salute!

As the name implies, this was a trysting-place in the days when the district was a famous hunting-ground.

The field-path passes the back of Comiston House with its rookery among the high trees. In the various stages of what remains of our pilgrimage ere we join the city highway at Greenbank, we have the gradual unfolding of a panorama of views that will make us cry out with Wordsworth, " Dull would he be of soul who could pass by a sight so touching in its majesty." Before reaching Comiston Farm we look upon the great military barracks at Redford, the City Hospital, Poorhouse, and Craiglockhart Hill, and the far views to the Highlands of the northwest. Through Cockmylane—the clachan to the north of the farm—the view of the city opens before us with the Castle and church spires standing out over the valley of the Braid Burn, and as the path by the valley side is traversed, the Braid Hills, Blackford Hill, Arthur's Seat and Salisbury Crags, and many another vista in turn will so uplift us that it comes as a shock to find ourselves once more among racing motors and tramway cars.

The last few miles of our walk from Swanston along this pleasant winding field-path by Comiston and the valley of the Braid Burn is a right-of-way much used by visitors to the " stilly hamlet " under Caerketton. At present it has no name. Some day it may be known as Edinburgh's " Road of the Loving Heart."

The road round the hills may be travelled in and by many different ways. The motorist may complete the circle in a few hours, but the walker may spend a lifetime upon it and not exhaust its friendship or find the continual gift of its offering slacken or grow stale. The route outward by the Lang Whang and homeward by the Biggar Road has been followed because the view-points in this course are more significant, and the unfolding views of the city and surroundings more wonderful when approached from the south.

CHAPTER II

THE KIRK O' GLENCORSE

IN view of the interest taken in the Old Kirk at Glencorse and its associations, and the pilgrimage there of many visitors from all parts, the following account, compiled from references to Presbytery Records and Scott's *Fasti,* may not be without interest.

MINISTERS IN GLENCORSE
SUBSEQUENT TO THE REFORMATION

1576	. . .	Lancelot Gibson (Reader).
1588-1589	. . .	Andrew Forrester.
1599-1602	. . .	Andrew Blackhall.
1612-1615	. . .	United to Penicuik.
1615-1647	. . .	United to Lasswade.
1636-1645	. . .	Alexander Robertson.
1645-1674	. . .	Robert Alisone.
1673	. . .	Mr Calderwood, an Episcopalian.
1674-1690	. . .	George Purvis.
1691-1695	. . .	John Fraser.

Church rebuilt, and burned before completion, 1695; completed, 1699.

1699-1757	. . .	John Wilson.
1758-1762	. . .	John Walker.
1763-1787	. . .	James Taylor.
1788-1836	. . .	William Torrence.
1818-1877	. . .	Alexander Torrence.
1878-1885	. . .	William B. Strong.

Present Church (designed by Sir R. Rowand Anderson).

1885-1928	. . .	William B. Strong.
1928-	. . .	Donald M. Begbie.

In 1811 the "Old" Church was renovated, and the tower, crowned with a neat belfry, added. An ancient baptismal font was found at this time among the debris of the fire in 1695, and is in the present Church, mounted on a modern pillared base. It is of a single block of stone, cubical in form, 19 inches square, with circular hollow basin 14 inches wide. A roll bede is worked round the top edge and angles: leaded socketings in the top give evidence that the font originally had a cover.

Andrew Forrester, "Reader at Lasswade and also at Clarkington," was admitted, 12th December, 1588, but after two months "he was ordained to provide himself at sum other Kirk in respect of the means of his stipend."

A Presbytery Minute of 15th January 1589 states that " Andro Forrester, Minister of Glencors, is destitute of ane place of residence at his awin paroch Kirk; and it was considerit be ye brethrene that the said Andro, at my Lord Mortoun's desyre, suld exercise himself in ye said Lord's house, provydit allwayes yt. he observe and wait upon his awin paroch Kirk at ordinary tymes."

The union of Glencorse Kirk to Penicuik is referred to in a Minute of 18th June 1612: " Ane requiest is made to ye brethrene of ye Presbyterie that seeing they had consentit to the union of Glencors with the Kirk of Pennycuik, and promeist to counsell for the plantation of the same, in respect yat Glencors is not able to interteine ane minister for the present as is allegit, desyring the brethrene of the Presbyterie to consent to the said union, ye said brethrene, on deliberatioun considering ye extent of ye said Kirk, that for lack of moyen, yai had been destitute of ane pastor, and that yai lie thrie or four myle fra the Kirk of Lasswaid unto the qlk. they are united be Act of Parliament,[1] and yt. yai are distant fra the Kirk of Pennyciuk

---

[1] On 3rd April 1593 the Laird of Roslin declared to the Synod of Lothian and Tweeddale that " he was nane of the parochinaris of Leswaid, but ane of the parochinaris of St Katherine-in-the-Hopes in respect of his residence in Logan House Tower."

twa myles at ze farrest: therefoir the Presbyterie consentis to the union of the twa Kirks, provyding yr is na houp of provisione for Glencors be itself, and that ye brethrene, ye commissioners . . . sie ane reasonable augmentation provyded fra Glencors for the present minister of Penny-ciuk and his successors."

While this arrangement continued for over three years, it did not agree with the desire of the Glencorse folk, who wished to have a Minister of their own, as the following excerpts of the minute book show:—

" 26 Oct. 1615.—Ilk day the folkis of Glencors com-peiring in grit number, and craving the benefit of the Word and Sacramentis, was referrit till ye day appointed for ye visitatioune of Leswaid, and was orderit to be present there.

" 9 Nov. 1615.—Reportit that ye parochiners of Glencors had given in ane bill conteining many poyntis controvertit between them and Mr. George [Ramsay, Moderator of the Presbytery], bot speciallie complaining of ye want of the Word and Sacramentis, *desyring most earnestlie ane pastor;* qlk. being read Mr. George desyrit ye sicht yairof to advise yairin, that he micht give answer yrto against Thursday come aucht dayes on the day the folkis of Glencors are ordeinit to be present at ye Presbyterie.

" Ilk day the brethrene considering ye great neid yt. ye Kirk of Lesswaid stude in of reformation in discipline, as also the suit of ye folkis of Glencors, thocht gude yt. thai suld have ane extraordinarie meiting at Dalkeith on Tuysday nixt. And all ye breither to be thair under ye paine of ane merk."

The question for the Glencorse folks was one of ability to provide the Minister's stipend, and a way out of the difficulty was found by appointing a colleague to the Minister of Lasswade. This appears from the following copy Minutes of the "Extraordinarie meiting," and the sub-sequent meeting of the Glencorse folks at the Presbytery.

" 14 Nov. 1615.—Ilk day the breither thocht guid to try gif there could be ane stipend provydit for ane particular minister at Glencors or not; quilk failing, gif their necessitie, togidder with yat of Lasswaid, micht be helpit be ane second and colleg to Mr George."

" 16 No. 1615, Thursday. — Compeirit ye folkis of Glencors, desyring ane answer to thair bill given in at Leswaid Visitation. The brethren assurit thaim of all diligence in ye same, as they wald be answerable to ye Generall Assemblie. Being askit quhat they wald give to ane Minister, answerit that qlk. they gave of auld, and yat yair was some Kirk Land and ruynse of ane house at Mylton. As to farder contribution they promisit to report yair mynd that day aucht dayes. Mr. George being askit of his resolution, give in ane answer mainteining his nondilapidatioun of ye benefice.

" The Presbyterie proponing to Mr. George yair that in caise yai could not find sufficient moyens for ane particular minister at Glencors that he wald be easit in adjoyning to him some holy breither quha micht be ane fudderance to him in discipline and word, als weill for ye necessitie of ye people of Glencors as they of Leswaid. The qlk Mr. George maist gladly admitted, provyding that in respect of his strict and grit necessities his stipend was not imparit."

The Presbytery visit Glencorse, and a Report is made of the visit.

" 23 Dec. 1615.—Ilk day the former brethrene reportit that on Friday last they went to Glencors, quhen protestation being maid that this thair visitatioun maid was not as ane paroche Kirk bot as ane pairt of Leswaid, wt.out prejudice to onie manis rycht; that they had inquirit of thaime quhat was the whole soume of provisioun qlk thai wald bestow on ane pastour, seeing thai were so desirous and instant to have ane. All in ane voyce renewit thair former offer of four akeris of land, togidder with some threetie pndis money: as for farder thai could not. The brethrene schaw thaim that nane wald, nor micht undergo zat wark under sik eyket chargis. The parochiners confessit ye same, and cravit yair awin advoyse how they micht be helpit; for they were destitute of word and sacramentis. The brethrene proponing this overture that thai wald be about to cause some holy and diligent brother undertake ye burden, to furder Mr. George at Leswaid in word and discipline as also to instruct thaim by preiching and catechising, yea, administer to thaim also the sacramentis in due and proper season in and at thair awin Kirk at Glencors, the breither proposing this, the parochiners of Glencors was hartlie weill content wt. ye same, and requiested thame to performe their overture. The breither efter this report was read, enterit into deliberatioun quhom they thocht meitest to supplie, as colleg to Mr. George, both ye necessitie of ye Kirk of Leswaid, and ye suit of Glencors; and efter due advysement, the haill breither, wt. full consent, made choise of Mr. James Porteous, Minister at Soutra; quha being removit, and efter posit, quhat he thocht of that requeist, referred himself into ye handis of ye Presbyterie, and besought God that he wald glorifie his maitie [majesty] in his wakeness. And lykwayes the breither thocht guid that some of the breither suld be directit to speik and deall both wt. those of Leswaid, and wt. the Heritours of Glencors."

The stipend was accordingly provided for by the heritors, including Lord Ochiltrie, Lady Bruchtoune, William Sinclair, Younger of Rosling, Lord President, Lady Craigmillar, Lady Ross, the Countess of Glencairn, Sir John Prestoun of Pennycuik, Knight, George Abernethie, Thomas Borthwick, Portioner of Greinlaw, Adam Bothwell of Hopesyde.

Glencorse was therefore under the charge of James Porteous during the years from 1615 till 1636. In that year (1636) " James Porteous, Minister of Lesswade related that for sa meikle as ye paroche of Glencors had been annexed to his Kirk thir many yeirs bygane, And he had been serving yaim according to his abilitie, bot now aige on his pairt, and distance of place and ye charge of his awin kirk makes him unable to repair thither, And yairfoir hes demitted ye said kirk to Mr. Alexander Robesoun, who hes resaved presentation yairto be ye Kings Majestie" (Charles I.) (Alexander Robertson, 1636-1645).

Mr Robert Alisone, Reader and Schoolmaster of Carnwath, ordained 1643, is next presented to the charge by Charles I. in 1645. Died 1674.

" Glencorse became a Parish Kirk in 1647 " (Presbytery Records). A Commission is sent to report on St Katherine's (site submerged by Glencorse Reservoir)—a 13th Century Chapel, dimensions 44 ft. 9 ins. by 20 ft. (Anc. Mon. Com. Report). Teinds of Bavelaw given to Monks of Holyrood for maintenance of Divine offices at St Katherine in Pentland, between 1220-1230, confirmed 22nd year of Alex. II, 1235-6 (" Munimenta Sancte Crucis ")—both St. Katherine's and Mount Lothian (St Marie's Kirk) belonged to Holyrood Abbey, prior to Reformation, 1560.

In 1574 St Katherine's under charge of Adam Letham (Lichton, Leighton), Minister of Currie (Scott's *Fasti*). " The Reader's Salary at St Katherine's to be payit out of the third of Holyrudhous by the taxmen of St Katherine's and Mount Lothian " (Reg. of Min. 1567, Reader's Stipends 1576). When Charles I. erected Edinburgh into a Bishopric with Prelatic domination over Midlothian (1633-8), St Katherine's came under Episcopal jurisdiction until 1635 when, along with Mt. Lothian, it was united to Penicuik, which accounts for the " Kirks Road "—Logan Valley to Penicuik, and explains the following:

Report of those who visited St Katherine's-in-the-Hoppes

Sept. 7 1648.

" The which day, reported the brethern that was appoynted to visit St. Katherines in the Hoppes that they had perambulet the whole bounds, and found (1) That the length of the said Parish wes 4 mylles and the bredth thereof two. (2) That there wes parishioners there betwixt 60 and 80 soules, besyde young ones. (3) They found by the peoples own deposition that they were *not able to come to Penicuik Kirk in the winter tyme, nether at any other tyme, unlesse that the weather of extraordinar temperat, and that for mountain and waters.*[1] (4) That there was sufficient of rent with in the said paroch for the mentening of an minister there. (5) That the outmost of these people was four mylles fro Penicuik, and the nearest two mylles and an half. (6) That there might convenientlie be biget a Kirk at *Erncraig*, it *being the middle of the paroch*, and manse and gleyb may be had there, And they conceavet if the Presbyterie would tak paines to setle an minister there, they should do an work not onlie acceptable to God, but comfortable to these poor people.

(This Report was approved by the Presbytery, who recommended it to the ensuing Provincial Assembly, but nothing further is heard of the proposed Kirks at Erncraig. The Site was somewhere up the Logan Valley, west of St Katherine's, but the exact situation is unknown.)

[1] The boundary between the parishes of Penicuik and Glencorse was marked by the March Burn. In winter time St Katherine's was sometimes in one parish and sometimes in the other, according as the water of the March Burn altered its course in heavy spates, when the neighbouring hillsides poured down their floods. The east end of the wall of the Chapel was nearly twenty yards from the March Burn, and the Logan Burn was about the same distance from the south wall. The *Edinburgh Courant*, 13th October 1842, states: "It is now nearly a century since the little graveyard was used as a place of sepulchre, and not less than two hundred years since the voice of psalms was heard in the church. Few of the numerous pilgrims who make annual visits to this quiet sequestered spot are aware that several fathoms under the surface of the lake are the remains of the Church of St Katherine, still quite distinct, and surrounded by the scattered monuments so long laid under its waves with the *Memento mori,* and the date 1623 still fresh on one of them." The ruins have been visible at various times when the Reservoir was dry.

The condition of the Kirk of Glencorse—1648

The Kirk is planted with an Minister. The bounds of the paroch is two miles of length and als much in bred. *The Kirk is situat in the middle of the parishin;* the number of communicants 180. The King is Patrone. *The Kirk was erected in Anno* 1647, and the minister hes the whole valued dewties of the paroch, which in the haill extends to 600 [merks?] and ten bolls and ane chalder half meall, half beir.

There is within the paroch an prebendarie of seven scoir of merks, payet of late to the Earl of Roxburgh, who is one of the heritors of the parish to one that servit at the Chappel Royall [Stirling], now vacant be the death of those persones who were presented yrto, and the dewties is lyand unpayet in the heretours hands, and must be payet to some for the securitie of his land: and we conceave he would be well pleaset to bestow the same upon pious uses wtin the said paroch. It wer not amiss that seeing there is nether an mentenance for an schooll, nether anything to uphold that pt of the fabrick of the Kirk that belongs to the King, nor anything mortifiet for the building or upholding of brigs, most necessarie for those who hes to serve God at His house, that some paines be now taken to sie if the Lords would appropriet the same for the forsd. uses.

June 21 1649.

The which day the Presbyterie being informet that there is an prebendrie of seven scoir marks within the parisch of Glencorse, payet of late for menteaning the organes and singers in the Chappell of Stirling, now vacant be decease of James Macail and James Crichtoun, last presentit thereto, therefore, seeing the Minister his stipend is deficient of what is allowed be Act of Parliament, Q'fore appoint our Commissioners for the Assemblie to supplicat the General Assemblie to recommend the same to the honourable estaites of Parliament, and desyre the said prebendrie may

GLENCORSE KIRK

be addit in augmentation as a pairt of the minister of Glencorse his stipend in all tyme coming.

November 7 1649.

Reported Mr. James Fairlie that he had spoken wt Alex. Bodwell of Glencorse anent the desyre of the brethren that he would give as much ground near to the Kirk of Glencorse as ane Schulehouse and Chalmer for the minister to retyre to betweyne sermons, since his manse was near half ane myle from the Church, and ane water qlk is sometimes impassable betwixt his house and the Church, and had no certene place to retyre to for to shelter him from the violence of the weather betwixt sermons, but that he had refused to give any ground for that use."

This family of Bothwells, descended from the Bishop of Orkney, and ennobled in the peerage as Lord Holyroodhouse, acquired the lands and barony of Glencorse by Charter of Charles I. in 1647. They had litigation with their neighbours—in 1687 with Deans of Fulford, in 1702 with Clerk of Penicuik, and in 1710 with Trotter of Mortonhall, and parted with Glencorse in 1809.

When Sir William Purves of Woodhouselee obtained a ratification by the Scottish Parliament of a Royal Grant of *inter alia* the patronage of the Kirk, he tried to change the name of the parish to Woodhouselee (it originally consisted of these two baronies, Glencorse and Woodhouselee), and for a time it was named " Woodhouselee or Glencorse," but in the end he was unsuccessful.

Lord President Inglis of Glencorse, in a pamphlet (26th Dec. 1877) printed in Watt's *Life of John Inglis* (1893), has pointed out that *Glencorse,* and not *Glencross,* has been the name of the parish, barony, and estate from the thirteenth century.

At Glencorse the 25th of Aprile 1650.

" The which day the Presbyterie keepet a visitation of Glencorse and preached Mr. Patrick Sibbald.

The which day Mr. Adam Penman, that had perused the Session booke, reported that he did find all things right and orderlie therein.

The minister Mr Robt. Alisone being interrogated (1) if he had preached twyse on the Sabbath all the year (2) keeped the Directory (3) Catechised weekly (4) visited families and pressed them to worship God (5) preached against the corruption of the tymes and did the rest of the dewties of his calling, Answered, he did. (6) If they had majistrates for punishing profanity according to the Act of Parliament, chosen by the heritors? Answered they had not got these yet, because they could not get the heritors for the doing thereof.

The minister being removed, And the elders examined upon oath, did approve him in his life and doctrine and everie dewtie of his calling.

June 6 1661.

The whilk day came a reference from the Session of Glencorse, the tenour whereof followes:—

Glencorse Kirk May 1, 1661.

The whilk day the Minister and elders having regraited before the heritors of the parochin of Glencorse the ruinous state of that part of the Kirk from the Eastern door to the Western door, which is holden up for the present by props of timber, notwithstanding whereof the whole side wall in that bounds is most like to fall, earnestlie desyring them to take some speedy course for the repairing of the same, that the administration of the Lords Supper be not still hindered, and that the people may not be still in a fear to resort to the kirk, William Purves[1] gave under his hand

---

[1] The arms sculptured on the South Transept are those of Sir William Purves of Woodhouselee, Advocate. The patronage of the Kirk of Glencorse was granted to him in 1669, when the Scottish Parliament ratified a royal grant in his favour. The coat-of-arms on the west side of the North Transept are those of Henry Bothwell of Glencorse (Lord Holyroodhouse), who was served heir to his father in 1734, and the adjoining panel contains

that he was content to repair upon his own chairges and to uphold in all tyme coming all that part of the Kirk which is already designed to him for his roome in the said Kirk by the Presbyterie and Sessione for his lands of Foulfoord and Woodhouslie within which designation that ruinous part of the Kirk is."

The following continued record of the Ministers of Glencorse gives the further story of the Church, with sidelights upon the times:—

The Church had an Episcopal Minister in 1673.

George Purvis, admitted by the Bishop of Edinburgh, was the next Minister in 1674. From Scott's *Fasti* we learn that " He gave in a supplication to the Committee of Estates shewing he had given obedience to the proclamation, yet certain persons had discharged him from preaching (1689), taken away the keys of the Kirk door, and the Kirk Bible, and the Laird of Glencorse was ordered to protect him." He was deposed in 1690, " though he objected against some of the witnesses as bearing malice against him, they having previously assaulted him in the pulpit with swords and staves." Died 1710.

John Fraser, ordained 1691, removed to Alness, Nov. 1695.

His career was an extraordinary one, as appears from the above-mentioned authority: " A native of the Highlands. Studied and was graduated at the University and King's College, Aberdeen, in 1678: proceeded to London and attended the dissenting ministry, till hearing Alex. Shields (1684), both were taken prisoners, sent to Leith chained together in the kitchen-yacht, carried to Edinburgh,

those of his second wife, Mary Campbell, eldest daughter of Lord Neil Campbell of Armaddie. Their family consisted of eight sons and seven daughters. There is an interesting version in the vernacular of the Bothwell motto, " Surgendum adversus urgentia," on the stone above the doorway of the lodge of Glencorse House —" Set a stout heart to a stay brae." This stone belonged to an old Scots house that occupied the site of the present Glencorse House.

examined by Privy Council, and under alarm of a commotion by the Marquis of Argyll, sent to Dunottar Castle, 1685. After a six days' journey and three months' confinement there, with fearful suffering and privations, which brought on a cough that continued through life, he was brought back to Leith, and banished with many others, by the same authority, and gifted to the laird of Pitlochie, who carried them to New Jersey, where he was released. He then went to New England, and being a licenciate, preached at Waterbury in Connecticut, till the accession of William and Mary, when he returned, and became Minister of Glencorse, 1691. From knowing Gaelic he was appointed by the General Assembly, 1694, to supply in Ross, Sutherland, and Caithness, where he received a call, which his presbytery rejected, and, that his services might be retained, a new Church was being built for him by the parishioners—[at Glencorse]. The distant call was renewed in the following year. The evening before an Appeal to the Synod was to be discussed, the Glencorse Kirk, which was almost finished, was destroyed by fire, and this determined Fraser to accept the call as an ordination by Providence. He was therefore translated to Alness."

The Church was rebuilt in 1699 in the shape of a cross, with accommodation for 200 sittings, when *John Wilson* was appointed Minister at the age of 23, and so continued for 58 years. Died 1757, age 81. The date 1699 appears over the traceried window in the Woodhouselee loft in the South Transept. The Transepts were added to the original structure at this time.

John Walker, the Minister of Colinton (see p. 113, *Colinton and Bonaly*) was Minister of Glencorse from 1758 till he was translated to Moffat, 1762. The *Fasti* adds that " besides his official duty [at Glencorse] he was partially fond of Botany, and had amply opportunity of gratifying his taste amid the soltiude and delights of the Pentland Hills."

James Taylor, Minister for 25 years from 1763.

William Torrence, Minister for 48 years from 1788. Died 1836, age 90.

Alexander Torrence (son, appointed assistant and successor). Minister for 59 years till his death in 1877.

The late minister, the Rev. William Baillie Strong, was appointed in 1878, and preached the last sermon in the "Old" Kirk on 5th Dec. 1885, when the present Church was built. When the Manse was built in 1816, two-thirds of the population of the parish was situated round about it. Proof of the disappearance of many of the cottages around Flotterstane and the movement of the population from the district is seen in the fact that to-day the Manse is two miles away from the same proportion of parishioners.

After negotiating the worn step at the unlocked wicket gate by which we enter the sacred precincts, we pass the small "Resurrection House," which had its uses like that of Colinton, Currie, etc., in bygone days, and was a shelter for the solemn calculating elders "watching the plate" placed upon the white-napkined stool outside.

A remarkable traceried wheel window, comprising two hearts intertwined, in the South Transept, is the only part of the ruins having any architectural value, and along with the mouldings in other parts of the building, is characteristic of the seventeenth century.

There are many old gravestones. One in the north-east corner to a Frenchman from Dunkerque: a plain round-topped slab, with a Latin cross and an inscription on the front—"Ici repose Charles Cotier de Dunkerque, mort le 8 Janvier 1807." The old mansion-house of Greenlaw (referred to in Chap. XVI.), stood near the site of the present Barracks of Glencorse, and was converted into a French Prison, and for a time was indeed the only French Prison in Scotland at the beginning of the nineteenth century. This Frenchman died in Greenlaw Prison.

On the left, as the visitor enters the churchyard, standing in front of the Somerville-Dalmore tomb and near Sir John Cowan's grave, is what R. L. S. calls "the most pathetic memorial I ever saw, a poor school slate in a wooden frame with the inscription cut into it, evidently by the father's own hand "—" Sacred to the memory of Catherine Ogg, the beloved child of James Henderson, 42nd Highlanders, who died at Greenlaw, on the 25th Oct., 1869, aged 7 months."

Near the south-east door of the Church is a flat lichen-covered slab on which appears the earliest date that is legible—1618. There is, however, another date, 1647, on the same stone, and as the latter date coincides with the year of building of the Church, it was most likely erected then, or soon thereafter. Another coincidence is that the two parties resided almost at opposite ends of the parish— " Here lieth Thomas Verner of Auchindinie, died 1st April 1618, and Gavin Verner, The Hous of Muir, died 29th Oct. 1647."

Mr A. W. Inglis of Loganbank, son of the Lord President, shared the opinion that there had been a Church and burial-ground on this mound long before 1647. He informed me that the date 1611 was once legible upon one of the slabs, and pointed out that the inscription upon the Verner stone is " Here lieth " Thomas Verner, who died 1618; and that the Baptismal Font dug up in 1811 belongs to a very early period. There was also a stone with a sword incised upon it, known locally as the " Crusaders' Stone," which stood near the edge of the graveyard, but it fell over the bank and was broken to pieces.

Stone coffins have been found near here, proving the place to have been an ancient burial-ground, while in the woods, not a hundred yards from the base of the mound, lies a stone with cup-and-ring markings, one of the most interesting specimens in Mid-Lothian, and, as previously mentioned, a stone circle stood near Marchwell.

Doubless Stevenson had Glencorse Kirk in mind when he wrote *A Lowden* [Lothian] *Sabbath Morn*. In *The Body-Snatcher* we have in all its horror a " resurrectionist " tale of Glencorse. The vicinity also enters into *Weir of*

Hermiston. "As to the Church where Archie Weir first beheld young Kirstie Elliot, R. L. S. heard, as he and his father neared Glencorse, 'the clinkum clank o' Sabbath bells,' and noted 'the solemn elders at the plate stand drinkin' deep the pride o' state.'" He also writes of it to Sidney Colvin: "On a Sunday in 1875 . . . I've been to Glencorse Church. It is a little cruciform place with heavy cornices and string course to match and steep slate roof. The small kirkyard is full of old gravestones. In Church Mr Torrence preached—his voice leapt like an ill-played clarionet from key to key—over eighty, and a relic of times forgotten, with his black thread gloves and mild old foolish face."

The Church, the Minister, and the whole surrounding district was fixed indelibly in Stevenson's mind when from Samoa he wrote to Crockett—"Do you know that the dearest burn to me in the world is that which drums and pours in cunning whimples in that glen of yours behind Glencorse Old Kirk? Oh that I were the lad I once was, sitting under old Torrence, that old shepherd of let-well-alone, and watching with awe the waving of the old black gloves over the Bible—the preacher's white finger-ends meanwhile aspiring through! Man, I would even be willing to sit under you—a sore declension, truly—just to be there. I shall never take that walk by Fishers' Tryst and Glencorse. I shall never see 'Auld Reekie.' I shall never set my foot again on the heather . . . Do you know where the road crosses the burn under Glencorse Church! Go there and say a prayer for me. See that it is a sunny day; would like it to be a Sunday; but that's not possible in the premises; and stand on the right bank, and shut your eyes; and—if I don't appear to you!"

Stevenson is remembered by several who attended this Church. They wondered who he was—the lanky lad with the velvet coat. Mr Inglis, who occupied the Glencorse loft, tells me that Stevenson sat in the Minister's pew just under the pulpit, and that he was "fairly regular in attendance—about every second Sunday." On entering the churchyard gate he would turn off the footpath to the right, and was frequently seen, just before the bell rang, looking over the tombstones or over the wall of the churchyard, looking down on the burn, where the road crosses. Doubtless he remembered many of the old man's sermons, and the expositions of Torrence's favourite text—" Though I speak with the tongues of men and of angels, and have not charity, I am become as sounding brass or a tinkling cymbal." And Stevenson, writing as a lad of sixteen about the opposite heights above Rullion Green, draws the picture of a scene that many a Pentland walker has looked upon and wondered—" The sun going down behind the Pentlands casts golden lights and blue shadows on their snow-clad summits, slanted obliquely into the rich plain before them, bathing with rosy splendour the leafless, snow-sprinkled trees, and fading gradually into shadow in the distance. To the south, too, they beheld a deep-shaped amphitheatre of heather and bracken—the course of the Esk, near Penicuik, winding about at the foot of its gorge —the broad, brown expense of Maw Moss—and fading into blue indistinctness in the south, the wild heath-clad Peeblesshire hills."

BONALY TOWER

CHAPTER III

SUNRISE FROM CAERKETTON

THE rising of the sun is one of the most wonderful sights in the world.

Yes, we say, and accompany our gesture with a smile! but it is only when tested by our own experience that the glories of the dawn come home to us with all the power of reality. And so it came about that on a midsummer morning I ventured forth at two o'clock to see the sunrise and the birth of a new day, from Caerketton's height. Principal Sir George Adam Smith tells us that in the East the sun does not " rise "; the word, he says, is weak for an arrival so sudden, the sun leaps above the horizon and bursts upon the city; but with us there is first a heralding of his coming, and then a gradual unfolding from one glory to another.

To walk abroad when all the earth is silent, and no one is about, begets the feeling of lordship and possession, which however entirely disappears when there has been witnessed the lordship of the rising sun, and his possession of the earth.

The morning was grey and the sky still held some of the sunset glow of the preceding evening. The atmosphere was warm after a day of heat, and refreshingly fragrant were the sweet scents of field and wayside flowers as one walked along the Greenbank path by the Braid Burn to Comiston Farm, and so by field-path to Swanston. From here it was a steady climb under the scarred face of Caerketton, through lush grass, heather and bracken, and the remains of the old fir wood planted by the Trotters of Mortonhall in 1766. As the snow-capped mountain tops in spring and winter beckon the climber towards the summit, so in the early summer morning the htill-tops looked cool and inviting, set as it seemed in a steel-blue filament of faintest gauze—the bloom of the early morning yet unborn—an ethereal beauty that stimulates both intellect and emotion, giving birth to that strange faculty we call imagination, which, as Shakespeare affirms, " bodies forth the forms of things unknown."

The top was reached an hour before sunrise. But often one stopped during the ascent to gaze over the city, which lay enshrouded in darkness; lights were burning in the City Hospital, while the revolving beacon on Inchkeith stabbed the gloom at regular intervals. With the field-glass, lights could be distinguished along the Fife coast. In the immediate foreground, the water in the new filter-beds at Fairmilehead gleamed like molten lead under the bordering trees.

But what was that strange sound high up among the rocks on Byerside Hill, a sound not unknown on the Pentlands—the sharp bark of a fox! Most likely he saw me, rather than smelt or heard me, for he was high up on the hillside, while I was in the hollow between the hills; and as I stood for some minutes he continued to bark, probably warning his mate, breaking the silence of the early morning, then when I turned to continue the upward climb he stopped, but began again when I stood still. This fellow was certainly in a neighbourhood where he could do much damage, a veritable land of plenty where:—

> " In earliest hours of dark, unhooded morn,
> Ere yet one rosy cloud bespeaks the dawn,
> While far abroad, the fox pursues his prey."

A recent round-up of foxes by shepherds and keepers around the Cairn Hills and the Cauldstaneslap resulted in a kill of thirteen and the discovery of a den with cubs.

A cock crew in Swanston Farm, and a dog barked some distance away. There was a faint attempt by a blackbird " with brief réveillé to summons all the brake," but Chanticleer must have deceived him, and his small signal did not " fill the grove with song."

At last the summit was reached. Nature was now fully awake, there were sounds on all sides, and the birds were ready to hail the dawn. A grouse called hoarsely "go-back," "go-back," "go-back"; whaups and pee-weeps—birds of the open spaces—sent their echoing notes along the lonely hillsides, and other lesser hill birds gave a chirp here and there, just to say "Good morning." There was yet no sign of the Dayspring.

The Glencorse and Loganlee Valley was filled with haze, and the tops of the Black Hill, the Kips, Scald Law, and Carnethy looked strangely beautiful as they stood out above the mysterious purple-rimmed hollow. In the deep blue above the peaks the morning stars were singing still. Then, very faintly at first, the Eastern sky began to blush, and

"The stars of heaven fell calmly away,
Like the flakes of snow on a winter day."

Above the violet-coloured horizon a soft pink glow was spreading quickly. The form of Arthur's Seat loomed up above the murky darkness of the city, and a bright rosy pink reflection, gaining in intensity, appeared on the horizon beyond. Cocks were crowing, the Inchkeith light winked on in rhythmic flash through the lighter haze, and now a breeze sprang up, and it grew chilly. Wonderful movements were taking place in the sky east of the Salisbury Crags: every moment there was a fresh advance, the colour changed to a bright crimson, it rose higher, patches of lavender-grey cloud were in turn illumined as with fire of gold and appeared with flaming head-dress. A lark began to sing, raining down his music from his airy blue home, then was silent, and again continued singing merrily from time to time. The colours of the red flaming heavens as seen through the glasses were now rapidly gaining in brilliancy, made more vivid because of the dull city haze beneath. All the eastern sky was afire, pulsating with life and energy, and in the process of higher transformation, till it seemed as if from some Vulcan forge in the Abyss beyond, this strange phantasmagoria was thrown up to adorn the skies in furious, riotous colour and design, to make a royal panoply for the coming of the King of Lights. It thrilled one to look out from the hill-top into the great silent space and watch this unfolding of beauty so rare and wonderful. One shut and opened one's eyes not only the better to appreciate the rapid gradations of light and tone, but also because nature may reveal glories that are sublime even to the point of pain. Then the burning of the crimson hues passed, the colours gradually faded, till all trace of the former magnificence had vanished.

All this was but the prelude to a more sublime colour display still to come.

The grey skies grew bright with translucent light. It was daylight everywhere. In ten minutes the scene had changed again. The cumuli and sharp-pointed rugged clouds that a short time before had been on fire were now lit up with a pearly whiteness, and through their fissures and lanes one gazed in rapt allurement, as it seemed into another world of pearl and gold, the Golden City far beyond, the land of Ossian's Elect. Gradually the whole heavens became radiant with this new light, and soft-toned clouds with golden crowns floated in a sea of palest blue—a beauty almost supernatural, with some secret as of Apocalyptic calm. It held one spellbound. To what fresh realm of Imagination would this nature revelation lead one next? To some diviner sphere—where life is crowned with Youth Eternal—for this did the sunrise seem to symbolise! At Heaven's Gate the larks were singing still—" sweet birds antheming the morn "—filling the silence and the distance with a divine harmony, and to their singing, at last, the King appeared, and his golden light flooded the landscape everywhere. Difficult would it be adequately to describe this scene of wondrous beauty that continued to unfold itself for over an hour. The awe and wonder of it stilled one into silence, then as with the larks it stimulated rejoicing, followed by the impression of thoughtful solemnity in the presence of such magic happening—a new day was born, in pearly hues and golden, to the accompaniment of the larks carolling.

CHAPTER IV

COLINTON AND BONALY

WILL H. OGILVIE and Robert Cochrane were walking over the Pentland Hills together one winter day in 1906 by Bonaly and Glencorse, and the charm of the hills, the varied views, and the exhilaration of " the clean winds blowing " made such an impression on the poet that the verses " In Pentland Wine," which appear on the title-page of the latter's invaluable *Pentland Walks,* were written to seal the memory of the occasion.

This is perhaps one of the best-known routes across the hills, and in winter-time no less than in summer it has a charm all its own. Moreover, Edinburgh folks have now an added interest in this part of the hill round Bonaly, through which the right-of-way passes, for in the spring of 1923 the Corporation purchased a stretch of 65 acres, comprising part of White Hill and Torduff Hill, for purposes of the city's water supply, and this pleasant rustic ground has been opened to the public, and vies with Hillend Park as one of the city's finest pleasure grounds. Here, among the heather and the whinny knowes, one may wander at will, and forget all about the decree of the Court of Session which enforced one to keep within a barbed-wire barricade, or, like Henry, Lord Cockburn, " seated 800 feet in air," behind Bonaly, read Tacitus from cover to cover!

It was in the view from up here about Torphin that Grecian Williams saw the likeness of Edinburgh to Athens —the Braid Mount on the right representing Brilessus; in the Castle, we have the Acropolis; in the Calton, the hill Lycabetus joined to that of the Areopagus; in the Firth of Forth, the Ægean; in Inchkeith, Ægina; and the hills of the opposite coast of Fife, Peloponnesus; and the resemblance is now more complete for the National Monument stands upon the Castle Rock and we have the Parthenon in the Acropolis.

But it is perhaps round about Bonaly House, and the hills immediately beyond it, with all the romantic association of the times of Lord Cockburn, that chief interest centres for Edinburgh visitors to this part of the hills, apart from the views and the rusticity of the scenes all around. Cockburn was an outstanding personality of his time. He was a lawyer, sharing with Jeffrey the leadership of the Scottish Bar; became Solicitor-General in 1830, Lord Rector of Glasgow University the following year, and in 1834 was appointed a Judge of the Court of Session, and died at Bonaly in 1854. The excellent work of the Cockburn Association is well known.

Here he gathered round him many of the noted men of his times, and although his was not the popularity of a great name like that of Scott or Jeffrey, or Wilson or Chalmers, he was one of the most popular men north of the Tweed, and all who knew the wiry, muscular, and athletic figure with the handsome face and capacious brow, and eyes that sparked like a hawk's when he was roused by energy or wit, were at once attracted to him. He spoke in the broad doric of his time, untinged with provincialism or affected by the language of the South, had a great fund of humour, and was as athletic at seventy as he was in early manhood, thanks in large measure to his exercise on the Pentland Hills, and his delight in the fresh breezes of heaven. There was not a recess in the valleys of the Pentland, not an eminence on their summits that was not familiar to him; and here it was, on the top of one of the Pentlands, " emblematic of the solidity of our foundation and the extent of our prospects," that Cockburn and Leonard Harner resolved to set about the establishment of the Edinburgh Academy. Brougham, Jeffrey, Scott, and Cockburn were all trained at the Edinburgh High School.

Among the many noted men Lord Cockburn gathered round him at Bonaly there might be found stern leaders of the Bar, and critics of the *Edinburgh Review,* of which journal Jeffrey—afterwards Lord Jeffrey—became Editor, who here unbent and became joyous and uproarious, playing bowls upon the lawn; and Cockburn tells us that in strolling through the rugged glens above his house with a troop of youngsters, lighting a fire with his own hands and making a rustic dinner, he found what yielded him more enjoyment than the brightest dreams or the proudest realities of ambition. One likes to think of Dr John Brown's description of him:—

"There is Harry Cockburn, with those wonderful eyes, melancholy and lonely, brown and clear, and deep as a muirland tarn, sparkling at times as if the sun shone on them, or oftener as if a star of their own twinkled from out their depths; but their habitual expression pensive to melancholy: what nature and fun and pathos! What a voice, what homely power! and his long country stride, and his leisurely flow of soul, rippling but strong, singing a perpetual and quiet tune, as if listening to himself and turning everything to his humour—as native, as inimitable, as unmade and exquisite as a roadside spring."

Then he goes on to tell the following story, which illustrates Cockburn's peculiar humour and his gift of witty repartee.

"One day, coming down the Mound from Court about 5 P.M., a friend met him and said: 'You're looking tired: have you been all this time in Court?' 'Yes,' he said querulously, 'it's that man——' 'Does he take up your time at that rate?' 'Time! he exhausts time and encroaches on eternity.'"

There was genius in that word "encroaches," said Dr John Brown.

But his heart, I think, was most often in the Pentlands, where he enjoyed life so thoroughly as witness his quaint letter to a friend when he was Solicitor-General. "It will be a great delight to receive Mr and Mrs Smith into our pastoral fraternity . . . I hope Mr Smith is aware that whatever Mr Cockburn was, His Majesty's Solicitor-General is a decorous person, arrayed in solemn black, with a demure visage, an official ear and evasive voice, suspicious palate, ascetic blood, and flinty heart."

" There is a fellow very like him who traverses the *Pentlands,* in a *dirty grey jacket, white hat,* and *long* pole. That's not the Solicitor-General, that Cocky, and Mr Smith may use all freedom with *him.*"

Although the Friday Club, which Sir Walter Scott and Lord Cockburn founded in 1803, held its weekly meetings in the city, the members would no doubt spend many a jolly field day on the hills and at Bonaly. It was a literary and social club open to those who were " supposed to combine a taste for learning and science with agreeable manners," with no written laws, no motions, no disputes, no ballot, no fines, no business of any kind except what was managed by one of themselves as Secretary.

But the Bonaly Friday Club was more closely identified with Bonaly House. This Junior Literary Society was an imitation of the Friday Club, and was originated by Lord Cockburn's eldest son and his five brothers with twenty-nine youthful friends. The members regarded the Club as if it were of great importance, as we learn from the amusing and grandiloquently written particulars of the Club's History, issued in 1842—in the writing of which it is thought that Lord Cockburn himself had a hand. Francis Jeffrey Cockburn, the youngest son, writing in 1892, tells us that the Club had a theory that Bonaly belonged to them, and that Lord Cockburn was their tenant whose privilege it was to provide everything they required on the days on which it was pleased to meet! " When the day was fixed," he writes, " the President sent a polite but formal note to the tenant informing him that the Club would meet at Bonaly on such a day, and requesting him, firstly, to vacate the premises, and, secondly, to provide what was needful for their comfort! "

The symposiums of literary wit and humour and farce

w,ere greatly enjoyed. Many members, like those of their parent Club, rose to high positions in their respective professions.

Lord Cockburn frequently invited his friends to spend a " hill-day " with him at Bonaly. On one occasion the party included Nasmyth, the inventor of the steam-hammer, and seven artists, among whom were Sir George Harvey, one of the original Associates and founders of the Scottish Academy, the celebrated D. O. Hill, and James Ballantyne, the reviver of the art of glass-painting, and author of *The Miller of Deanhaugh*—in which Colinton is referred to— and several other Scots songs, including " Ilka Blade o' Grass " and " Castles in the Air."

They climbed far up the hills, sat down on a semi-circular hollow in the hillside, made by the sheep, with Cockburn in the middle, and after they had regained their breath, and let the view have its stimulating effect upon their artistic temperament, Cockburn entertained them in his own humorous and witty way, with his marvellous powers of conversation, for he had great understanding of men and books, this fine old type of Scottish gentleman. Cockburn went to the true fount of wisdom when he wanted informa- tion about the hillside business. He consorted with the shepherds of the hills and learned his lessons. One day he was having a " crack " with a shepherd, and seeing some sheep lying down in a rather exposed place, he said to him: " John, if I were a sheep, I would lie on the other side of the hill "; to which the shepherd replied, " Ay, my Lord, but if ye had been a sheep ye wad hae had mair sense." Sydney Smith, who was the original projector of the *Edinburgh Review*, had not the spare athletic figure of either Jeffrey or Cockburn, and it must have gone ill with him if he ever climbed Bonaly. It was to " a most delight- ful old lady, that perfect type of a Scottish gentlewoman," Miss Stirling Graham, that he made the famous joke about the hot day that " he wished he could put off his flesh and sit in his bones, and let the wind whistle through them."

Dean Ramsay tells the story of how Lord Rutherford was rebuked by a shepherd up here at Bonaly. He was complaining about the east wind and the mist blowing over the hill, as many a Pentland walker does now, but the shepherd saw it from a different point of view—" What ails ye at the mist, sir, said he: " it weets the sod, it slockens the yowes, and, forbye, it's God's wull." Which reminds me of the answer given by a Pentland farmer to my inquiry as to how he was getting on with his ploughing—" Na," he said, " the grun's ower weet, it's seek wi' sap, ay, an' soor."

And dear old Professor Blackie, who walked over the wilds of Argyllshire till he wore the soles off his shoes, and had to bind them on to his feet, loved the Pentland Hills, and burst into song over the Bonaly Burn.

And no doubt when Chalmers and Jeffrey were out visiting Cockburn at Bonaly they would look in and see Henry Mackenzie in his thatched cottage at Colinton. In his time he was the Nestor of literary Edinburgh, which then included men like Hume, Robertson, Adam Smith, and Blair. He wrote *The Man of Feeling*, a book but little read in these days, but which Burns carried about with him in his pocket when ploughing, and so frequently perused it that his thumb-marked, worn-out copy had to be replaced by another. " I prized it next to the Bible," he wrote to his schoolmaster. He founded and edited the *Mirror* (1779-80) and *Lounger* (1785-7), the first periodicals of their kind in Scotland, and in the latter had the glory of introducing Burns to the Edinburgh wits and wider circle of its readers. Mackenzie was a man of wonderful virility, and at the age of seventy-three he was one of the most active sportsmen in shooting parties at Abbotsford, along with Scott and Sir Humphrey Davy; while we are told that at the opening of Edinburgh Academy, when he was nearly eighty, ' he made an animated address, exulting in the rise of a new school upon a reformed system." The length of the day seemed to be too short for him. Lord Cockburn narrates that about this time he appeared one day at Bonaly for breakfast, played bowls most of the forenoon, had a party to dinner in his own house, and " when I left him was predominating in full talk to a larger party at eleven." One of the amusements of the sentimental novelist was cock-fighting! He died in 1831, at the age of eighty-six.

Many interesting personalities have lived in and around the quaint old village of Colinton, now growing out of all recognition. Of the Ministers connected with the parish there was the Rev. John Walker, D.D., in 1783—formerly of Glencorse and Moffat, who was known as the " Mad Minister of Moffat," and whose parishioners thought him demented as he tramped around the Pentland countryside with his insect-net. He was also keenly interested in botany, and found in the pursuit of his scientific inquiries a convenient way of getting outside and away from his Kirk members, for his appointment, under the patronage of Lord Lauderdale, was very unpopular on account of the absence of any reference to the feelings and wishes of the people, who formerly had been consulted, even under his lordship's patronage, when an appointment was made. Feeling ran high, and a secession of members took place, notwithstanding the highly respectable character of the Minister chosen. One record runs that he " was nearly jostled out of the Gate by the gown tails." The story is told that when catechising a Presbyterian he asked " who made Paul a preacher," and was met with the quick-witted rejoinder: " It wasna' my Lord Lauderdale! " He was punctilious about his personal appearance, and wore a nicely curled wig, and the good ladies of Colinton, when they saw the insect-net hanging out of his pocket, thought he must have a pair of curling tongs there also!

He was an M.D. of Glasgow University, and in 1779 was nominated by the Crown, Professor of Natural History in the University of Edinburgh, a post which he held concurrently with that of Minister of Colinton, and which he adorned with the same high standard of efficiency as that which characterised his work for the Church, of whose

General Assembly he was appointed Moderator in 1790. He married Miss Wauchope of Niddrie.

His successor—the Rev. John Fleming—formerly of Carrington, was appointed in 1804, and was not so careful of his personal appearance. He was a big, burly, farmer-like fellow, and when not engaged in clerical duties was dressed in a coat of Galashiels blue cloth, with very large buttons, and top-boots. Prior to his appointment to a pastoral charge he was Factor to the Earl of Rosebery. He left funds to endow Chairs of Political Economy in Edinburgh and Glasgow Universities, when that science was only in its infancy, and gifted books to the Parish Library in the days when Free Libraries were unthought of. And after him came the well-beloved Lewis Balfour, the grandfather of R. L. S., who although he may have lived in what to the youthful mind appeared a very dark room surrounded by a library of " bloodless books," must have had a quiet humour also, when, as narrated by a former Minister, Mr Marjoribanks, he sent his lady collectors round the parish to collect funds for the new Kirk bells, with collection-sheets having printed over the top—" For the Bells of Colinton by the Belles of Colinton."

Lewis Balfour (1777-1860), D.D., Glasgow, 1853), son of John Balfour of Pilrig, before his presentation to Colinton by the Earl of Lauderdale, was minister of Sorn, 1806-1823, the parish identified with Alexander Peden, the famous Covenanting Minister and friend of the Boswells of Auchinleck. He married (1808) Henrietta Scott, daughter of Rev. Dr George Smith, Galston, who in Burns's " Holy Fair " " opens out his cauld harangues on preaching and on morals." The twelfth child of the family of thirteen, Margaret Isabella (1829-1897) married Thomas Stevenson, C.E. (1818-1887), also one of a family of thirteen, and became the mother of R. L. S., who was born on 13th November, 1850.

Many notable families have been resident in the parish and its surroundings: Foulis of Woodhall, Forrest of

Comiston, Otterburn of Redhall, Lords Woodhall and Dreghorn, and Sir William Forbes, the Banker, who built Colinton House, and preserved the old Manor House or Castle, built in 1450, whose son married Miss Wilhelmina Belsches, the lady of Sir Walter Scott's choice; Lord Dunfermline, Speaker of the House, son of General Sir Ralph Abercromby of Aboukir, was also a resident in Colinton House, and was succeeded by the second Lord Dunfermline, father of the Hon. Mrs Trotter. Colonel Trotter, the last proprietor, died in 1925. Nor shall we omit the pawky old snuff-makers of Spylaw, and the generous gifts of James Gillespie in founding and endowing an hospital and school, or the poet Malloch—who changed his name to Mallet, that Englishmen might be able to pronounce it correctly—who was tutor at Dreghorn to the sons of George Home, proprietor of the Castle in 1720. Here he composed the ballad of " William and Margaret." He studied at Edinburgh University along with Thomson, and influenced the poet to collect his fragmentary pieces and connect them into a regular poem; thus " Winter " was published in 1726, to be followed later by the completed " Seasons," the writing of which began a new era in English literature, so far as the description of nature in poetry was concerned. In 1740 Thomson and Mallet wrote the masque " Alfred," in which the song " Rule Britannia " first appeared.

Law, Literature, and merchandise were for centuries identified with the old families of Colinton.

Yes, it may be interesting to ruminate about all the wonderful folks, the old gentlefolks of the Colinton and Bonaly of other days, for Colinton will not now sit for long as a genial old man full of happy talk and jovial memories —these days are past and over; but we like to think that it was the hill wind, and " the wine that the hill wind brings," of which Will Ogilvie speaks, that helped to fire the spark of personality, and make it gleam and burn brightly in all the interesting folk who have made the associations of these places so rich in all that is sweet and ennobling.

CHAPTER V

THE COUNTRY OF "THE GENTLE SHEPHERD"

CARLOPS AND NINEMILEBURN

CARLOPS lies towards the south-western corner of the Pentland range, thirteen miles from Edinburgh, in a circling wind-sheltered fold of the lower hills that slope down from the higher Pentland peaks; and to the eastward stretches the moorland of Harlawmuir and Auchencorth Moss, 800 feet above sea-level, with the rolling Moorfoot Hills in the distance.

Up among the Pentland heights, near Harper-rig Hill and the Boar Stane Pass, the North Esk River has its source, and winding down through the heathery moorland, passes into a lovely hill loch, and flowing round the base of Spital Hill and Patie's Hill, tumbles over a waterfall at the Carlops Mill. Bustling and brawling it thereafter passes under Carlops Brig, then meanders through the green valley under the Scroggy Brae, Roger's Rig, and the Girth Hill, on through the deep wooded gorge of Habbies Howe and the elfin-haunted demense of Newhall, and ere it enters the woods that environ the grounds of Penicuik House, skirts the old historic Castle of Brunstane.

This picturesque river has inspired the muse of some of Scotland's best poets—Drummond of Hawthornden (1585-1649), so keenly sensitive to the beauty of natural scenery, and the first in Scottish poetry to record the beauty of a mountain height shining in the snow; and Allan Ramsay (1686-1758), the scenes of whose Pastoral Comedy, *The Gentle Shepherd*, are laid around Carlops, Newhall, and Habbies Howe. Sir Walter Scott also found inspiration here. It was to Lasswade, on the Esk not far from Roslin, that he brought his bride; and here he began *The Lay of the Last Minstrel,* and laid the foundation of his fame.

Here also he was visited by Wordsworth and his sister Dorothy, who praised the " easy flowing energy " of the *Lay*, and to whom he recounted the historic and legendary associations of the beauteous vale. For him it was bound up in a thousand happy memories:—

> " Sweet are thy paths, O passing sweet!
>   By Esk's fair stream that run
> O'er airy steep, through copsewood deep,
>   Impervious to the sun.
>
> Who knows not Melville's beechy grove,
>   And Roslin's rocky glen,
> Dalkeith, which all the virtues love,
>   And classic Hawthornden? "

John Leyden also came to see Sir Walter at Lasswade, bringing with him some old historical tale or ballad that " The Wizard " might add to the *Minstrelsy;* while Lockhart has described the valley as affording " some of the most romantic scenery that Scotland can boast."

The village and district has had associations with witches and fairies from the earliest times. The etymology of the name—Carlops, or " The Carlops," as it is properly and commonly called—has given rise to much speculation. In view of its situation Gaelic scholars hold it is " the little fold in the hills," from Cathair, a hill, and Luban, a little fold; others, the town of Lupus—Caer Lupus; the popular derivation is " The Carline's loup," from the legend of the witch who, with her cat and candle on her broom, was believed at nights to make her loups or leaps across the great rocks, which at one time formed an almost complete archway[1] over the road at the southern end of the village, and to bound and frolic across the mouth of the glen, near which she had her " cruve." It was an eerie place on dark nights, with the winter wind howling among the hills and

---

[1] The romantic appearance of this archway was unfortunately long ago destroyed when the rocks were used as material for keeping the Old Road in repair.

whistling through the Windy Gowl, and many a terrified shepherd lad fled quickly home when he saw the witch at her gambols. So the place came to be called "The Carline's loup," modified to "The Carlops."

In the Menzies Charter of 1315 the name was le Kerlinglipis," in later Charters "The Lands of Kerlingleps" (1467); in Timothy Pont's seventeenth-century maps it is "Karlinghoups," and "Carlinhops," and so on; but "The Carline's loup" is the form of the name that is earliest known, and in it is enshrined legendary lore and tradition, which in such matters we do not set lightly aside.

In the Parliament held at Perth, 1425-6, a complaint was made by David Menyhes (Menzies) of Bogry that Sir James Douglas, Lord of Dalkeith, overlord of the lands of Carlops, which Menyhes had possessed in peace for twelve years and more, had in the vassal's absence, given them to Alan of Erskyne in right of his wife, "against law and to no small hurt of the complainer. The Lords Auditors having fully heard the cause, gave for sentence that the lands of Karlinglippis should, without any delay, be ' recognosced ' in the hands of the Lord of Dalkeith, and should then be delivered in pledge to Menyhes as their lawful possessor " (*Origines Parochiales Scotiæ,* pub. Bannatyne Club, 1851). In the seventeenth century the feudal superior-in-chief was the Earl of Morton, and the immediate superior the Menzies of Weems in Athol, who sold the lands to a family named Burnet.

The lands of Carlops were purchased from Archibald Burnet, the last of that family, and added to the Newhall Estate by John Forbes of Newhall, Advocate, son of Sir David Forbes, Knight, of Newhall, uncle to the celebrated President Duncan Forbes of Culloden, who befriended and introduced to public notice the poet Thomson (of "The Seasons"). John Forbes was the friend and patron of Ramsay—the "canny" Mr Forbes, as the poet called him. He was also joint-author with Dr Pennecuik of the *Description of Tweeddale.* Other proprietors were the Browns of Newhall, of whom Robert Dunmoor Craufurd Brown, Advocate, began the building of the present village of Carlops in 1784. He also edited both Pennecuik's *Tweeddale* with copious Notes, and the Scenery Edition of *The Gentle Shepherd,* in two volumes, printed by Abernethy & Walker, Edinburgh, in 1808, and illustrated by David Allan, the " Scots Hogarth," and wrote several historical dramas and poems in Scots, without putting his name to any of these publications, or claiming any recognition. He is described as " A Lawyer, little in practice, small estate, but very independent," in a sort of Scots *Who's Who* of 1788, entitled *The Political State of Scotland,* a curious and illuminating volume compiled by Adam of Blairadam for Henry Dundas, who was supervising Scottish affairs on behalf of Pitt. The last of this noted and respected family of lairds was Robert D. C. Brown's grandson—Horatio Robert Forbes Brown, an Honorary LL.D. of Edinburgh University, and author of several works on Venetian life and literature, who died at Belluno, Italy, on 19th August 1926. Newhall House, and the several farms on the lands of Carlops, have now passed into the hands of individual owners.

Many a quiet and unpretentious country village loses all records of the historical, literary, and industrial lore circling round its name when there is no chronicle in a permanent form of the part that the inhabitants played in the drama of national affairs, or reliable record as to how they lived and thought, worked and played, in times so different from our own, and posterity is the poorer for the loss. A note of village history, custom, or humour, with the story of the quiet contented life of the " forefathers of the hamlet," is often a grateful antidote to the materialism and the strain of modern life, stirring the fancy and enlivening the memory concerning the interesting days and no less interesting personalities of long ago. Yet this information is frequently difficult to obtain, for much of it was oral, consisting of fireside stories and old folk's reminiscences, and traditional tales are often all that have been left to us. But Carlops was fortunate in this respect, because it had its Chronicler in Robert D. C. Brown, the above-mentioned laird, and from a humorous poem written in 1793, entitled " Carlop Green or Equality Realised," we gain much insight into the life and history of the inhabitants of this Pentland village.

The poem, we are informed in the Introduction, is composed as to subject, scenery, character, and rustic gaiety, in the same style of humour with that which prevailed so much in Scotland among the leading wits before the Union with England.

We are introduced to the various inhabitants about the Green and in the town, and the attendants at the Fairs: Mass John the Minister; Lettergae the precentor, who " let's-go " (gives out the tune); Jonny Jow, the beadle, that rings Mass John's kirk bell; Israel, a man who lived at Canaan, Morningside, near the lands of Egypt and the River Jordan, in 1792, and whose children were known as " the children of Israel "; next come Elder Sam, the joiner-gentleman of Ninemileburn; the miller, a miser who " grudges whan he works, because it gars him hearty eat "; the smith, the smuggler, the weaver who works a still among the birks on the brae-side in a hole at a well; showmen, tinkers, and spaewives, and Tabitha with her tabby cats, who

> " Warlock stories tells sae weel
>   O' ghaists and goblins lean
> At Barrie's cove, the caldrons, craigs,
>   Or Carlops hill or dean.
>
> O' dwarfs like ancient painted Peghs (Picts)
>   Lamentan' o'er their urns,
> And whiles o' Fairies green about
>   The glimmeran' glens and burns ";

then comes Squirt the postman from *Beinn-na-Cuachaig*, the Hill of the Cuckoo, Penicuik, " wi' Gowk-hill-news sick fu'," eager " that he may get within the Toll, before that aught gets out," to tell his budget-fu' o' tales to the waiting weavers, of the progress of the French Revolution—

> " In state to tell the wabsters round
>   Was razed the proud Bastile,
> With it, that all were levelled now,
>   And everything gaed weel.
>
> That Louis' self was guillotined;
>   The people bore the sway;
> That here, too, each would soon be free
>   To eat and nothing pay.
>
>   .   .   .   .   .
>
> That all were to be fraternized,
>   Were to have bonnets red;
> And were to serve, each man himself
>   Without another's aid,"

and so continues his oration on the blessings of Equality—

> " That a' will pasture where they please,
>   Like Lot and Abraham;
> The lands will a' be commons then,
>   For horse, cow, sheep, and lamb.
>
> Th' embrace fraternal will go round
>   Love will our thoughts engage;
> Then humblings, toil, and tax will cease,
>   As in the Golden Age."

He repeats the news everywhere, and to every one, as he goes along the Linton Road.

The recruiting sergeants come to Carlops Green and call on the youths to enlist in defence of their country against a French invasion. James, an Edinburgh dealer, meets John, a neighbouring farmer, at the Fair. He buys John's fat yeld cow, and they settle the bargain over a friendly glass. A fife and drum band passes by, and this introduces politics. James, who is a Friend of the People, gives a lecture on Equality:—

111

" I'm for Equality,' cries he,
  ' I've read all Thomas Paine,
And, lest a word I should forget,
  I'll read him o'er again :
What right have those they call the rich . . .
Come, here's to you, Friend John,—
What right have they to more than we?
  I answer surely none !'—

' What would you do then, tell me James?'
  ' Oh, by all means *divide!*
I'd like, if 'twere but from mere spite,
  In Crœsus' coach to ride.'

          .   .   .   .   .

' Your equal purse would soon be gone,
  All would be as before;
Some would pick up what you had lost,
  And add it to their store;

Ere lang, this sure would be the case,
  And what would you do then?'
' Why, what else would I do,' says John,
  ' But just divide again!' "

John defends the British Constitution, founded on a distinction in riches and rank, with equal rights. James pro-
poses a division of property—the proposal is overheard by
two begging sailors, and they ask for a share of the cow,
and her price; and the answer gives rise to John's story of
an English squire and his man who, travelling from the
South to Edinburgh Races, got no farther than the Carlops
because of the excellent fare provided at the Inn:—

" The Carline's head—the Carline's loups—
  These charming boils and roasts—
The mutton of the Carlop Hill
  Shall ever be my toasts."

While John is telling his story, the sailors realise James's
doctrines and carry off and divide the cow and price.
James returns to Edinburgh without either the price or the
cow, a convert to good order, comforts, and security, and
the distinctions in rank and property, with equal rights:

" Quoth John to James, ' What think you now?
　　Is't this you call *Equality?* '
Quoth James to John, ' It surely is;
　　Though't won't do in *Reality.*'

Ere James got back to Edinburgh town,
　　Without or cash or cow,
He'd got his fill of *Sans-culottes,*
　　And *levelling* I trow.

The *Requisitions* that were made
　　At ance opened baith his een,
And sent him hame a wiser man,
　　That day, frae Carlop Green."

NEWHALL

Gae farer up the burn to Habbie's How,
Where a' the sweets of spring and simmer grow
Between twa birks, out o'er a little lin
The water fa's and maks a singand din;
A pool breast-deep, beneath as clear as glass,
Kisses, with easy whirls, the bordering grass.

　　　　　　—The Gentle Shepherd.

The study of an old " Map of the Scenery of Allan Ramsay's *Gentle Shepherd,* from a plan of the year 1770, with additions from a survey in 1808," throws the glamour of a great romantic interest around the district of Carlops and Ninemileburn.

The district is well known to Edinburgh folks and Pentland walkers. Here, it is now agreed, we have the scene of Ramsay's Pastoral. Ramsay was a frequent visitor in summer, often staying for six weeks at a time, at Newhall, where all the literati gathered. These included the poets Thomson of " The Seasons," an open-hearted and keen observer of nature, whose interpretation of its æsthetical enjoyment was among the first of its kind, and Gay, who wrote *The Beggar's Opera* in 1727, two years after the publication of the *Gentle Shepherd*—the " sonsy Gay," as Ramsay calls him, lively, good-humoured, and inclined to corpulency, like Allan himself, the protégé of the Duke and Duchess of Queensberry, who were intimate friends of Sir John Clerk of Penicuik. Here also the Worthy Club met in summer. A picture by David Allan let into the ceiling of the Club Room shows Ramsay reciting his poem to a full meeting of the Club, and the charming Mrs Forbes bringing in a steaming bowl of punch.

Many of the places in the district bear the names of characters in the poem—Mause's Cottage, Patie's Hill, Roger's Rig, and some others, but how are we to account for such names as Monks Burn—now Ninemileburn, so named because it is nine Scots (but over eleven English) miles from Edinburgh—Monks Rig, Friarstown, Spital House, St Robert's Croft?

Prior to the thirteenth century the site now occupied by the mansion-house of Newhall is supposed to have contained a monastery belonging to the Cistercian monks. This religious Order was founded in the eleventh century by Robert, Abbot of Molesme, a Benedictine, who was born at Champagne in France in 1018, and adopting a life of devotion and prayer, lived for a time in the forest of Molesme. There he and his followers built an oratory in honour of the Holy Trinity in 1075, and lived in cells made of boughs of trees. Afterwards they settled at Cistercium, an uninhabited forest, covered with woods and brambles and watered by a stream, five leagues from Dijon. St Robert's Croft at Ninemileburn, which stood at the confluence of the Spital Burn and the Monks Burn, was doubtless named after the founder of the Cistercian Order.

No written conveyances of Newhall exist prior to 1529, when it was possessed by the family of the name of Crichtoune, and was in the form of an irregular Castle, with walls of great strength, and having a prison, chapel, and chapel-yard. The prison was used at a later date for disorderly coal-miners on the estate. The name "New Hall" probably originated when the new mansion-house was built upon the site of the old Convent, which would have a hall in which the Courts for the tenants were held. The Cistercians were great employers of labour.

Monastic establishments, such as Newhall, usually erected smaller houses near by, called hospitals, houses for travellers and for the sick and aged. They were the inns of those days, and the present farm of Spital is the site of one of these inns. The remains of another on the other side of the Spital Hills, on the Esk side, is also to be seen, called on the map—"Ruins of the Back Spital House." Weary and benighted travellers found rest here, and through all the centuries this right of shelter has continued in the neighbourhood, and down to 1800 one of the buildings of the Spital House was allotted for this purpose. This custom survives even yet in the district, and gangrel bodies are seldom denied a night's shelter and food, as I have witnessed several times. This Hospitium or 'Spital, which remained until the Reformation in 1560, was modernised about 1750, and in lieu of the 'Spital there was built a new inn, called the " New House," on the main highway, about a mile south of the Toll Gate at Ninemile-burn, above the cottage called " Honeybrae." The present Inn at Ninemileburn is really the successor of the Monks' Inn of these far-off days.

The road by which the monks passed from 'Spital, along the hillside, over the Monks Rig to Gap Law and the right-of-way at the Kips, can still be traced, and the " Font Stone " on this track through the heather is referred to in the walk over the Monks Rig to Ninemileburn.

It is well to state, however, that there is another theory which accounts for such names as Monks Burn and Monks Rig, namely, that they were called after General Monk, afterwards Duke of Albemarle, who it is said, while at Dalkeith House on the North Esk, sent a detachment of his troops to the neighbourhood, where they had a skirmish with some Royalists, in the time of Dr Pennecuik, who was a contemporary of Cromwell, Montrose, Monk, and Charles II. The fable or plot on which Ramsay's Comedy is founded is said to have been communicated by the Doctor, and Ramsay introduced Monk into the Pastoral—

> " Now Cromwell's gane to Nick, an' ane ca'd Monk
> Has played the Rumple a right slee begunk,
> Restored King Charles, an' ilka things in tune,
> An' Habby says we'll see Sir William soon."

" Sir William Worthy," modelled upon the character of the laird, Sir David Forbes, is represented as having fought under Montrose against Cromwell, and recovered his estate with the Restoration of Charles the Second by Monk. He also speaks of a hollow called Charles' Nick, marked on the map near the Carlops village and burn connecting the scene with the Restoration of King Charles.

The late Horatio R. F. Brown[1] stated that he had " doubts as to the truth of the Monastic tradition " of Newhall, doubts which his grandfather evidently did not share.

A Crown Charter of the lands of Newhall in the barony of Penicuik was granted by King Robert III. to Lawrence Crichtoun, dated about 1405, and there is a tradition that the reddendo was a pair of silver-gilt spurs. There is a doubt as to this, however, the original Charter having been lost, probably through the sinking of the ship by which Cromwell intended to convey such archives to London in 1660; but a Latin Index in the Register House and Robertson's English Index indicate the contents of the lost Rolls. The lands passed through the families of Fairlie of Braid, Hay of Forresterseat, Scott of Drumsheugh, and Patrick Baxter, till in 1634 they came to David Crichtoun, younger of Lugton, " and others." Alexander Pennecuik, on his return from service as Surgeon-General to the Scottish Auxiliary Army in England, sold the estate of Pennecuik, which he had inherited, to Sir George Clerk,

---

[1] Article in *Scottish Historical Review*, vol. xvi.

and along with his first spouse Janet Leslie, acquired the property of Newhall in 1646, from a George Watson and his wife. Pennecuik obtained a Crown Charter, the tenure being a quit rent of a silver penny. On the decease of his first wife he married the daughter and heiress of Murray of Romanno, became possessed of that estate, and settled there. Dr Alexander Pennicuik, who succeeded his father in Newhall, presented the estate in 1702 to his eldest daughter, Mrs Oliphant of Lanton, who sold it to Sir David Forbes, Knight in 1703, after which Allan Ramsay was a frequent guest at Newhall. John Forbes, Advocate, succeeded his father, and died about 1750. After passing through various hands it was purchased from the Hays, in 1782, by Thomas Dunmore of Kelvinside as an investment for the fortune of his ward and grandson, Robert D. C. Brown. From Robert Brown it descended to his son and grandson, Hugh Horatio Brown and Horatio Robert Forbes Brown, respectively.

The kindly interest taken by the benevolent laird, Sir David Forbes, in his tenants is thus portrayed by Ramsay in his Comedy:—

> " Nor wad he lang, wi' senseless, saucy air,
> Allow our lyart noddles to be bare.
> ' Put on your bonnet, Symon;—tak a seat.—
> How's a' at hame?—How's Elspa?—How does Kate?
> How sells black cattle?—What gies woo this year?'
> And sic-like kindly questions wad he spier."

Laird Brown mentions in Dr Pennecuik's *Tweeddale* that " the command of Freestone, Whinstone, Lime, Sand, Wood, Water, Coal and Peat, with a turnpike road running through their centre, induced the proprietor of the lands of Carlops to begin building a village on them A.D. 1784, at which there is now a woollen manufacture, and also to ornament and enrich that part of the county with a number of new and neat farm-houses." It was the modest Robert Brown himself who began the building of the village as we know it. In his day there was a mansion-house near the site of what is now called Carlops Mains—a small white-washed house with architectural designs over the door, which stands beside the Carlops Rock, not far from the highway—an inn, a turnpike gate, and a few cottages. He established the hand-loom weaving industry, and the primary object of the building of the village was to accommodate the weavers. There was a flax-mill at Marfield, another near Harbour Craig, a fulling-mill and dyehouse at Monkshaugh, as well as a powder-mill, a bleach-field at Gladsheugh, and a carding-mill above Carlops Brig, subsequently a meal-mill, now forming part of the buildings of Carlops poultry farm.

The late laird, H. R. F. Brown, said he remembered hearing the clatter of the looms in 1860. The last Carlops weaver was working at his loom until 1894. Carlops, therefore, in the end of the eighteenth and early part of the nineteenth centuries, was a busy, manufacturing and industrial centre.

The weaving industry was hard hit by the application of steam power and gradually died out, but two mail-coaches continued to pass through the village daily, this being a main highway to Dumfries and the Lead Hills, to Glasgow by Carnwath and Carluke, and to Lanark and Hamilton. The Carlops carrier is the last surviving relic of the romantic days of this old highway.

The first experiment in Scotland of raising a potato crop in pure peat earth was made at Newhall in 1750, with successful results. It was also discovered at Newhall that carrots grow luxuriantly in pure peat earth, freed from water. While these trials were being carried out on the southern side of the hills, the Earl of Stair at New Liston on the northern side, was raising turnips and cabbages in open fields for the first time. Before that time turnips, cabbages, and potatoes had been grown only as garden plants.

Carlops as a thriving weaving village had neither policeman nor kirk, so that it was said there was neither " law nor gospel" in the Carlops; but the village had a Sunday School as early as 1830, and a Free Church congregation the year after the Disruption, which at first met in the loft of the Carlops Mill, and afterwards in a cottage that served both as church and school, upon the site of the present building, which was erected in 1850. In 1846 there was a population of 370, many of whom were employed at the lime-kilns and Deepsykehead Quarry. The Parish Church hall was not built until 1900.

Among all the historical, literary, and industrial curiosities of this district, the earliest historical event is perhaps the most interesting of all. It comes with all the force of a shock to be told that for a time the boundary line between Scotland and England ran through Carlops. This fact is recorded in the *Orygynale Cronykil of Scotland*, by Andrew of Wyntoun, which he completed in 1424, where, relating the Battle of Durham or Neville's Cross— 17th October 1346—a dark day in Scottish history, when King David was captured and sent to the Tower of London, he goes on to narrate that the boundaries between England and Scotland were fixed first at Cockburnspath and Soutra on the Lammermoors, and then at Karlynglippis (Carlops) and Corscryne, a hill on the borders between Lanarkshire and Peeblesshire, in Kilbucho parish. (It was upon this hill that the English army lay encamped before the Battle of Biggar.)

The historian tells us, that following upon the Battle of Neville's Cross, the English captured the Castle of Roxburgh, and overrunning Tweeddale, the Merse, Ettrick, Annandale, and Galloway, their temproary successes enabled them to boast that the new boundary of Scotland was from " Coldbrandispethe to Soutra, and subsequently to Carlops and Crosscryne." The territory was recovered within a few years, but for a brief period Carlops was on the Border line.

The Glen or Pass in which the village of Carlops is situated must have been considered a place of military importance at one time. Patie's Hill is the traditional site of a Fort where there has been found a battle-axe and two iron spurs of uncommon design. There were also military works in Carlops Dean, where another battle-axe was found, near some old foundations. In the Dean there is a hill with a flat summit, named Dun Kaim, originally called Dun Cam, the fort on the crooked hill, the Dun being the most rude as well as the most ancient of the Celtic Forts. Carlops Hill, like Patie's Hill, was also fortified, and military works are said to have existed on the opposite side of the Pass on the banks of the Back Burn, and at Whitfield, two miles to the south-eastward. Other traditional British Forts are situated above Castlelaw Farm, and between Lawhead and Turnhouse Hill, and at Camp Hill near the Kirk Road at Silverburn.

In view of this apparent military connection of the Carlops, of whatever period it may have been, the derivation of the name from the Gaelic Caer, contracted to Car, a fortified town or camp, and lop or lip, the "s" being frequently omitted, derived from luib, a winding hill, giving us Carlop, the Fortified Town of the Winding Hill, forms a suitable alternative for those who disbelieve in the Carline's Loup, and expresses precisely the situation of the village as we know it to-day, tucked away in the fold of the winding hill.

But this village of Carlops, hid in the fold of the hills, with its few cottages on each side of the spacious highway, its old village Well, whereon we read inscribed "God's Gift," its Kirk and market green, its post-office, sweetie-shop, and store, its tea-houses and Inn, no longer resounds to the rhythmic movement of the weavers' cob and shuttle. Its two attendant spirits seem now to be Peace and Humanity, although these may not be so easily recognised or appreciated by the numbers who arrive in motor vehicles in the time of summer, attracted by the hilly environment and the poetical associations of Allan Ramsay's Pastoral; but the walker and the wayfarer who rejoice in tramping over the hills in winter, in early spring, and in autumn, and entering the lonely but snug little village when it exhales an atmosphere native to its rural surroundings, will be able to interpret and to understand something of this spirit, quiet and elusive as the wisps of blue smoke that rise tremulously in the still frosty air from cottage chimneys, and of the attendant spirit of Humanity that welcomes and cheers and satisfies at the Inn.

For the visitor with a few hours at his disposal, there are sections of the old historic road at each end of the village from which characteristic views of the countryside of Ramsay's *Gentle Shepherd* may be obtained. There is also the charming walk up by the Old Mill and Waterfall and the banks of the Esk, with bordering shades of brackens and rowans, and moss-covered rocks, and with many an inviting pool, then across the log and turf-covered bridge, and along the birken glen where the primroses grow, to the farm of Fairliehope. This pleasant ramble may be extended farther into the hills to the North Esk Loch, and to the cottage where dwelt the genial shepherd Willie Tod, born at Spital, son of "Honest John," the Swanston shepherd, who was born at Friarstown near-by, and who taught R. L. S. "all he ever knew of that Hillside business" *(Memories and Portraits)*. The circle may be completed in returning from Fairliehope by the road that, while winding and gradually descending from the hills, opens up to our view an extensive panorama of the Moorfoots, and enters the village at the scene of the Carline's loups and the old mansion-house of the lands of Carlops.

THE HARBOUR CRAIG

The Harbour Craig lies in a valley that borders the rolling moorland of Harlawmuir and Auchencorth Moss, east of Carlops and south-east of the North Esk River, Newhall, and the Habbies Howe, and was so called from the protection which the great perpendicular Crag or Craig with its crevices, rising to a height of about fifty-five feet above the valley, gave to those Covenanters who here found refuge after the Battle of Rullion Green. The valley is shut off from the Pentlands by the wooded glen of the Habbies Howe, and is so sheltered that but few sentinels would be required upon the surrounding hills to guard its approaches.

Nevertheless from the Craig there is a full view of the chain of Pentland heights stretching from Rullion Green to the Black Hill above Silverburn, with a foreground of valley, stream, and woodland, which is surpassed only by the fuller view from Harlawmuir.

It was on the edge of the moorland not far from this spot that the supposed skirmish took place when General Monk's troops were following Charles II. to Worcester.

Laird Gifford of Linton was one of the number of those who here found refuge after the Pentland Rising, and his name and the year 1666 are engraved upon the rock, along with other names and initials, lichen-covered or worn by storms of wind and weather.

Many of the dates are prior to 1666, and in the 1808 edition of *The Gentle Shepherd* the dates 1612 and 1640 were said to be legible. It is probable that the rock came to be known as " The Harbour Craig " after 1666, although it was known by shepherds and hinds both before and after that date as the " Lover's Loup," and as such Ramsay uses it jocularly in his comedy.

During the whole of the persecution, and up to the year 1680, frequent Conventicles were being held in this Pentland countryside, and the Harbour Craig was a favourite resort not only because of its security, but because it formed a suitable rostrum from which to address a gathering in the green haugh below.

From 1811 till 1829, when the Rev. Robert Renwick was Minister of the Lintoun Secession Church, meetings of commemoration were held at the Harbour Craig, and at intervals thereafter until in 1867 there was begun, on the first Sunday of August, the long series of annual Covenanting Memorial Services which have been held at this place down to the present time. Eager hands have in turn passed on the torch, which has been kept burning, and in all the quiet village kirks among the hills every year sees some memorial celebration, and young hearts touched by the inspiring and impassioned appeal of the voices of the past. So here, and at many another Conventicle by Rullion Green and Dunsyre, the music of the old Scottish Psalms and Paraphrases rises in the still summer air in the glen, while the curlews' notes and the bleat of the sheep add to the reality of the worship of the Unseen in the spirit-land amidst the Pentland Hills.

In the centuries now long gone, the hill folks around Logan House and Bavelaw, and many another place out-by, tramped by the Kirk Road over the hills to Penicuik to worship in God's house there. That right-of-way is still well marked from the head of Loganlee Valley up and over between Scald Law and Carnethy, and down by the Grain Burn. And to-day, the same religious zeal still burns in the hearts of many who come from far distances to attend the annual services at the Harbour Craig, where the Carlops Minister with reverence and devotion sees that all things are done decently and in order, as his predecessors have done for over a century.

"ROBIN TAMSON'S SMIDDY"

Ninemileburn, like all the other villages round the Pentland Hills, had its Smiddy, but few smiddies have found a permanent place in Scottish Song like "Robin Tamson's Smiddy."

The humorous song with the lilting tune is known and delighted in wherever Scotsmen gather. It tells the story of the young ploughman who was sent by his mother to get the mare shod, and makes love to the daughter of the Blacksmith, "wha ne'er wad let her tak' a man, tho' mony lads had socht her." The young man carries her off, and when the Smith " came to our fire-end, and fand us baith thegither," Quo' I " Gudeman, I've taen your bairn, an' ye can tak' my mither "—

> " Auld Robin girn'd and shook his pow,
> ' Gude sooth,' quo' he, ' you're merry,
> But I'll just tak' ye at your word
> An' end this hurry-burry ';
> So Robin an' our auld wife
> Agreed to creep thegither,
> Now I hae Robin Tamson's pet,
> An' Robin has my mither."

The song was written by Alexander Rodger, who was born at East Calder across the Pentlands on 16th July 1784, and lived at Haggs Farm, Dalmahoy, and at Midcalder, Edinburgh, and Glasgow. As a boy he probably visited the Smiddy that stands beside the burn, and as with all boyhood impressions, he never forgot the scene, and came to write about it sometime between 1820 and 1832. He was doubtless also familiar with *The Gentle Shepherd*, and with the poems of Robert D. C. Brown, the Laird of Newhall, in whose ballad, " Peggy's Mill below the Carline's Loup," the following verse occurs:—

> " Will was auld Symon's cottar's son;
> Bess was Glaud's cottar's dochter,
> A virtuous widow's only weane,
> An' mony a herd had socht her."

I am told by one who remembers the Smiddy as it was in 1863, and also by the son of the Smith himself at that time, that " the Nine " Smiddy, like most village smiddies, was the centre of the life of the district, where all the news and gossip of the countryside was exchanged. And Robin Tamson's prototype might well have been " a walthy carle," for work meant money, and he had work in abundance, much of which was necessarily done after nightfall, and had to be completed ere morning. The horses of the neighbouring farms had to be shod; ploughmen brought in broken and blunted coulters; loose harrow-teeth, blunted spades, and many other implements of husbandry had to be repaired; and there also came quarriers from Marfield, and miners from the coal-pit on Brunstane Moor with their various implements, and there were cheery gatherings at "the Nine" Smiddy at all times. Conversation went on despite the incessant and deafening ringing of the anvil and the blowing of the bellows. Larger gatherings than usual would take place about New Year time, when all the lads had a hand in "the dicing"—throwing the dice, at threepence a time, for shortbread, cakes, and currant buns.

The Smith's house, adjoining the Smithy, was at one time used as an inn. On the other side of the burn stood the joiner's shop, with saw-mill and water-wheel. The wheel, which could be seen from the highway, was the successor of a smaller one that existed sixty years ago. The Smithy stood just off the road that goes down to Marfield at the entrance to the "Habbies Howe." This road crosses the present highway at Ninemileburn, and is a continuation of the cross-road that connects the present Inn with the highway from Edinburgh to Carlops.

The original tack of the Smithy subjects was granted by Sir John Clerk of Penicuik in 1795, and the old Smithy buildings with the thatched roof ceased to exist as such about forty years ago. Among the mighty men of the hammer who reigned here were the Robbs and Johnstones, Rankin and Davidson. A modern cottage now stands upon the site, in the possession of a family who have owned a neighbouring cottage since 1820.

The burn is the Monks Burn, that comes down from Pentland's "towerin' taps" with many a purl and "singand din," and "whimples through the clachan," a fit accompaniment with the lowing of cattle standing knee-deep in the lush grass that grows by the burn side, and the crowing and cackling of cocks and hens, to the stamping of horses and the ringing of the anvil; and into the picture there came the Blacksmith's daughter, and the inspiration of the humorous lyric muse, adding another attraction to the district of Allan Ramsay's *Gentle Shepherd*.

THE ARCHITECT OF THE SCOTT MONUMENT

George Meikle Kemp, whose artistic genius designed the famous monument, was born in 1795, and had an intimate connection with this rural countryside.

The first fourteen years of his life were spent around the family homestead on the Newhall Estate—Glaud's Cottage, referred to in *The Gentle Shepherd,* where the scene is thus described—

> " A snug thack house, before the door a green;
> Hens in the midden, ducks in dubs are seen.
> On this side stands a barn, on that a byre;
> A peat-stack joins, an' forms the rural square.
> The house is Glaud's;—there you may see him lean,
> An' on his divot-seat invite his frien'."

His father was employed as shepherd by the laird, and here the boy assisted in the care of sheep, and for one year acted as a herd at a neighbouring farm. His work took him out to the moors and hills and streams around Newhall and Ninemileburn, and we can see the lad with thoughts not occupied overmuch about the flock, but caught up in the fascination of nature study—birds, animals, wild flowers, and all the attractions of nature in mountain solitude and among the mysterious rocky ravines of Marfield and Habbies Howe. The streams and burns attracted him, for here it was he tried his miniature water-wheels. We can see him sitting under the lee of a knoll upon the hillside eagerly working with his penknife, fashioning a waterwheel, then with a long look up the hill, and down the holm to see that all was well with the sheep, moving across to the hill burn, and fixing the wheel, watch it birling at the water's edge. Out of bits of black oak found in the moss around Newhall and Harlaw Muir he carved ornaments of skilful workmanship, an accomplishment which he developed in later life and applied in practical demonstration of larger architectural ornament and design. About the age of ten he first saw Roslin Chapel and Castle, and the effect which these buildings had upon the impressionable mind of this delicate yet intelligent boy never left him; and his emotions of that hour, when he later came to understand them, he described as those of " tremulous surprise." In his leisure hours he found relaxation in the reading of Allan Ramsay, Fergusson, and Burns, and in the local legends and songs of his native countryside. And like every other native of his day around Newhall, he could play the fiddle, and sing to his own accompaniment.

There were two occasions on which he stood in the presence of Sir Walter, with whose name his own was to be so honourably linked. The first was when tramping one warm summer day to his new situation in Galashiels, that, near Elibank Tower, Walter Scott stopped his carriage and bade his coachman ask the young man with the bundle of tools how far he was going, and gave him " a lift " beside the driver. On arrival at Galashiels Kemp learned with interest that his benefactor was none other than " The Shirra."

On the second occasion Kemp was sketching in Melrose Abbey when Sir Walter entered with a party of friends. He came forward and was quickly interested in the drawing, comparing it closely with the part of the building delineated, when, alas! Sir Walter was called away by the momentary excitement among members of his party caused by the too demonstrative " Maida," his dog, and Kemp's opportunity of conversation with the great man was lost, a circumstance which he never ceased to regret.

Kemp was a born walker. He attended a committee meeting in Glasgow in connection with the proposed restoration of Glasgow Cathedral, and walked from Edinburgh and back again. While residing in Lancashire he travelled fifty miles to see York Minster. It was night

127

when he arrived, and he was weary with the journey; but in a moment all sense of fatigue had vanished. Before him towered the stately edifice, so varied in its styles of architecture, the outlines silhouetted against a moonlit sky, and partly hid in mysterious shadows. It had a strange and wonderful effect upon him, holding him as by a spell all through the silence of the night. It was daylight when he left the Minster.

His journeyings on the Continent were all on foot. " I chose this mode of travelling," he says, " as both the cheapest and most informing, since none of the country along the roads we take is likely to escape our view, and by lodging in houses unfrequented by fashionable travellers we see the manners of the people without disguise." To this thoughtful man with the sensitive poetic soul, with a culture and humility that were native to him as his own Pentland Hills, we can imagine the effect which the grand design and gorgeous decoration of the Cathedral buildings of the Continent had upon him—it was all a new discovery to him.

He was once asked if he never wearied in his long walks, and replied, " Oh no, when the slightest failing of mental activity comes on I at once apply to my favourite poets, Chaucer or Spenser. I always carry a copy of one of these for immediate reference." Sometimes when overtaken by darkness in his long walks, he made his bed among the brackens, by the side of a running stream, with the starlit sky for canopy, and when the morning dawned in what to him was elfin-land, all the wonder and the power of nature's work in earth and sky filled his soul with pure delight. Memories of his boyhood days around Newhall often came to him, and his emotions were frequently translated into verse.

When he fell in love, it was to Ninemileburn and the scenes of his boyhood that he often came. It was the place he loved best. Here the lovers sat, and discussed their plans. Here he unfolded to Elizabeth Bonnar all his

Conventicle at Harbour Craig

prospects, and promised that he would build a house for her, upon this spot, so linked with sacred memories. But like many another sweethearting couple around the Pentland Hills, they tarried too long, on one occasion at least—the coach went off without them, and they had to walk home to Edinburgh.

Kemp was of a shy and thoughtful disposition, and seldom was communicative. One who worked at the same bench with him in a Border town was asked what sort of man Kemp was, and replied, " Weel, he's a guid tradesman, but I dinna think there's muckle in him, for him an' me have been workin' thegither for the last fortnight, an' he has hardly opened his mouth to speak a word a' that time."

In due time his genius found expression in the masterpiece that was to make his name famous. His design for the Scott Monument was accepted, and the foundation stone was laid on 15th August 1840, by Sir James Forrest of Comiston, Bart., Lord Provost and Lord-Lieutenant of the city.

For six years (skilled) craftsmen laboured (enthusiastically), while Kemp superintended its erection. Standing upon solid rock, it towers 200 feet high, and is founded 52 feet below the level of Princes Street.

Unfortunately he did not live to see its completion (August 17, 1846), his death taking place two and a half years previously (March 16, 1844), and the top stone of the imposing structure was placed in position by his son.

Sixteen of Scotland's poets adorn the vaulted roof of the Gothic Temple, and sixty-four niches are filled with statuettes of the famous novelist's characters. The marble statue of Sir Walter is by Sir John Steell.

The (chaste) tablet at Redscaurhead between Eddleston and Peebles, where in the carpenter's shop of Andrew Noble he worked as an apprentice, forms a pleasing memorial (dedicated October 1, 1932).

CHAPTER VI

AN APRIL DAY

AN April morning—clear and bright, sunshine after rain, and the birds singing; just sufficient of winter in it to make exercise exhilarating, and a promise of summer for the mind's contemplation.

Our journeys into the more distant parts of the hills are usually planned and thought our for some time before the adventure is to take place, so that when the morning arrives, our plan completed, we set forth in the mind of the man who wrote, " Ye shall go out with joy, and be led forth with peace: the mountains and the hills shall break forth before you into singing, and all the trees of the field shall clap their hands." I think the author of these words must have been a walker, so accurately does he picture the mood of the man rising on an April morning, with a full day's holiday before him to tramp across the countryside and among the hills, where the birds are singing as they wheel in the sunlit sky, and the wild untended trees are clapping their hands for very joy of the springtime. And all his leading through the day is in peace.

So it was on this day—morning train to AUCHENGRAY, and a day's tramp across the hills and moors, by moorland streams and fir-woods, to West Linton, where the Biggar bus would take one home at evening.

Auchengray Station serves a wide district, cross-roads radiate everywhere, and the village, sitting on rising ground above it, half a mile away, would seem in country fashion to keep a watchful eye upon all travellers. Only one passenger emerged from the station and took the road to the left, climbing to the village, knapsack on shoulder and cromak in hand, while the larks poured forth their song and the cries of the curlews filled the air, and a skein of geese passed high overhead. The church, the school, the inn, the farm, the smithy, and the motor-garage, with a few old cottages, are all the passer-by sees of Auchengray, but from its elevated situation there is a wide view of the farm lands and peaty moorlands surrounding. Beyond the village there is a sign-post directing the way to the right, and we do not travel far before we crest the hill, and there rises up before us the long sweep of the Pentlands, with Tinto Hill on the right. At a bend in the road three farms cluster—Easterhouse, Loanhead, and Greenfield—beyond which lies the village of Tarbrax, and the heights of the Cairn Hills in the distance.

Love for nature and the far spaces, boundless freedom, fresh air and exercise make the walker interested and alert; the senses speak to the mind, and his sympathies become one with the landscape through which he passes; he can be happy alone, or in company, and so it is that the thoughtful freeman has in most cases a generous outlook on men and things, and welcomes every new adventure on the road, along which he seldom travels far without seeing something of interest or experiencing some fresh impression.

In Auchengray a gang of navvies are laying pipes for a water supply from the Lyne Valley Reservoir, and a request for a match affords the walker an opportunity for conversation with one of them, and the Irish brogue falls soft and musical upon the ear in strange contrast with the rugged exterior of this hardy son of toil; the milk boy comes next, then the blacksmith looks up and invites conversation; after that the postman—the man who is welcomed everywhere—and here comes a miner, who looks up from the blue-covered " Report of the Coal Commission, 1926," which he is reading, and is so perplexed that he too must stop, and talk. Then he points to Tarbrax —" one of these non-paying concerns, shut down!—that

131

building on the right among the trees is the Educational Authority Hostel," "expensive to run," he adds, "and that's a doo cot beside it. The Oil Company owns the land round about, and runs the farms," and so one gets in a nutshell all the country's troubles, and on a spring morning too! with the sun shining and the birds singing! and one turns perhaps thankfully to a shepherd lad in a field near-by whistling to his dog manœuvring a flock of sheep. The road-mender is next met—he is an interesting fellow to chat with. He reminds us always of Michael Fairless, who wrote that well-known book *The Roadmender*—you remember him, watching the birds—" the robin cocks his tail with a humorous twinkle of his round eye," "two wrens search diligently on a fallen tree for breakfast, quite unconcerned when I rest for a moment beside them," and it was this philosophical road-mender who learned in his work to understand dimly the truth of the three great paradoxes—" the blessing of a curse, the voice of silence, and the companionship of solitude." Companionship such as this is reserved for the walker in country places. He takes and gives much.

At Dykehead Farm the road turns to the left, and leading through open moorland the Lang Whang is soon reached—four miles from Auchengray—where the right-of-way over the hills begins. Many a track, like a well-intentioned man, starts well. This one does so. How good it is to get off the hard road, and to go swinging along over the soft, springy turf of the track, winding through the reedy grass, making straight ahead for the brown rolling hills in the distance. One forgets all about the marshy places. After all, this is no place for daintily shod folk—strong boots with tackets in them are required; and with this twin feeling of freedom and security, the walker soon ceases to choose his steps, but marches forward with high heart, buoyant and playful as the April wind upon his cheeks, blessing nature for her cleansing and elevating power.

132

Many Pentland walkers are of opinion that this end of the hills is marshy and dangerous, and only to be visited in winter, when the ground is frostbound, or in mid-summer, when it is dry. There are marshes and bogs and peat hags, it is true, but the real walker delights in all wild and difficult places, and the forbidding and the sinister attract his attention, and minister to his innate curiosity.

On our right we pass an old march dyke, fast becoming levelled, alongside which flows the Dryburn, that ultimately joins the Clyde. Later we shall cross another Dryburn that goes to the Tweed. The light spring wind, warmed by the sunshine, with soft sweet savour, is as a " beaker full of the warm South," bringing with it that well-known perfume—the tang of the moorland, so good to inhale, as we tramp on for mile after mile over withered tufty grass and heather; and just as we top the rise a magnificent panorama of mountain landscape opens out before us. At the same moment there comes the sweet-smelling incense of heather burning. These Pentland Hill panoramas with their wild moorland settings, peaks and passes, rocks and rivers, are known only to the walker: they cannot be seen from the road. It requires walking, often hard and toilsome, to get there if you are not in good form, but the wild grandeur of the view is well worth all the effort. It was Ben Jonson who said in another connection, " How near to good is what is fair!" but Thoreau would say, " How near to good is what is wild."

We are now on Henshaw Hill; before us lies the Garval Syke, a great cleft in the hills, through which flows the Medwin Water—part of which will reach the Tweed and part the Clyde—guarded on each side by the Pike (1283 ft.) and the White Craig (1425 ft.) respectively. On the right runs Darlees Rig (1462 ft.); Craigengar (1700 ft.) rises majestically on the left, and through the Syke appears Byrehope Mount (1751 ft.), Fadden Hill (1526 ft.), and Catstone Hill (1470 ft.). On the right foreground is a peat bog, on the left the right-of-way post by the dykeside, where the Harburn route by Crosswood joins this route from Auchengray. Along the dyke runs the boundary line of Lanarkshire, which after crossing Cobbinshaw Loch and the Lang Whang at Maidenwell, mounts Henshaw Hill and follows the course of the Medwin and the Garvald Burn to Dolphinton.

The hill-crossing from HARBURN by the Garvald Syke is a route favoured by many who love a day's tramp on the hills. The distance to the post near Crosswood Farm on the Lang Whang from the station is about three miles, through an interesting countryside, in which we pass the site of a camp or castle which tradition says Cromwell fortified to repress the depredations of the moss-troopers; and Castle Gregg on Camilty Farm, with remains of a camp where the fragments of Roman pottery and coins of Vespasian, Hadrian, and Marcus Aurelius were found, indicating a date about A.D.170. On leaving the Lang Whang and following the track, which goes to the right at the farm-house, we make for the cottages at Mid-Crosswood, and the clump of trees on the hillside, after which there is little difficulty in following the path through the valley to the gate and the post on the slope of Henshaw Hill near the Garval Syke, six miles from Harburn.

The track from this point where the two rights-of-way from Auchengray and from Harburn meet, does not exist. And after all this is to the walker's advantage. Even the following of a track may be difficult, but to find it after it has been lost may often be more difficult still. The hills inspire us with a new feeling of liberty, they also give to us wisdom and fortitude and calmness, and mountain air breathes romance, so that we contemplate without anxiety the loss of the track. A sense of direction is all that is required. A map is a necessity, and a compass a useful adjunct.

The Medwin is crossed by a sheep bridge, and the stones at the ford are scraped and worn by many a drover's and shepherd's tackets. After passing through a gate or over it, and climbing the heathery slopes of the White Craig, we reach the top of the Rig, where another of these spacious views of the hills opens out. If a west or south-west wind is blowing the full force of it will be felt here; you will hear no curlews, and you will seek the shelter of one of the shepherd cairns dotted about, to consult your map. " In the multiude of counsellers there is safety," but probably when you are on the top of Darlees Rig you have no counsellor but your map. And in the multitude of paths there is no guide, for the paths run about here in all directions, many of them hard and dry, but in the valley below there are marshy places. The map or compass will keep you right; make straight for the Covenanter's Grave, keeping the valley of the Medwin on the left, and the mass of the highest hill—Bleak Law—on the right, and with a little luck you should be sitting by the grave of the Covenanter about lunch time. It is not so very difficult to find, provided that on your first visit you are persistent in your search. The stone is several feet high, standing on a hillside facing westwards, with Bleak Law in front, and the valley of the West Water between. In seeming reverence the heather refuses to encroach upon the encircling grass; and on this April day it is a pleasant place to be; the air is filled with the cry of the whaup and the singing of the lark:—

> " High in the blue, with eager outstretched wings,
> Till the strong passion of his joy be told."

There is a wildness and a solitary grandeur about this amphitheatre in the hills—a melancholy grandeur if the mood suits you—amid the " enveloping silence." The place has many visitors in the summer days—and even the wild winter storms fail to drive away all traces of their visits—and new direction posts are of assistance to wayfarers over the hills at this point. Many a walker here for the first time has been glad to come upon the house of Medwinhead, and to ask the shepherd there to tell him where he is. But the shepherd, good-natured man, will probably answer your question by asking you another, namely, where you wan to go to. A reference to the map will show that there is a choice of several routes either to Dolphinton or West Linton. This wild, hillocky, heathery moorland may appear a dreary place to the walker who thinks he is lost, but to him who has been here before it is one of the most charming places in the hills, fresh and full of variety and agreeable surprises like mother nature herself. There are two streams to guide you, the Medwin and West Water. To explore the former with its long winding valley and rocky banks and trout pools is a summer day's delight, while the latter is like a Highland corrie burn with sweet-smelling banks, white boulders, sparkling water, cascades, and a merry song, and if we follow it we shall come to a picturesque camping place where the purple heather blooms, and where the two streams meet, near Walton Cottage. Turn left, and the road from Garvald Home Farm leads to Dolphinton Post-office, where the Biggar bus will convey you to Linton, Carlops, or Edinburgh.

From Medwinhead there is a path to Fernyhaugh Farm, where the road to Dolphinton by Garvald Farm may be joined. But if we have lunched at the Covenanter's Grave, it is unlikely we shall wish to descend upon Dolphinton. There is a fine old drove road from Medwinhead to West Linton, a friendly path: it will go with you all the way. Moreover, it is a right-of-way, and you need have no fear of trespassing. There is still another route. From Medwinhead follow the road through the woods and the heather to Fernyhaugh Farm, where a right-of-way path to West Linton branches off to the left at the post near the farm cottages.

On this April day, the last-mentioned route is taken. From Fernyhaugh it accompanies a pine wood[1] for some distance, a pleasant path, well marked, and at the end of the wood we pass the Nether Cairn on the left, and the Garvald Burn, winding through the valley on the right. Our track is high up above the valley, over the opposite

[1] This wood has since been cut down.

side of which rises the shapely Mendick Hill (1480 feet). A little farther on we come to the Upper Cairn, another of these mysterious collections of stones found among the hills, of which there is no known history. One may climb to the top of the grass and heather-covered mound, and view the route that lies in front to the woods around North Slipperfield. A visit should next be paid to the Rumbling Well on the right, the source of the Garvald Burn, a copious flow of spring water coming out of the hillside with a low rumbling tone. Like " Rumbling Tam," the well at West Linton, it is clear as crystal, cold as ice, and refresh-on a summer's day.

Fir-woods are characteristic of the Pentland landscape, and from the wood we are now approaching, there comes the cooing of wood pigeons, and from a topmost branch a blackbird is pouring his rapturous melody, singing because he is glad, with the blue sky above him, and the green hills around him, and in his delight in simple things making glad the heart of the walker also. Still in fancy I hear him singing, in the clear, sweet-scented air of spring-time.

After crossing the second Dryburn we soon arrive at the right-of-way post where the hill path from Medwinhead is joined, and from here we walk to North Slipperfield, and so by the Golf Course to West Linton.

This walk from Auchengray or Harburn to West Linton —about fifteen miles—is full of interest; and if the paths do disappear at times, a general sense of direction, with the aid of the invaluable " Bartholomew," will see you through without difficulty, bringing to you an increased love for the quiet fascinating places of the wild.

The right-of-way paths in these lesser known and unfrequented regions of the Pentlands are being overgrown with heather and moorland grass, and becoming lost; many of them cannot be discerned, but now that the eastern end of the range with two public parks and well-known paths is becoming more popular every year, walkers in search of the wild and solitary and varied crossings at the western end will doubtless become more numerous. These quiet places among the hills, so little known, yet through which pass the rights-of-way, will appeal to walkers, old and young—to the older school for the memories awakened by the atmosphere of spring and summer airs, the walk on the hill-top, the path by the stream and the wood, and reminiscences of the days when first they knew the hills, when through youth's magic casements opening on nature's wonder and mystery they heard their name whispered uopn the hill-top, and knew that they were friends with the silence and the solitude of the hills; and to the younger for the adventure that enters into a tramp across an unknown moorland country that means blazing the trail for oneself; and to all it brings experience in a feast of reflective thought and impression that will often come back in other days.

The ministrations of this April day had been many and varied. All day long the whaups and the peewits had been calling, and the air had been filled with bird-song; where there were hedgerows many a sprightly chaffinch, singing his bright lyric, gave question and answer, and with a flutter and a flash of white-barred wings flew off to another twig, to begin his song again; there was the music of the fountains in the high places and of the rivers in the valleys, but most of all one loved the sweet-scented moorland air. What was it brought the perfume, so characteristic of the spring-time?—was it the moor burn first met earlier in the day, or the moorland tang that haunts the memory of the rover, the moist grass being warmed by the sun, or had the scent been gathered from nut-scented whins on the hill-sides and from cottage gardens round the hills? All contributed to spice the clean fresh winds of spring. So the going out with joy, and the leading on in peace, had all come true, as did the words of the wise man who said that the mountains and the little hills shall bring peace. At any rate it somehow finds a place in the heart of every wayfarer as evening brings his day's adventure to a close.

CHAPTER VII

A SNOWSTORM ON THE HILLS

A NEW YEAR'S DAY EXPERIENCE

HE believed in beginning the year well. But that was not the only reason that sent him out on the hills on this first day of the New Year. He had recollections of similar firsts of January, and these prompted in him a desire to renew the experience.

Ten o'clock saw him footing it out to Colinton and up Bonaly Hill. The ground was frost-bound, the air sharp and keen, and soon he reached the end of that ugly barbed-wire barricading that prohibits quiet, hill-loving folk from wandering from the beaten path, lest haply they should consider the hills their own property. Once past the boundary wall, and on the Pentlands proper, one breathes more freely, quickens one's steps, and often bounds across the drain-pipe gullies like a man practising the hurdles.

This Glencorse right-of-way is one of the most popular and interesting of all the hill-crossings. There is first the ascent from the village of Colinton to the Tower of Bonaly, then the climb along the side of a rocky ravine to the hill-top, after which the path winds through a glen formed by the Harbour Hill and Capelaw, presenting different viewpoints at every turn, till the splendid range of Carnethy, Scald Law, and the Kips breaks upon the view, with the waters of Glencorse gleaming through the fir-trees. Every visit reveals some new aspect of the hills.

Climb to the hill lochan under Capelaw on a wintry Saturday afternoon, when the " withered hills " are grave and austere, and nature is mute save for the cry of a startled grouse or the wind among the bents, and here you will experience all the balm of solitude that your heart may desire. But the scene is changed when you pass through the glen in the blush of a summer morning, when the green hillsides are sparkling in the sunshine, and the air resounds to the singing of birds and the bleating of lambs. Or see it on a local holiday, when crowded townsfolk flock to the purple hills and howes, for freedom and fresh air, and it is then that the hills and valleys echo back the joyous shouts of the merry throng.

When he came to Glencorse a strong " nor'-easter " was raising the loch into billows like a sea, and every portent of the sky was threatening. Loganlee was hardly reached about one o'clock, when the snow began, and soon it was blowing up the valley with the strength of a hurricane, and lashing the waves into spray as it flew. He had often wished to experience a snowstorm in the Pentlands, now his wish was to be granted. The original plan was to tramp over the East and West Kips and along the hillside to Carlops, where a cheery welcome, a roaring fire, roast beef, and plum-pudding, awaited at the Inn. By the time the head of the Loganlee Valley was reached all the hillsides were covered with snow, and he listened to a voice which said, " Why not climb a peak, and see how it feels up there in a snowstorm?" The opportunity was too good to let slip. He began the ascent of the BLACK HILL, so called because at no time of the year does it present any other appearance than black, except on such a day as this, when it may be truly called the WHITE HILL! Taking shelter behind a dry-stane dyke for a breather, he looked over to where Threipmuir Reservoir ought to be: " it lies just over there, probably frozen," he said to himself; but no part of it could be seen. The Kips were also invisible, as well as the summit of the Black Hill. Then began the climb. Snow lay heavily upon the heather, and at every step it fell into his shoes—stupid fellow to wear shoes on the hills—but what of that! How different it all was from the hot September afternoon, when near the same spot he had thrown himself down on the sweet-scented heather, and listened to the pleasant hum of busy bees. In the silence the snow fell steadily; he was here on the hill-top alone.

140

Have you ever, O young man, sung and shouted for joy? Ever flung yourself against wild nature's stormy elements, when the wind roared, and the hail and the rain battered you and stung you hard? Ever filled your lungs and stretched your arms and sung all the songs, and every bit of song that ever you knew? Have you ever felt this strange fascination to climb a snow-white mountain peak, or gathered sufficient will to rise with the lark and welcome with the full-voiced chorus the wondrous breaking of a new day?

If not, there are some rare experiences in youth which you have missed, and you will not understand the joy of the man who delights to company with nature and to share her secrets in her intimate and varied moods.

But to return to our friend: he climbed round the back of the Black Hill intending to cross Dens Cleuch that lies 800 feet below and reach the right-of-way that runs through the Maiden's Cleuch between Bell's Hill and Harbour Hill. In the darkening winter afternoon Dens Cleuch looked more like a mountain gorge, so strangely do the hills and glens alter in appearance under gloomy skies and wintry weather. I remember this gorge well, for once a keeper climbed from the bottom to the top of Bell's Hill after me, and was astonished when I asked him if he was after me, to which, he breathlessly replied, that he " waas thinkin' aboot it," whereupon he sat down beside me, and smoked my tobacco. The enthusiastic hill-walker is never satisfied with climbing one peak, he must climb another and still another, and knows no greater satisfaction than when he can walk along the hill tops by a connecting ridge. This keeper seemed to have unwillingly caught the hill-climber's enthusiasm, for he had been chasing folks off the hills all day—it was a local holiday, and they were damaging his dykes and disturbing his sheep; and having turned off about a score of trespassers, he thought he would add yet another to his list by capturing the fellow on the hill-top. But I think he felt rewarded. It was more pleasant to " crack " in a friendly fashion and to smoke a peaceful pipe than to scold; and when we parted he had made up his mind to climb no more hills that day, nor chase " ony mair o' thae toun's-folk."

To cross the gorge on this New Year's Day was by no means an easy task. The hail and snow began to blow hard and it was painful to push on against it; and so, knowing that the Malleny shooting-ranges were near by, he crossed over stretches of long rank grass covered deep in snow and reached the ranges by Craigenterrie. Here he emptied his shoes of snow and water, and began the tramp to Currie; but ere Currie was reached the snow had turned to lashing rain, and he was no longer a white man, but a very wet one. Every one seemed to be indoors as he passed through Currie, Juniper Green, and Colinton. The storm was now raging in all its fury, and perhaps some who looked out of windows pitied the man who tramped along the muddy road, wet through, squelching water out of his shoes at every step. It required hard going to keep up the circulation, but in due time he arrived home, very wet, but very happy. And then a warm bath, and dry clothes, and dinner, when the blinds were drawn and the fire burned bright. With understanding he could repeat the words of W. H. Hudson—" Better days than those spent in roughest weather on the hills I could not well have known." What a splendid day it had been! It was worth while braving all the elements for the joy and exhilaration the experience had brought to him. He had begun the New Year well.

CHAPTER VIII

WINTER WALKS

THERE are many who know the Pentlands only in summer time. There are a few who love them best in winter, when the air is cool and invigorating and good for exercise, and when all the uncommon beauties of the hills are most apparent; and if the daylight of a winter afternoon be short, the experience may be all the more refreshing and the impressions more vivid and intense, even within the period from mid-day till we reach our objective—say Carlops or Ninemileburn—as the winter sun drops down behind the hills and fills the sky with its ruddy splendour.

Wind and rain do not affect the true walker as determining influences in his going for a walk: on the contrary they are frequently responsible for certain varied experiences which he would not willingly forego. It is not without interest to learn that in Edinburgh 56 per cent. of our wind comes from a westerly direction; that half-a-century's observations tell us of the pleasant and equable climate we enjoy; that the difference between the temperature of the three coldest months of the year and the three warmest is under 19° F., and that winter and spring, which are probably the best seasons for walking, have the least rainfall, which is greatest in summer and autumn, April being the driest month, and July and August the wettest of the year.

1. Balerno to Carlops

By the Boar Stane

The week had been bitterly cold, with rain and sleet showers, and intermittent sunshine. We had read of snow in various parts of the country, but we were eager for the hills, and soon after midday we were seated in the bus that in forty minutes conveyed us to Balerno.

The sun shining from a clear blue sky, with here and there a trailing cloud, the sound of running water, green woods and pastures, soon make us forget the din of the city and the daily task, and it is not long before we get settled down to the enjoyment of our walk. The road we have chosen is that which strikes west from the village— the Cockburnhill and Buteland road. The first stretch brings us to John's Burn, where the spreading branches of the trees meet overhead, and mansion-house, cottage, and smiddy stand cheek by jowl; but it is Saturday, and the smith's work is done, so that to-day no ring of the anvil accompanies the music of the burn that gives the clachan its name.

There is a double bend in the road here, then it straightens out again, and we can see far ahead. Long straight roads are usually tiresome and uninteresting, but not so this one, for we pass several farm-steadings, and there is a beech hedge that is a source of continual interest. It is the delight of many birds, and the red berries of the hawthorn are shining in the sun. Robin greets us as we pass along, Tom-tit is far too busy to pay any attention, and Mr Blackbird is terribly annoyed at being disturbed.

The sight of the snow-capped hills in the distance, and the knowledge that in an hour or two we shall be up amongst them, brings a fresh inspiration, and gives a lightness to our step. Our way is not by Cockburnhill, but by Buteland Farm, so we turn to the right where the road forks, and pause for a moment at the Cock Burn, for it speaks to us every time we pass, in its clear sparkling waters and laughing eddies. We first catch sight of it as it comes gliding peacefully through a wood, then it brawls and hurries under an old stone bridge and blunders into the opposite bank, and then, as if remembering with a smile that there is a sharp turn to the left, it rushes off

EASTSIDE, SOUTH BLACK HILL

again. It is a kindly human sort of burn, this Cock Burn, and it seems to laugh outright at those who could call it " Coburn."

As we approach Buteland Farm we notice that the bark of many of the roadside trees has been nibbled off: perhaps it is because these trees are so handy to Bunny, who lives just underneath them, and he may be feeling the effects of the winter; but the ferns in the sheltered ditches under the hedges have not yet lost their leaves. The first recorded observation in Mid-Lothian of that rare bird—the Hoopoe —was made here in 1923.

Look out now for a fir wood on the left, just opposite the old Temple House, where the shepherd lives, and at the side of the wood there is a five-barred gate leading to the right-of-way over the hills by the farm of Listonshiels. It is now a straight walk to the Boar Stane, and we can see the clump of trees on the horizon, three miles away. But three jolly miles—there is not a dull bit in the whole stretch of it, as it crosses moorland and heather, and there is a fine aroma rising from the tufty grass moistened by the sun, which we always associate with this tract of pasture-land that opens up a view to the westward, of the Cairn Hills and the Cauldstaneslap. It would of course be a strange track that did not pass something of interest. These bent gnarled thorn-trees betray signs of having withstood many a wintry blast, and in the adjoining field the sheep have made a muddy place where they stand licking a lump of rock-salt. Curiosity led us to examine it, with the result that a fragment of it has since formed a useful weather-glass, for when rock-salt becomes moist and wet, rain is not far off. Above and around us the sea-gulls are whirling and circling in the sunshine. But it is when we lean against the gate in the march dyke overlooking a pleasant undulating green haugh, and look up towards the hills, that all the wonder of the fine panorama dawns upon us. How characteristic of the Pentland Hills it all is. On the right rise the steep Cairn Hills, glistening in the sunshine, and on the left the pointed Kips, Scald Law, and the North Black Hill, with clumps of fir-trees in the foreground and on the white hillside above Threipmuir, and the red-roofed cottage at West Bavelaw.

One never grows tired of this walk up to the Boar Stane. The path winds about through the bracken and the heather, and we cross the amber-coloured Bavelaw Burn by a turf-covered bridge, and pass the Baron's Cleuch. It is well defined and marked by posts, and although there is snow on the ground to-day, the sheep have been over the track and made it plain. At last we gain the top—1300 feet above sea-level—joyfully extolling the virtues of winter walking upon the hills on such a glorious day. There is a far view of the Moorfoots on one side of the pass, and the Lomond Hills and the Ochils and the white peaks around Ben More and Ben Lomond on the other, weaving their spell upon the memory, and making us forget the chilling effect of the frosty air, which requires us to keep moving.

The Boar Stane is the name given to the outcrop of rock under the fir-trees to the west of the right-of-way path, and this name, like that of Deerhoperig adjoining, and the Wolf Craigs at the source of the Baddinsgill Burn, points to the time when the wild boar, wolf, brown bear, and reindeer roamed the Pentland Hills and were hunted there. Not far off we have the old Estate of Boarland, now named Boreland or Bordlands, which at one time was connected with Spitalhaugh. Many of the place-names in the hills are of ancient origin, and even the present-day configuration of the rocks at the Wolf Craigs and the Boar Stane suggests these as likely places for the dens of wild animals.

R. D. C. Brown of Newhall, Carlops, writing early in the nineteenth century in his historical pastoral drama, "Mary's Bower, or the Castle in the Glen," describes a hunt upon the Pentlands:—

" From Harper-rig's collected cone
The Eagle long ago has flown;
From out its caverned crags below
Has reynard issued, stealing slow,
And wolves, by hunger wak'd, to prowl
The Pictland range for deer and sheep,
Already unresisted, sweep
Its southern strone, between
The Lyne and Carlop Dean
About the pass at Windy Gowl."

Among the three hundred bones found in a rock-fissure at the Green Craig, Howden Glen, in 1886, constituting part of the lair of some carnivorous animal, were identified those of deer, wolf, fox, and horse, and the evidence of bones of reindeer which was found was considered " the most conclusive evidence of the existence of the reindeer in Scotland in prehistoric times that has ever yet been shown " (*Transactions*—Edinburgh Geological Society).

In imagination we can picture these Pentland valleys filled with stately glaciers that passed out eastwards to the sea—nature's primeval forces of frost and ice and flood— carving the hills and glens into the forms that now afford us so much delight. In the course of the ages the great pine forests grew, providing a home for the wild animals that roamed free and unmolested until the early Celtic colonists arrived and began to hunt them.

The remains of a large oak have been found in a peat moss on the summit of the Spital Hill, 1500 feet above sea-level; and similar traces of very old oak-trees have been discovered in the vicinity of the West Water. Tradition asserts that such places among the hills as Logan Tower, Bavelaw, and Fairliehope were hunting seats in bygone days, and the two 'Spitals—the Fore and the Back 'Spital— built by the monks of Newhall as appendages to the Monastery there, prior to the thirteenth century, possibly served, among other purposes, as places of refuge from the fierce attack of wolves. 'Spitals or hospitals for this pur-pose existed in Yorkshire during the reign of Athelstan, and as late as the sixteenth century wolves were common in many parts of Scotland, and similar places of safety were required not only for travellers, but also for flocks and herds and their owners.

After we have examined the Boar Stane, we take our way down the valley to Carlops by the side of a fine old drystane dyke that forms the boundary line of Peebles-shire, and as we near the Henshaw Burn we cross several water channels that the winter storms have deepened and enlarged, and find them decorated under the overhanging banks with nature's handiwork in drooping icicles of delicate formation; and as we stand meditating upon the mystery of their rainbow colours and varied beauty, a flock of snow bunting rises from the burnside, the white feathers of wing and tail showing conspicuously as they fly up the hillside to settle again as abruptly as they had risen. It is only occasionally that one sees on the Pentlands these winter visitants from northern regions.

It is very still in the glen, and becoming colder, the high hills shutting out the westering sun, but as we crest the top of the path the North Esk Reservoir comes in view with the sunlight filling all the upper hillsides and touching the tops of the trees that bield the keeper's cottage. But what is all this unusual stir—a great motor-wagon, laden with metal tanks, and a dozen men moving about? Some one has seen us, and waves his hand: it is our friend the keeper; then the motor moves round to the cottage door, and soon we learn all about it. The loch has been restocked with two-year-old trout, and the local fishing club are congratulating themselves on a good day's work, for the motor has travelled from Stirlingshire to-day with its precious freight of Loch Leven trout, which it is hoped in days to come will provide the best of sport.

This sequestered place, embosomed in the hollow of the hills, is beautiful at all times; but on this still winter's afternoon with the surrounding heights clothed in snow, it has a sublime grandeur that touches the deep places in us.

148

THE WOLF CRAIGS

As we take our way to Carlops we frequently pause to look back upon the steading by the lochside and the fascinating view of the high hills surrounding it.

We can hear the rushing sound of the Esk as it passes the ruins of the Back 'Spital on our left, and, in front of us, standing upon an eminence overlooking the meeting-place of three narrow glens, is the old hunting seat of Fairlie-hope, which when viewed from the slopes of Mount Maw resembles a Highland shooting-lodge set upon a pine-clad hillside whose base is washed by two singing corrie burns. In 1374-5 King Robert II. granted to Sir James Douglas and his son James the whole barony of Lyntounrotheryk, which included the land of Fairliehope; and on 14th May 1536, Jams V. confirmed a Charter of this land granted by James of Douglas, Lord of Dalkeith, to James Forester of Medofield, in return for homage and service, which land Alexander Forester of Corstorphine had resigned.

At the end of the seventeenth century the proprietors were the Browns of Braid, and in the sixteenth century the adjoining lands of Newhall were possessed for a time by the Fairlies or Fairleys of Braid.

Moles are common on the Pentland Hills, and this after-noon we have seen many evidences of these curious creatures. Cowper humorously refers to the mole as the miner of the soil who, " not unlike the great ones of man-kind, disfigures earth, and plotting in the dark, toils much to earn a monumental pile, that may record the mischief he has done." At one time mole-catchers were numerous around the hills, but to-day they have few successors. One of the last of the " old school " was Sandy Farquharson, who lived at Lanely Bield on Newhall Estate, a personality fondly remembered by the old folks of the countryside, for he was one of Carlops' minor poets, full of drollery and pawky humour, whose fiddling made every kirn a great success, and visits to the Lanely Bield events to be long remembered.

On the occasion of an immigration of many rough-legged

buzzards to the hills—October-December 1903—several of which were shot, they lived largely on moles, which at the time were very abundant. One of the birds when fired at dropped a mole, and two partly devoured were found on the ground over which they had hunted.

We have the choice of two roads to Carlops from Fairlie-hope, the one down by the Esk-side, a rocky path winding up and down along the hillside and entering Carlops near the Waterfall and Patie's Mill; and the other, a farm road that brings us to the Carline's Rock. Choosing the latter, we continue our journey, but we do not hurry, for the sun has set, and gorgeous colours are reflected in the sky. Sunset among the hills is a sight to linger over, but soon it passes, and through the shades of twilight there shines the evening star.

Walkers have many happy recollections of their experiences. Once when we passed this way, the ploughman was busy with his team, and as we drew near he seemed to anticipate a word from us. Country folks are sensitive to impressions, and they do not quickly forget a new thought or person they meet. The plough gear slackens and rattles, and he says something to his horses in language which only they can understand. "Aye, I'm on the last rig noo, then I'll be feenished wi' the lave o't." And he would be only just in time, for already the fine mists of grey and amethyst blue over the freshly turned, sweet-smelling earth, were getting blurred, and the dark Carlop Hill was making twilight of the day that soon would turn the gloamin' into mirk; and so amid " the mystic shadows dim, which round the car of twilight swim," we enter the village, where we are to enjoy that much-talked-of meal—a ham-and-egg tea, and we are not disappointed. The memory of it is with me as I write—how good it is to hungry walkers.

There is a starry sky and a moon to-night, grateful company on the homeward way; and the walk to Penicuik upon the hard frosty road is a fitting completion to the tramp across the hills, the bracing and health-giving effects of which, together with the quiet peace that the silence of the great hills always brings, will be with us all the week.

(The distance from Balerno to Carlops by the Boar Stane is about nine miles, and from Carlops to Penicuik five and a half.)

2. BALERNO TO CARLOPS

By the Green Law and Patie's Hill

The autumn tints had lingered long, and in many places there was still a riot of glowing colours—mellowing reds and russet browns, golden orange and purple. It was on such a day that we passed through the village of Balerno, and were soon in the open country. Beneath the hawthorn hedge on each side of the road the leaves lay thick, as if some elfin hands had plucked them off. The beech hedge was becoming a sombre brown, and robin redbreast was not so easily seen.

As we approached the moor at Marchbank[1] on the way to Threipmuir we spied a magpie busily feeding among some brushwood. As we watched him we became conscious of how still the day was; there was not a breath of wind, not a sound, except a cock crowing in a neighbouring farmyard. Over the Forth, and along the Fife coast, the afternoon sun was shining brightly, and we could pick out a yacht's sails in the Firth, and the old monastery on Inchcolm.

Our path to-day, so far, is a right-of-way. From Balerno we make for the Kitchen[2] Moss, turning to the right when we come to the top of the Bavelaw Avenue, and then to the left, through the gate, where the post indicates the path to Ninemileburn. A fine scene opens out here. We are now on the moors, and a new-born breeze from over the hills carries the Pentland wine. Yes, it is good to be here, and this glorious panorama satisfies all our hill-hunger; but

[1] Originally called Rummelbank farm house.
[2] Kitchen was a common surname in the Pentland area.

when we get to the Moss and are shut out from the city-ward view we are cought in an even more fascinating prospect, for here we see the line of Pentland tops from Carnethy to the Cairns " standing round like kings."

We cross the Logan Burn, amber-brown with peaty water, and continue on this path until it makes a sharp turn towards the Kips; and here we leave it, and get on to the tussocky grass, making a bee-line for the top of the Green Law in front. Now we are off the right-of-way, and there is no path, but sheep-tracks only. Law-abiding hill walkers must use discretion—in winter-time the solitary walker will usually have the hill-tops to himself, and must have a better excuse to offer than R. L. Stevenson, who pleaded that " the offence is now covered by prescription."

We continue along the top of Spital Hill, from which the view in all directions is full of interest. Frequently we pause, and look long towards the west, for here there is a fine tumble of hills with the peaks of the Cairns, Wether Law, The Mount, Craigengar, Byrehope Mount, and, nearer us, Mount Law, all showing strangely weird in the dying light of the brief day. It is perhaps from the summit of The Mount that the best impression of the spaciousness of the Pentlands is obtained. A blue haze is beginning to rise from the valleys, and soon only the peaks will be visible. But the impression remains long with us—

> " these beauteous forms
> through a long absence, have not been to me
> as is a landscape to a blind man's eye :
> but oft, in lonely rooms, and 'mid the din
> of towns and cities, I have owned to them,
> in hours of weariness, sensations sweet,
> felt in the blood, and felt along the heart."

Wordsworth: *Tintern Abbey.*

Far below us on the right lies the North Esk Reservoir. We can see the smoke rising gently from the cottage, set picturesquely among the trees at the loch end. The good-wife is making tea—but not for us. We are on the hill-tops, and the exhilaration we draw from the heights precludes any thought of descending to the valley. Here are rare delights unknown to the road walker of the plains, in the stimulated senses and kindled imagination that the intoxicating air of the hill-top brings. We wish to keep to the tops, even though the going may be difficult in the long white tufty grass, making it necessary to watch our steps for fear of ankle trouble.

A march dyke brings us up, and we cross the path that runs over the hills down to Spital Farm and Ninemileburn. Then we mount to the top of Patie's Hill. The hills in the quiet of autumn time have a strange beauty; their great slopes covered as with a garment of many colours. Nature is a wonderful artist in her pictures of autumn colour on the Pentland hillsides, with a harmony of tone that delights us. There is a bloom upon the pine-tree tops above Fairliehope, and it blends with the waters of the infant Esk that are flowing down the valley.

As we near Patie's Mill we begin to descend. But we are loath to break away from the lure of the hills, and again, with rekindled imagination, we stop—just to listen, and to bathe our souls in that silent balm which every hill-lover knows.

The only sounds we have heard this afternoon have been the call of grouse, the bleat of sheep, the gurgle of the Logan Burn, and the song of the Esk at the waterfall by the Carlops Brig, and we had seen no other walkers. We are now nearing the road, and the hoot of a motor horn brings ue back to the life of a noisy world. It is with a sigh that my friend remarks: " I'm sorry our walk's finished for another week."

Soon we are set before the savoury meal in the lamp-lit room, beside the cheery fire, and with the shepherd in " The Noctes " declare: " I'm nae glutton—nae gormandeezer—but a man o' a gude, a great appeteet—and for the next half-hour I shall be as perfectly happy as ony man in a' Scotland."

To-night it is very dark, no moon or stars. Seen through the trees, as we take the short cut through the woods to Penicuik, the twinkling lights seem specially bright and friendly. And as the bus rolls on, taking us homewards, it is not of our fellow-passengers we are thinking—our thoughts are far away—on the hill-top, for we love its silent friendship, and fain would carry that with us.

3. CURRIE TO NINEMILEBURN

By the Kips and Monks Road

A strong fresh breeze is blowing out of the west as we leave Currie village, and begin to climb the Kirkgate in the direction of the hills. It is a strenuous beginning for our afternoon's walk, but we take it leisurely, and frequently stop to admire the view, and to refresh ourselves with great draughts of the cool hill wind—the walker's champagne—whose after-effects are altogether beneficial. And we are amply rewarded for the climb, when on reaching the top we turn westward, and gaze on one of the finest prospects to be obtained in the vicinity of our lovely city. Standing out clearly before us are the three cantilevers of the Forth Bridge, with the Ochil Hills behind, while the panorama extends far to the eastward with the Lomond Hills for background.

At Harelaw Farm we turn sharply to the left, and make for Harelaw Reservoir, along the banks of which we take the pleasant Scots fir-bordered path, continuing along Threipmuir to the ruins of Redford. Here nature has been " busy with a hand of healing," and all the desolation of the cut pine woods that marred the loveliness of the landscape is being covered with green sedges, mosses, and brushwood, and soon a new fir plantation will take the place of its stately predecessor that existed for over 150 years, and was cut down in 1919-20. In the thick tops of the pines nested the long-eared owl, the tawny owl, and the kestrel (when permitted), and a capercailzie was shot here forty years ago. The grey hen and sandpiper also nested here; and in the centre of the wood grew patches of the Prince of Wales' feather moss.

As we begin to climb Bavelaw Avenue, we marvel at the perfect artistry of the wind, for it has carried the fallen autumn leaves from off the roadway into the channels on each side, and the effect—so accurately has it been done— is that of two straight lines of burnished copper, running parallel with the green grassy borders.

On reaching the top we follow the direction of the post on the right, and soon find ourselves among the heather, making for the Kitchen Moss and the base of the West Kip. This route, so far, is well known to the Pentland walker. He never tires of it, for the views are magnificent, and the everchanging atmospheric effects are a delight for mind and eye. To-day, the peaks standing round the Logan Valley like sentinels have each a distinctive colour- ing. Only now the purple shades have all merged into browns, the moors are like so many sections of most delicately coloured Eastern carpet, and the hills are as if covered with exquisite tapestries. The clear air of autumn gives the hills a distinctness and nearness that appear preternatural. It almost seems as if we ourselves had changed, so keen is our vision, so light and free our move- ments, so full of joy our hearts. Above and around the gulls and the peewits are flying, the skies are more " summery " than those of summer, and the Pentland air is as good as that of Braemar.

We have now arrived at the 1500-feet level under the slope of the cone-shaped Kip, where the right-of-way post points the paths to Penicuik and Ninemileburn. That to the left down the valley by Eastside Farm joins the Biggar Road near Saltersyke, and a delightful cross-road by Silver- burn hamlet leads to Penicuik. There is no difficulty in following this route. That to the right leads to Ninemile- burn by the wooded west side of the glen, above the keeper's cottage at Westside. Watch the map and follow the path, for here it turns sharply to the west or right, over Braid Law, then—directed by posts—over dyke stiles, along well-marked paths, and across a field, we find ourselves at the old hostelry by the wood and waterside—a pleasant ramble at all seasons, in which you may imagine yourself anywhere but in the vicinity of a city, although you are only eight and a half miles from Balerno. The Biggar bus will convey you back to town, for it passes the road-end at Ninemileburn. We shall, however, take neither of these roads to-day. Let us imagine ourselves to be monastic pilgrims, and travel by the Monks Road. It is not a right--of-way, but it was certainly traversed centuries ago by the monks on their way from Newhall as they journeyed to Queensferry and Dunfermline, or in their walk from one cloister to another in their errands of mercy, and the part of it that runs from Spital and Ninemileburn to the base of the West Kip can still be followed. Let us take this walk, of which impressions made on a glorious late autumn day linger in my memory. Just before we reach the post at the West Kip we strike off to the right, bearing in mind the axiom that height gained should never be lost, and the path will soon be found. It winds along the top of what is called Gap Law and the Monks Rig, and in a short time we should come to the socket of a cross, but commonly called the Font Stone, lying among the heather, a block of Silurian grit 3 feet by 2 feet 8 inches, and 10-15 inches high, lying due north and south, having a cavity in the middle 20 inches by 12 inches and 9 inches deep, with two indentations on the wide eastern edge, perhaps meant for the knees of the worshipper at a cross, which originally stood in the centre, but which has long since disappeared, although in the Laird of Newhall's notes in the Scenery Edition of *The Gentle Shepherd* it is stated that the orna-mented top of the cross was " still lying at the bottom of the rig " (see *Socy. of Ant. Proceedings,* vol. 33).

Whether it was a Font Stone, a wayside shrine, or a land-mark commanding all the country to the south for the

Logan Valley from the Lovers Loup

pious friar as he journey over the hills to Convent or 'Spital, who can tell? but there it remains to-day, and as we stand and medidate upon it we link ourselves with a visible symbol of the time when the white-robed monk was a familiar figure on the Pentland Hills.

In 1833 two shepherds, John Tod and James Aitken, turned over the stone with levers, and found under it a few copper coins. It is said that on the east side of Scald Law, in a dry green hollow between it and the South Black Hill, called the Cross Sward, there was another similar stone with a socket in it, in which a cross was formely fixed as a religious landmark, but this stone has disappeared; perhaps it now forms part of the dry stane dyke near by.

The view from here is extensive—from the rolling plains of Haddingtonshire, right along the Moorfoots till the eye rests on the peaks of the Border Hills in Peeblesshire. From the Monks Rig we see the Inn at Ninemileburn, and as it is now over four hours since we left town we descend the hill as the day draws near its close. Below the Rig the wind seems to have died away, an atmosphere of quiet peacefulness pervades all the countryside, a dog barks at the Spital Farm, homely smoke rises from the cottages along the old stage-coach road by Honeybrae, and as we come to the Inn we are reminded of Allan Ramsay by the verse on the sign above the door—

> " Gae faurer doon the burn tae Habbies Howe,
> Where a' the sweets o' spring an' simmer grow,
> An' when ye're tired o' prattlin' side the rill,
> Return tae Ninemileburn, an' tak' a gill."

It is of course doubtful if the famous Allan penned the latter couplet, but that there was an Inn in this part in his day, when he was a frequent visitor at Newhall House, is certain. The Inn here is really the successor of the old Monks' Inn of those far-off days, although one of its predecessors was called the New House Inn, and stood about a mile south of the toll at Ninemileburn. Some of the local folks who gather at the Inn will tell you all about it, and about the Monks Road, and the Pillar Knowe, and the Quarrel Haugh, where disputes were settled, the old stage road, and Allan Ramsay's *Gentle Shepherd,* and all such news as " will kittle yer mind wi' joy." But even monks must often have felt the effects of the bracing mountain air in and around these parts, and we believe that they dined well; Allan Ramsay, too, would be no exception— " the joyous Ramsay," as Sir Walter called him—for he roamed about the Pentlands in winter, as we are reminded in the verse in one of his imitations of Horace—

> " Look up to Pentland's tow'ring taps,
>   Buried beneath big wreaths o' snaw.
> O'er ilka cleugh, ilk scaur an' slap,
>   As high as ony Roman wa'."

And did not Laird Brown of Newhall, a hundred years ago, anticipate what succeeding generations of Pentland walkers would like best when they come down from the hill-tops, when he wrote—

> " With this good bacon, ham and egg,
>   Of that cold fowl I'll have a leg,
>   Of running birds the leg is best,
>   Of those that fly, the wing and breast." [1]

" An inn restores us to the level of nature, and quits scores with Society," wrote Hazlitt, and a Pentland appetite is a common bond which has united monks, lairds, and tramps at the Inn at Ninemileburn.

---

[1] " Mary's Bower, or The Castle in the Glen," Act. II.

CHAPTER IX

A GREY DAY

MIDCALDER TO PENICUIK

*By the Cauldstaneslap, West Cairn Hill, Craigengar,
Covenanter's Grave, Medwinhead and West Linton*

THERE are times when to the mountaineer and the
hill-walker the hunger for the high places and the
open spaces comes hard upon him. He may be tied
to the city by day, and in the quiet of the evening he will
find peace and satisfaction in going over old numbers of
his Mountaineering Club *Journal*; then, shutting his eyes,
memory and imagination will bring to him the vision of
the hill-tops, clear and splendid, and all the joys of other
days are his again.

But for Edinburgh men there are always the Pentland
Hills. " Ah yes," says the old fastidious campaigner who
will be satisfied with nothing but the Grampians and
Lochaber, Breadalbane and Skye, " but the Pentlands are
only the Pentlands." Very true, but they are none the less
wonderful to some of us who love them well, and many
a time the tonic of a day upon the Pentland Hills has
helped us to regain life's true perspective, and enabled us
to see life steadily and to see it whole, by the power of
their miraculous alchemy to clear the brain and restore
the soul.

It was a grey frosty morning in midwinter when we made
our way to the Old Lanark Road by Belstane Farm from
Midcalder Station. Hoar-frost lay upon the sides of the
winding road, and under hawthorn hedges green leaves
lay in abundance. Moreover the robin piped his song.
It was not of love he sang, unless it were love of life. The
robin, like the mountaineer, counts the winter months good

to sing about, as well as the days of amorous spring, and memory and hope play their part in his song, as well as in that of the mountaineer.

At the old Toll-house on the Lang Whang we join the right-of-way for the Cauldstaneslap.

The sight of the open moor, the Cairn Hills beyond, and that tang of the moorland breeze are as a draught from the well-known spring, and we press the tufted grass beneath our feet with a feeling of satisfaction and well-being, knowing that at the day's end all the restless hunger for the hills will be satisfied once more. The path runs by the side of a dry-stane dyke to the Water of Leith, which we cross by stepping-stones: then the friendly path leaves us, and we begin the approach to the hills over heathery moorland. It is biting cold in the Cauldstaneslap to-day. Through this old-time Pass, drovers from West Lothian, Stirlingshire, and the North of Scotland came with their droves of black cattle into Tweeddale, the Southern counties, and England, and the track is a continuation of the road called farther south at Stobo and Manor, the Thieves' Road, ironically so termed from being the usual pass of that formidable plundering banditti the Moss-troopers. Immunity from their depredations could be purchased by a payment of blackmail or yearly tax to one of the gang. A tradition exists that along this road in early days the barons themselves were Mosstroopers; and that when the proprietor of a Castle or peel-house in entertaining his vassals or friends found his provisions exhausted, a plate filled with spurs was placed on the table, at which signal horses were mounted and the country scoured for a fresh supply, and on this being obtained the revel began anew. This Pass, then, through the hills was at one time a main drove road from the north to the south, and the hard wild life of the drover, which caught the imagination of R. L. S., was as full of adventure as any mountaineer could wish. It is good to be up here to-day, and the exhilaration that comes after a couple of hours' walking prepares us for the climb up the West Cairn hill. This Hill (1844 feet) is only some fifty feet less than Scald Law, the highest peak of the range; and although the Cairn on its top is of considerable size, it is not so large as that on the East Cairn Hill, which is surrounded by very large slabs and boulders, while the Cairn itself measures thirty yards round the base.

Turning westwards we tramp along the tops of the Cairn and Colzium Hills until we reach the top of Craigengar, passing on our left a curious outcrop of rocks called the Wolf Craigs, and the Ravendean Valley, where the hunted Covenanters held their Conventicles in the time of Charles II. On our right lie the lochs of Crosswood and Cobbinshaw like leaden sheets in the distance, with Cairns Castle at the end of Harper-rig, once the home of the Warden of the Slap. That entrancing view to the north, so well known, and the peaks so well loved—Ledi, Venue, Lomond, More, and all the rest, are shut out from us on this dull grey winter day, but the measure of the greyness was not the measure of our spirits. There's a hunger for the hills that the hill-lover knows that can find no satisfaction until he stands upon the tops. The hill-tops have a strange fascination for the climber, and this hunger of the spirit urges him forward and upward, for it is up there that the mystic voices speak and nature's wondrous story is unfolded; and the ascent of one peak but begets the desire for the next. Let us for a moment forget the Highland hills, " a wild kind o' warld by themsells," as Bailie Nicol Jarvie called them. Here is the Highlands in miniature, where the hills " stand round like kings," a score of them, all over a thousand feet, a great wild tumble of heights and howes, woods, streams, lochs, and moors, a glorious array before us and around, and our spirits rise far above the elemental greyness. The Pentland Hills—the friendly hills of home—are wonderful hills to those who know and love them in their varied moods. Descending Craigengar with its cave, we pass down dark Ravenscleugh, the burn at the foot of which joins the Medwin Water. Medwin is a tributary of the Clyde, and it is interesting to note that within a diameter of a mile from this spot we have the source of the Crosswood Burn, a tributary of the Linnhouse Water and the Almond, which enters the Forth at Cramond; and the Baddinsgill Burn, which joins the Lyne, a tributary of the noble Tweed; while at the junction of the Ravenscleugh Burn and the Medwin the boundaries of three counties meet, Mid-Lothian, Peeblesshire, and Lanarkshire. A rock on the hillside goes by the name of Roger's Kirk, a relic of Covenanting times, and here we climb the Black Law in search of the lonely Covenanter's Grave. In this wild and open spot upon the hillside the grey slab stands facing westward in memory of the sturdy son of freedom who, wounded at Rullion Green, sought to return, ere death should overtake him, to his native country in the West, but in vain. The well-preserved inscription tells the story: " Sacred to the Memory of a Covenanter, who fought and was wounded at Rullion Green, November 28, 1666, and who died at Oaken Bush the day after the Battle, and was buried here by Adam Sanderson of Blackhill."

The story of this Covenanter has often been told, and never fails to touch the imagination of the many hill-walkers and visitors from Dolphinton and Dunsyre who visit his lonely grave upon the hillside, rising in the centre of the encircling hills and moorland. That he should have travelled so far along the hills from Rullion Green to the banks of the Medwin, on the dark November night, with a wound that proved mortal, was a token of his heart's desire to get home again; and his refusal of shelter at the farm of Blackhill, to which he came at dead of night, lest Adam Sanderson, the farmer, and the other occupants should suffer harm at the hands of the dragoons in search of fugitives, showed a manly Christian spirit, unquenched by his enfevered frame. The farmer did what he could for the dying man, and took him to a sheltered place under an oak bush near the West Water. Before he died he expressed the desire to be buried in sight of his native Ayrshire hills, and this request was carried out by Sanderson on the spot where the present tombstone stands—although local tradition says he was first buried by the side of the West Water—from which spot, over 1300 feet up, through a gap in the hills to the north of the Bleak Law, it is possible to see hills in Ayrshire, eighteen miles away as the crow flies. The tombstone was erected about 1841, and a service, at which between fifty and sixty people were present, was conducted by the Rev. Dr Manuel, acting Minister of Dunsyre, who was largely responsible for its erection. Memorial services are held here at intervals, but not so regularly as at Rullion Green and Harbour Craig, Carlops, which are more easily accessible.

The view from here is majestic, and, in the darkening winter afternoon, awe-inspiring. Here indeed is glorious solitude—" Peace is here or nowhere, days unruffled by the gale of public news." A whole day may be passed among the Pentland Hills, without meeting anyone, or seeing signs of human habitation. A few hours' walking may bring us to as wild and romantic a countryside as we may desire, and the delight of coming across a shepherd's cottage we have never seen before is as good as striking El Dorado. And so it was that as we descended the hill from the Grave of the Covenanter in thoughtfulness and quiet, and passing the ruins, centuries old, of Adam Sanderson's farmhouse at Blackhill, we came suddenly upon the sheep farm of Medwinhead, with a combined shepherd's cottage and shooting-lodge set against a background of pines with far views of the Peeblesshire and Lanarkshire hills.

The proprietor of this little moorland estate of Medwinhead, who erected the buildings, was James Faed, the mezzotint engraver, who died in 1911 at the age of ninety-one—one of the three famous artist brothers born in a millwright's cottage at Gatehouse-on-Fleet.

The shepherd, from the Argyllshire hills, described the varied prospect that stretched out before us, and spoke of the "cauld wuntur and the blashy wuthur, but hoch aye! Spring wad soon be here again." All lovers of the country places know how good it is to talk with shepherds and farmers, ploughmen, keepers, blacksmiths, country post-ment, and fishermen. How often we find rich personalities there, whose experiences have brought to them a rare philosophy of life, men who company with the far spaces, and work mainly in silence with nature and her bounty. Was not Stevenson taught by the byre-man's philosophy that "him that has aye something ayont need never be weary," meaning that a man with a definite aim in life should never be cast down?

The shepherd also directed us to the drove road that runs past his door to West Linton, four miles away, an old road that brought drovers and cattle in days gone by through Lanarkshire to the trysts at Linton. Originally it would be a sheep track, hence the manner in which it skilfully engineers all difficult places, and it is possible to imagine what it would be like in those far-off days, but now it is just a friendly path that winds up and down and over the hills, one of those paths beloved by all true walkers. Footpaths are part of the intimacy and friend-ship of the hills; we even bless them and venerate them, for we remember how much has gone to their making, centuries of time, and successive generations of shepherds and quiet country folk, and it is good to know that there are so many of these friendly footpaths over the Pentland Hills that can never be closed. The old paths are best, so declared Jeremiah. "Thus saith the Lord, Stand ye in the ways, and see, and ask for the old paths, where is the good way, and walk therein, and ye shall find rest for your souls"; and the walker knows how this has a literal as well as a symbolical application for him. We only know a country in proportion as we are acquainted with its foot-paths. The walker who knows his paths, and is ever on

164

The Lyne and Mount Maw

the look-out for new ventures, knows the heart of the country, for they cross hills and valleys and streams, and pass by woods and springs and through farmyards, to all sorts of pleasant places, the joy of the walker's heart.

Suddenly the surrounding hillsides were bathed in a soft pinky sheen, and looking back we saw that the sun had suddenly dropped into a blue stratum of the sky, and just before setting was suffusing every hill and vale and wood with a rich glow of surpassing beauty. The cold greyness of the day was all forgotten in the glory and the splendour of the sunset. The woods upon the hillside and the rising ground radiated the glory as of some other clime; and as we turned to go, the sun behind us seemed like the good fairy setting her children on the path that led to home, ere the evening shadows fell. Long afterwards we could feel the spell of it all, and quieten our restless spirits in its remembrance.

The wind that had spoken in many voices all the day was now at rest, and in stillness the earth received her benediction. Then, as if from nowhere, so quickly did it happen, the hills drew down their night-caps of grey wool, and passed into the keeping of the eternal silence. It was dark when we passed from Slipperfield to Linton, but to think of time in the wild and open countryside, or to speak of distance, is to break Dame Nature's wizard spell. There were still ten good miles to Penicuik by the moor road, but we footed it cheerfully with shoulders back and down, and saw it under unique conditions. Great black clouds floated as in a pageant across the sky, and the silent moon and stars played hide-and-seek. At one moment Harlaw Moor lay covered in inky blackness, and going was an adventure. At the next it was lit up with a weird and fitful light, yet kindly, showing us the way, shining out of black and mysterious surroundings.

We do not know how far we had walked, but we knew that the day had been good. The tonic was effective. We had inhaled " great draughts of space," found a cleansing in the blowing of the wind, refreshing in the greenness of the grass, and shared the intimacy of the talking stream in quiet places. A grey winter's day upon the Pentlands has its surprises no less than a week-end among the Highland hills in the glorious days of spring.

CHAPTER X

AN AUTUMN DAY

My hand to my staff, and my face to the weather."
" And light as a bird give my foot to the heather,
PROFESSOR BLACKIE

IT was in this spirit that we set off one wild blustering
October morning to make this crossing, one that can
be recommended to all who love to tramp the heather
over a well-defined track, with little climbing, but just
enough of adventure in it to make it interesting, and a
series of fine landscape views.

A nor'-wester was blowing as we left the train at Auchengray. It was a day in which any sort of wild weather
might be expected. A few days previously the conditions
had been summerlike, and one had basked in the sunshine
on the top of " The Mount " and " Mount Maw." This
was followed by a gale that swept the country for a night
and a day, then came an ideal October day, still, bright and
warm, and a frosty evening. But to-day still another
variety of weather was expected. Pictures of the hills so
often depend upon the sky pictures. Details in the landscape will stand out more vividly and the harmony of
colour become intensified under a luminous cloudy sky and
a rainy atmosphere, and a strong beam of light may reveal
interesting contrasts in the countryside, of white cottages
among green fields, and a grey road winding across a
bracken-covered hillside, leading to the farm-steading. All
uncommon sights and effects are dear to the observant
walker, and he knows that some of the rarest views are to
be had on stormiest days. He fortifies himself against the

167

chances of weather, he is well shod and suitably clothed, and finds himself in harmony with the spirit of the elements when the nor'-wester blows, and " blashes " of rain sweep the hills and moors between the intervals of blue skies and sunshine.

The westward turn is taken at the fork of Auchengray road, and half a mile farther on we take to the left to King's Inn Farm, a relic of the hunting days of the Jameses and their frequent visits to Carnwath and Cowthally. Still keeping to the left the road traverses an open moorland till we reach the farm of East Yardhouses ("East Yardies"), standing over 900 feet above sea-level. Yardhouses means Earth Houses, relics of the Picts. Here we enter upon an interesting old right-of-way that served the King's Inn long ago, and takes us over the foot-bridge across the North Medwin to the Old Lanark Road at Boston Cottages. But the Boston Cottages do not exist locally, although they do on the map. They are a heap of ruins, and are known in terms of their ancient usage as the Old Coachhouses, where the horses of the Edinburgh to Lanark stage were changed.

A post directs us to West Linton, and we begin to follow the right-of-way with feelings of misgiving. Will this path continue to be so well marked, or will it lead us to a point where it spreads out into half a dozen sheep and coney tracks, and all trace of the original road be lost? Ah! not so; for this is more than a moorland track, it is an ancient road upon which wheel traffic has left distinct traces, not unlike the old " Herring Roads " in the Lammermoors. It goes straight over the heather and the reedy grass till we come to the Westruther Burn, where there is a foot-bridge. Swampy places abound here and there in wet weather, but these may be avoided by short detours. With water-tight boots the tramper will be little disturbed. On he will go, rejoicing in the exhilaration of the snell hill wind, the perfume of the wet mosses and grasses of the ditches, complimenting himself on the easy-going, and musing on the wonder and the interest of the far-spreading westward view. Hills need not be high to command fine prospects. Any quiet bit of country may yield surprises of happiness to the seeing eye; while, as Richard Jefferies tells us, " Every day has its different clouds—the fleets of heaven that are always sailing on and know no haven "—a never-ending source of interest to every hill-walker.

A gate in a dry-stane dyke brings us to a pause, and as the next squall is almost upon us, we here find shelter. From this point we may travel to West Linton by a drove road that goes east between Bleak Law and Mid Hill, and so by Medwinhead to Slipperfield. Bartholomew's Map is an excellent guide; and the paucity of guide-posts is positive gain!

On the present occasion we follow the well-defined road by Stoneypath Farm and join the Newbigging to Dunsyre road near Anston Farm, two miles from Dunsyre village.

There is no place of refreshment at Dunsyre, nor indeed in any of the surrounding villages between Carnwath and West Linton, and unless you are lucky enough to have friends among the hill folks, you will require to provide for yourself.

We choose the old road between Dunsyre and Medwin-head by Easton, which passes through one of the most charming bits of the Pentlands, along the banks of the Medwin, to its junction with the West Water. The West Water and the Medwin are two of the most fascinating streams in the hills. The walk from Medwinbank to West Linton or Carlops will complete as fine a Pentland walk as the most fastidious rambler may desire.

Every walk has its own variety of weather and experience, and apart from the stormy morning and the calm bright afternoon of this October day, the conspicuous features of this crossing we found to be the entrancing views into the hill country surrounding the Upper Ward in the section between the Lang Whang and Dunsyre, and the sylvan beauty of the woodland scenery between that village and

Medwinbank; while in the later stages we take to our heart the homely Pentland peaks of Mendick, Mount Maw, and the Scald Hill, well tried companions in many a glorious day's tramping.

THE CRANE LOCH

There is always a spice of adventure in searching out the lonely and out-of-the-way places among the hills. The Crane Loch is one of them. The first time I found it was on a frosty Christmas morning. A motor-car conveyed me to Dunsyre, and a Pentland walker is not long in this vicinity before the summit of the Hill of Dunsyre, or Hill of the Prophet, calls him. It dominates the landscape, and affords the vantage-point that the roamer is always in search of. So Dunsyre Hill was climbed, passing on the way the spring that is affected neither by summer heat nor winter frost, in supplying the village with sparkling water. There is a cairn on the top, the circumference of the base of the original tumulus measuring 150 feet. But it was the far view that appealed most, the view of the Cloich Hills, and of the Pentland range, Mendick, Catstone, and Craigengar, and the woodlands around Easton and Medwinhead, with the bloom upon the fir-trees. Big views expand the mind, give wings to the spirit, and refresh the memory.

One sniffed the frosty air, and set off in search of fresh adventure down the hillside by the old quarry, across the heather, and up the slopes of the Bleak Law. This is another good view-point, and by facing due north there was discovered on the left hand, just over the shoulder of Weather Law, the snow-covered Crane Loch gleaming out of its grey surroundings. As one watched, large snow-flakes fell at intervals, borne on the grey wings of the north wind. The moorland between Bleak Law and the loch is very marshy, with clumps of tufty grass and wet spagnum mosses, and this part is best traversed when the ground is frozen.

This irregularly shaped loch is an eye in the far-stretching moorland, and its appearance may be either drearily grey or blue as the skies. Once upon a time it was a mile in circumference, but this Christmas Day 450 yards was the measurement round its borders. The loch is silting up at the western end, and it may ultimately disappear. Its waters were frost-bound; two wild ducks rose from the reeds as I approached, and downy feathers were scattered round the edges. It is the only natural loch in the Pentlands that has not been turned into a reservoir, and its moorland setting far from all human habitation makes it a haunt of moorfowl, wild ducks, wild geese, and herons, and in springtime black-headed gulls nest around its shores and in the surrounding marshes. White hares were abundant on the high ground, and a congregation of golden plovers rose from a rugged water-course, uttering their sharp shrill cry of " three-three." But it is a place where wild nature keeps her secrets to herself; and the origin of its name seems to have been lost. Even the stories connected with this elfin lochan and the moorland sykes that the Covenanters knew have faded away with the old generation of hill folk. " Aye, I've heard my faither tell stories aboot the Cran loch, but, losh! I dinna mind them." So are the old stories lost.

Taking a straight line back to Dunsyre Hill we cross the Westruther Burn near Burngrange—the site of the Dunsyre Markets—and the Anston Burn, and there are fine views here of the soft-flowing sweep of the contour of the hills rising amidst the rich deep brown colour of the heathery moors. Amid the stillness that falls over the hills at the closing of the short winter's day one listens to the tinkle and the talk of a hill burn on the lower ground. It is the only sound that breaks the silence of the moors as darkness falls.

CHAPTER XI

A BLUE AND WHITE DAY

WEST LINTON TO NINEMILEBURN
By the Cauldstaneslap and Hill-tops

RICHARD JEFFERIES said there were two periods in the year when the country with its far spaces, its hills, and mystic sounds subjected him to the migratory impulse. Every year from boyhood he felt it in the month of March, and often so powerfully as to be quite unable to resist it. " Go I must," he writes, " and go I do somewhere."

Many Pentland walkers know the call, and for them also it is a case of go they must. As I looked from my bed-room window towards the hills mantled in white and sparkling in the morning sunshine under a sky of deepest blue the call came; there was no denying its clarion note, and it was responded to joyfully.

A great boon has come to the Pentland walkers in the motor-bus service that now plies along the hill road between Edinburgh and Biggar by Carlops, West Linton, and Dolphinton; and in the space of less than an hour I was conveyed to West Linton, than which one can wish for no finer jumping off place for a day's tramping on the hills. This bus service will be the means of opening up a new world to those whose tramps on the hills have hitherto been confined to the more frequented walks around Bonaly and Glencorse, Balerno and the Boar Stane, for now the Cauldstaneslap and the Covenanter's Grave are brought within easy access by virtue of the start which may be made from West Linton or Dolphinton; and great as is the charm of the former walks, the hills farther west have a greater fascination still. One visit to the Covenanter's Grave can never satisfy, and one must visit it in all seasons

172

On the Baddinsgill Burn

to catch the magic spell of its romantic setting amid the
hills around Dunsyre and Medwinhead.

Alighting at the Gordon Arms, we cross the bridge over
the Lyne, and take the first road to the right for the Cauldstaneslap route. It takes us past the Golf Course, and
when the Avenue is left behind the view opens out upon a
spacious landscape bounded on all sides by shapely hill-
tops, and revealing interesting nooks in the rolling folds
and valleys, as each new elevation is reached and at each
succeeding bend in the road. Mendick Hill, on our left,
stands up like a sugar-loaf in crystalline whiteness; while
on the right, beyond the Windy Gowl, like sentinels guarding the valley, rise Mount Maw, The Mount, and Wether
Law. It is a delightful moorland road that takes us into
the very heart of the hills. Wakefield Farm is passed on
our right, and the inviting entrance to Glen Fly on our
left, after which the road descends to the Baddinsgill Burn
that has its source beyond the Wolf Craigs, three miles
away, a cheery stream in every stretch of it, that comes
rollicking down through one of the most charming glens
in the hills. As we cross the wooden bridge the frost
crystals by the burn side sparkle in the sun, and we pause
to photograph the snow pictures among the overhanging
bushes and among the woodland surroundings of Baddinsgill farm; while under the blue sky and the snow-covered
slopes of Mount Maw lies the mansion-house at Cairn-
muir, beaking in the warm sunshine, lulled by the music
of the Lyne in the foreground, and beilded by pine woods
and fir plantations under Colin's Rig—an attractive scene
that we fain would linger over on this pleasant winter's
day. Half a mile farther on we come to the Kennels at
Baddinsgill Cottage, well known to every hungry and
thirsty Cauldstane tramper who has started on his day's
outing at Midcalder, for when the cottage is passed he
knows that Linton is not far away. To-day we meet the
keeper, and have a chat with him about many things—the
new bus service that is the talk of the countryside, his new

wireless set, and the wonderful things he hears up there among the hills; the new reservoir that has been formed in the Lyne Valley, whose waters cover the site of the neighbouring herd's cottage at Hareshaw; and of this old road to Baddinsgill that was constructed as a turnpike over a century ago, which has now lost the characteristics that endeared it to the heart of generations of Pentland walkers. The future road may be in some respects a better one, but its surface may never be so kindly as the old one we have known.

From the *Records of a Family of Engineers* we learn that R. L. S. knew the Lyne Water, which he visited along with his father; but it was as a young man of artistic feelings that he looked upon the river " as a pretty and various spectacle," not as a prospective engineer, as his father wished him to see it.

The old road stops at the Kennels, and the track over the hills begins—covered deep in snow to-day. It is wise to keep to the track if possible; one has only to lose it several times and get caught in a drain-pipe gully, to know its full value. After a few miles of this ascent we come to the Ravendean Burn which comes sparkling down through the hills over a pebbly bed and between banks of brown sand. The sun is hot on this March day, and the air is still in the valley, and the only sound, as we lunch by the water-side, is the soft singing tones of this little hill burn. It is a time for reverie, and fancy can weave strange mono- logues, but the resting hill tramper on such a day is not far from his land of pure delight, the music of the stream finds an echo in his heart, and his thoughts are upward borne on wings of song. Such moments of insight at their best must, however, be brief; the " voice of strange com- mand " over-rules us better than we know, and calls us to resume the upward way. And so refreshed and reinvigorated we set off again on the track that winds through heather and between boulders leading to the snow- covered horizon and the gate in the middle of the slap.

Ye gods, but the sunshine is welcome indeed after the grey days of winter! Blue and white everywhere, and a silence that can be felt. How good it is to be here on this clear frosty day, with all the fascinating beauty of the sunlight flooding the white hills and valleys on every side, when we feel that the beauty and the harmony of nature around are at root one with our own joy.

Like a miniature Alpine peak the clear summit of the East Cairn Hill beckons us; and with alacrity we obey her call, and get nearer the blue sky by another four hundred feet. General Smuts was right when, in unveiling the Indicator on the summit of Table Mountain as a War Memorial of the Mountain Club of South Africa, he referred to the mountain as the ladder of the soul. When we reach the summit we feel a new freedom, the soul is released from the things that weigh it down, and becomes dominant over the things of sense. An exhilaration of body and spirit realises itself in an ecstasy of joy.

Here was all the fascination and delight of the Swiss winter sunshine, and we were glad that we had obeyed the morning call, and found in the day an increasing revelation of the wonder and the beauty of the snow-clad Pentland peaks, that never look more alluring than when clad in white; glad to find ourselves in such a day's silent devotion of the spirit, impressed and awed by the majesty and beauty of our surroundings.

A day spent on the hills without any time-table or pre-arranged programme may be as full of surprises as any other slice of life, and so we found it. Our first idea was to make for Listonshiels and Balerno, but that meant leaving the hills. No, we could not contemplate that on such a day of winter sunshine. This sun-strained air was life and health, and we turned our back upon the direction of the plains, and made over the hills again for the loch at the base of The Mount.

There are no rights-of-way when the hills are snow-covered! Grouse may give the warning note now and again, but otherwise one tramps on in good conscience, rejoicing in the exercise, and at peace with the world.

Then came the happy thought. It was tea-time, and the blue smoke was rising from Tod's cottage. So down the hillside we went as fast as the uncertain going in the snow-covered ravines would permit, and rapped on the door. We had the usual hearty welcome, lots of hot tea and a happy half-hour. The obvious way home from the North Esk was by way of Carlops, but we were greedy for the hills, and climbed the hillside above the reservoir between Spital Hill and Patie's Hill, and descended by the right-of-way upon Spital Farm and Ninemileburn, counting upon the Linton bus to take us home. But again, another surprise. There were more than a hiker or two, some sheep, white hares, and grouse on the hills: a party with skis were packing up at Spital, and stowing away their gear in a motor-car, and good-hearted understanding people that they were, they offered us a " lift," and in half an hour we were back in town, just as the sunlight was saying good-bye to the day that had treated us so well.

Every hill-tramper knows the satisfaction of heart and mind that seems to come flowing in to every cranny of his being when he gets back to his fireside after a day upon the hills. Joyful as the thrilling experience of emotion and vision upon the hill-top may be, it is when the day's adventure is over and the matured impression becomes a personal possession that the light breaks in fullest radiance. Freedom has come when with the Psalmist he can say: " He restoreth my soul."

EVENING ON HARELAW

CHAPTER XII

A RAMBLE ROUND THE RESERVOIRS

THE varied and picturesque scenery of the Pentland Hills is greatly enhanced by the presence of no fewer than eleven reservoirs—large sheets of water like natural Highland lochs set amidst the romantic scenery of old castles, ruined towers, heather-covered hills, and plantations of Scots fir, the home of numerous birds and wild fowl, and the centre of attraction to anglers. Nature has so mellowed the immediate surroundings that under certain aspects of lighting and colouring these hill lochs present pictures that are often idyllic, and prove that even utilitarian schemes of this nature planted in the midst of the hills may also play their part in beautifying the landscape.

In the course of the following walk of about twelve miles —nearly half of this distance being by the water's edge— we shall visit Torduff, Clubbiedean, Harelaw, Threipmuir, Loganlee, and Glencorse.

Leaving Colinton, we proceed along Woodhall Road to Fernielaw Avenue, where we turn to the left in the direction of the hills. This avenue takes us to the valley or haugh near the Tower of Bonaly, which was the site of old Bonaly village.

Picturesquely situated between the hills named Torphin and Torduff lies Torduff Reservoir, whose waters reflect an olive-green colour beneath the rocks which rise sheer from the loch side, and among which a sparrow-hawk nested for many years. A cave in the hills, and a tree near the waterfall, are locally known as " Cockburn's Cave " and " Cockburn's Tree."

The valley with its sparkling stream and waterfall connecting the waters of Clubbiedean and Torduff is a particularly attractive spot, either in winter when snow is on the ground and the frost-encrusted reeds by the burnside in all their wonderful artistry of shape and design are sparkling in the sunlight, or at other seasons, when the fragrance of the moorland comes down through the pines and the whins, and Cockburn's Seat is decked with the red berries of the rowans.

There are many hill springs—marked by iron indication-posts—between this point and Colzium, eight miles to the westward—each with its own little collecting well and branch pipe leading to the larger branches and main aqueduct, yielding a minimum flow of four million gallons a day, and along with the Torduff supply providing water for (1) the higher districts of Morningside, Bruntsfield, and Merchiston, and (2) the storage tank at Firhill, Craiglockhart, where the water mixes with the Talla supply filtered at Fairmilehead. Torduff and Clubbiedean were constructed to store the surplus flow of the Black Springs in winter, and they also have each their own natural drainage area. Bonaly Reservoir, which takes the place of two small old reservoirs, was built to supplement the supply from Swanston or Torduff as required.

The walker will experience a real sense of freedom and a quickening of interest as he walks along the shores of Clubbiedean, which is on the same level as the top of Arthur's Seat, with the fine prospect over the open waters to the rolling slopes of the Pentlands melting into the Cairn Hills in the distance. Here the air is strong, and the spring wind carries the scent from the fir-trees on the opposite side of the loch, where an ancient Fort lies hidden; and however much we may love the winter time for walking, the glamour of the earth is strongest when the April days come. Spring comes early to the sheltered nooks that are warmed by the sun, and it is up here, around the lochs and farms and woods, that the thrushes sing their most passionate and captivating songs.

Following the farm road to East Kinleith and the Poet's Glen, our progress is now out of sight of the waters for a mile or two, and between Mid and West Kinleith we cross the road from Currie, commonly called The Kirkgate, leading on to the right-of-way to Glencorse and Penicuik by the old Malleny shooting-range, the Maidenscleuch, and Clachmede. The next farm-steading on the road is Hare-law, where we turn sharply to the left and make for the reservoir, guided by the peak of one of the Kips on the sky-line. Along the banks of Harelaw and Threipmuir we have an interesting stretch of country with many fine views embracing a combination of water and wood in the fore-ground and the hills and peaks beyond, with colour and graduation of tint and tone in the landscape, and all the wonders of the open sky. Here we shall delight in the solitude of these lonely lochs among the hills, the haunt of wild birds and water-fowl.

No water for the city is taken from Harelaw, Threipmuir, Harper-rig, and Crosswood. The first two supply com-pensation water to the Bavelaw Burn, a tributary of the Water of Leith, and Threipmuir was increased in size in order to retain more of the winter floods to augment the flow of the Water of Leith in summer, while Crosswood supplies the Crosswood Burn, Linnhouse Water, and the River Almond to compensate for the spring water taken away for the city.

Threipmuir is always interesting to lovers of wild life, especially in the breeding season. It is the home of the moor- or water-hen, with her brood swimming about her, and of that excellent diver the coot, easily identified by the white patch on the forehead, and all the commoner water-fowl. The shoveller, one of the more uncommon members of the duck family, whose distinctive feature is a broad bill, breeds here regularly, the first recorded observation being in 1898.

In the upper reaches great numbers of black-headed gulls breed, and it is an interesting fact that a few nests occur annually in stunted fir-trees at the upper end of the marsh. The eggs, which are about two inches long, are of a soft greeny-brown colour, spotted with dark brown, and the nests are built of sedges, coarse grasses, and reeds along the marshy sides of the water. In summer the head or hood is of a dark chocolate brown and the bird is easily recognised. The young birds run about the reedy marshes, but soon gain strength of wing and become active and alert. The babel of the black-headed gulls may be heard a long way off, and often astonishes the walker, who may be unaware of the presence of " the gullery." There are " gulleries " also on Harper-rig and Cobbinshaw Reservoirs. The one on Auchencorth Moss has existed since the eighteenth century, when gulls (maws) were a noted feature of the Moss, the northern part of which was called " Flow Moss," and the southern part " Maw Moss "—hence the derivation of the hill-name Mount " Maw " near Carlops, overlooking Auchencorth and Harlaw Moor. On the hill-sides we find the redshank, snipe, grouse, woodcock, and plover, and herons are frequently seen.

There are two birds in addition to the cuckoo that all hill-walkers know, and whose notes they love to hear—the CURLEW and the PEEWIT. The curlew or whaup is easily identified by its long bill. The upper parts of the body are brownish, glossed in faint purple, with the under portions a whitish colour. The eggs are of pale green ground shading into an olive green with brown spots. It is an attractive bird, and its whistling cry—a long bubbling kind of whistle in ascending scale—among the lonely hills is beloved by all. The very thought of this bird's cry will often bring on " hill-hunger," and R. L. S. has echoed the feelings of us all in the lines:—

" Blows the wind to-day, and the sun and the rain are flying;
  Blows the wind on the moors to-day and now,
  Where about the graves of the martyrs the whaups are crying—
  My heart remembers how! "

Our other friend—the peewit, otherwise lapwing or teuchit, is known to everyone, and his notes haunt the memory of every Pentland lover—a mysterious lonely sound, as if blown through a reed—long drawn out when used as a call-note, and short when the bird is alarmed, with an April call-note of will-o'-wit, peew-weet or " dix-huit "—the Pentland sound that R. L. S. hoped to hear in his last vision of the hills of home—" the call of the pee-wees crying, and hear no more at all." It is a beautiful bird, the head feathers forming a crest which is black with a glossy green tinge, hence the " green-crested Lapwing " of the poet. Under the eye from the beak passes a streak of white often marked by spots of black or brown, and the throat and breast are black; the back and wings are olive green, the latter shaded in purple and brown, and the sides and back of the neck, underparts, and tail are white.

Most hill-walkers have noted the antics of the bird in its devotion to its young, how when disturbed it runs a short distance, then rises and circles round with short sweeps, alighting now and again to tempt you away from the nest, all the time crying plaintively. It is, however, a debated point as to whether the bird rises straight off its eggs, or runs some distance before rising, and it may be that, as it is very quick of eye and ear, if it knows itself to be dis-covered when you are some distance away it will run before but if it be suddenly alarmed when you are close upon it, it will rise suddenly off its nest. Its flight is heavy, and the rounded wings make a musical humming noise which can be heard some distance away. But how he loves his sport of flying. Listen to that fine naturalist, the late W. H. Hudson, speaking of the peewit—" Rising to a considerable height in the air, he lets himself go with the determination apparently of breaking the pee-weet record, that is to say, of rushing downwards in the approved suicidally insane manner, with sudden doublings this way and that, and other violent eccentric motions designed to make him lose his head, and finally to come at fullest speed within an inch or as much less than an inch if he can, of dashing himself into a pulp on the ground below. Compared with man he must have a wonderful heart and brain and nerves to do such things, purely for the fun of it."

In the woods around the hills are found all the commoner wild birds, and occasionally we get a glimpse of the golden-crested wren with his exquisite ways. Pied wagtails have nested at Redford ruins, and here also have been seen tree pipits and spotted flycatchers. Two capercailzie were observed at Bavelaw in 1906. The kingfisher, that most brilliantly coloured of all our native birds, is not nearly so common nowadays as he was at one time on the Water of Leith, and although the nightjar is a stranger his hissing notes, rising and falling rhythmically in the still air, have been heard at Bonaly, where a former proprietrix had installed an aviary. A pair of goldfinches were observed near Dreghorn in 1897; quail have frequently been heard calling at Swanston; the cairn on the summit of South Black Hill provided a view of the greater wheatear in 1911, and a brent goose, not often seen far from the sea, observed first near West Linton, was afterwards shot near Drochil in 1912.

The badger has been seen at Boghall, and one was caught at Newholm, Dunsyre, and transferred to the estate of Sir Simon Lockhart at Lee. Otters have been seen at Torduff, Glencorse, and on the Medwin. I have observed few squirrels, but have frequently seen roe-deer around Garvald and Fernyhaugh on my way to and from the Covenanter's Grave, and on 30th April 1927, after a heavy snowfall, I saw five feeding in the grounds of Newhall, Carlops, between the mansion-house and the public highway; while foxes are numerous, and their bark is often heard.

The Redford ruins by the side of Threipmuir are reputed to have been the hunting stables of James VI., and a path in the Bavelaw policies is known as the Queen's Walk, after Queen Mary. That ardent huntsman James IV., who knew these hills from end to end, held " the Bavillawis " for a time in ward, and among the sixteenth-century holders were the Mowbrays of Barnbougall, Dundas of that Ilk, and Lord Blantyre, while Laurence Scot of Bavelaw was fined £2400, in 1662, for having espoused the cause of

Cromwell in the days of the Commonwealth, and in 1679 was summoned by the Kirk-Session of Penicuik to pay £28, 8s. " as a penalty for his sins," he having defied both Presbytery and Session: This family held the estate and castle until the close of the eighteenth century. Bavelaw Castle, like Merchiston Castle, was originally a keep, consisting of a rectangular tower with one wing, built like the letter L.

Sir Henry de Brade, who was owner of the Braid Estate in the second half of the twelfth century, also owned Bavelaw. The second Sir Henry gave to the monks of Holyrood the teinds of Bavelaw Estate for the services of the Chapel of St Katherine's-in-Pentland. This grant was confirmed by Pope Gregory IX. in the tenth year of his episcopate. We learn from an old parchment that an Inquisition was held in the chapel in August 1280, to consider the question of straying sheep on the Pentlands. The laird of Bavelaw for the long period of fifty years before then had been in the habit of exacting what was called " punlyn," or a fine of eightpence for each strange sheep found wandering on his land. The other farmers, who were King's tenants, held that they, as the tenants of His Majesty, had not only an equal but a superior right to exact " punlyn " for the stray sheep belonging to Bavelaw. The parchment does not give any clue as to the result of the Inquisition, but doubtless both parties agreed to be fined, and the shepherds would have the usual lively times at the " getherin's "!

Among the names of those attending the Inquisition can be distinguished those of present-day Pentland farms familiar to frequenters of the hills, such as Harleaw, Braidwood, Cotis (Coates), Walstone, Buteland, Listonshiels, Maleny, Bonaly, Balerno, etc., and as the inquiry took place in the thirteenth century, it is a proof of the antiquity of the place-names still existing in the Pentlands. This has also been noted in respect of the names of some of the peaks.

In 1381 the lands of "Bavillay" were held by Fairley of Brade. Here also at Bavelaw—spelt "Bevelaw" locally seventy-five years ago—was held the Rouping of the Pentland grazing lands, when, as one who attended expressed it, there was dispensed "most lavish hospitality—and aqua fortis distilled in the neighbourhood passed round in a goblet of bone that lacked nothing in originality."

It was upon a similar goblet that Byron inscribed the lines beginning—

> "Start not—nor deem my spirit fled;
> In me behold the only skull
> From which, unlike a living head,
> Whatever flows is never dull."

From Bavelaw to Loganlee the track is well marked, and this route to Glencorse vies with that from Bonaly as the most popular in the hills, and in summer time picnic parties here enjoy all the delights of life in the open.

If Threipmuir is interesting to the naturalist, the walk from Bavelaw to Loganlee is equally so to the geologist. At Bavelaw Castle the base of the Upper Old Red Sandstone rises to the surface; beds of sandstone and conglomerate may be seen in the burn to the east. To the south are Silurian rocks in which are two small quarries. In the Green Cleuch are the upturned edges of the Silurian rocks, and beds of nearly horizontal conglomerates are seen in contact with the vertical Silurian. An outcrop of a great instrusive mass of felsite or micro-granite, of which the mass of the North Black Hill is constituted, may be noted: nearing the waterfall we see a big boulder of mica-schist—a stranger to the district—well chiselled by collectors, which in the great Ice Age must have been carried from the direction of the West Highlands, and the scratched and polished pieces of rock which abound in the glacial drift bed above the boulder show the effects of the ice pressure. The geology of the Pentlands has been the subject of much authoritative research. "The Pentland Hills," a chapter in

The Geology of the District around Edinburgh, by Dr Robert Campbell, Edinburgh University, published by the Geologists' Association, London, in 1914, is a good guide, and is largely based on " The Neighbourhood of Edinburgh " (*Memoir, Geological Society of Scotland,* and Sheets 31 and 32), 1910, and *The Silurian Rocks of Britain,* vol. i., Scotland, also *Memoir, Geological Survey,* published 1899. These contain references to nearly all the earlier papers. There is a good sketch of the " Glacial Geology " by the late Dr Peach in Cochrane's *Pentland Walks.*

Continuing our walk by the side of Loganlee, we pass the ruins of " Hoolets Hoose," which may have been so named by the local folks centuries ago as being the habitation of owls. But all history of it seems to have been lost. It may have had some connection with the Chapel of St Katherine's farther down the glen in days long before the gentle waters of the burn were chained up in a reservoir. In vol. xxxiii. of the *Proceedings of the Society of Antiquaries,* in a Note by F. R. Coles, it is stated that " in all probability Howlets House was a chapel and the abode of a priest." The green plot adjoining may indicate a small garden or burying-ground, and there is evidence of a road leading to the house from the south side. The masonry corresponds with that of old Logan House, which is our next point of interest as we near Glencorse Reservoir.

This house is described in vol. xiii. (1879) of the above Society's *Proceedings,* which states that although it originally consisted of a single tower, there was built in the fifteenth century an additional tower on the north side of the original one, with a deeply sloped base—a feature introduced from France about that period—and an enclosing wall forming a courtyard. This tower was probably erected by William, third Earl of Orkney, as it was of the same character as the additions made by him to Roslin Castle. But both the courtyard and this tower have been removed, and a shepherd's cottage adjoins the ruins of the original Peel or tower, upon which " there has recently been cut the date 1230, which appears to be about the proper date of the building." Occupying a commanding position upon a knoll above the valley, strongly built, and consisting at one time of two stories, it probably served as a place of safety against attack, similar to the Towers of Fulford, Craiglockhart, and Liberton, and as it is in the neighbourhood of Bavelaw and the hunting ground favoured by the Scottish kings, it is not unlikely that at a later date, when the additional tower and courtyard were built, it was a hunting seat. In 1593 Logan House Tower was still owned by the St Clairs of Roslin (see Notes on Glencorse, p. 79), and continued to be their occasional residence until 1681, when they sold " Logan House and Kirkton lands, with tower and fortalice." The Fergussons of Raith and the Cowans were subsequent holders.

Following the winding road round the Glencorse Reservoir, with Carnethy towering on the right and Castle-law on the left, we come to the point where the Bonaly right-of-way joins the road, opposite which is the site of the submerged chapel, and an ancient drove road round the base of Turnhouse Hill. A soft grassy path, though not a right-of-way, runs round the base of Castlelaw to the farm of that name, a pleasant relief from the hard road, for those who care to join it. From the farm a good idea is obtained of the wooded countryside stretching away to the Moorfoots, and the farm road takes us to the Biggar Road at Glencorse Manse and Crosshouse Farm opposite the, entrance to the Bush Mansion-house. The island in the reservoir with the bank of dark firs and bushes surrounding the east end of the loch, the keeper's cottage, the rising height of Turnhouse Hill and the others that close in the valley on all sides, combine to form a picture that is worthily admired of this—to many—" Queen of the Reservoirs."

Glencorse was connected in 1914 with the Talla Aque-duct, so that it now acts as a service reservoir in connection with the Talla Scheme. It may therefore never again be

wholly dry, nor the site of the ancient Church of St
Katherine's again become visible.

At Flotterstane the bus will take you back to town.
Others may prefer to continue along the highway to the
first cross-road on the right leading through musical sylvan
glades by the Old Church of Glencorse to Milton Bridge—
a road full of interest to nature lovers and of quiet delight
that will bring peace to the heart of the walker, who out
of the vastly solitudes of the hills passes through this leafy
cathedral space to the main highway, forgetful of all the
fatigue of his " Ramble round the Reservoirs."

EDINBURGH WATER SUPPLY
Thirty Million Gallons per Day

Behind these smiling reservoirs lies the long and often
troubled history of the anxious striving of the City Fathers
to meet the growing city's need for a plentiful supply of
fresh water. Originally the Edinburgh Water Supply was
obtained from pit wells in the Cowgate, often insufficient
in quantity and impure in quality. In 1598 the supply was
increased by the water of the South Loch in the Meadows.
This loch was partially drained in 1722, and the Meadow
Walks became a favourite resort of the citizens. Lord
Cockburn says: " There has never in my time been a single
place in or near Edinburgh which has so distinctly been
the resort at once of our philosophy and our fashion.
Under these poor trees walked and talked and meditated
all our literary and scientific and many of our legal
worthies."

In 1621, the inhabitants applied to the Scottish Parliament for power to bring in " sweet water from the country."
The power was obtained, but nothing was done for over
fifty years. It was proposed to levy a fire-hearth tax to
defray the expense, but this " scheme of oppressive
exaction," as the citizens termed it, was not gone on with.

George Sinclair, a Leith schoolmaster, discovered certain

springs that rise in the valley of the Braid Burn, north of Hunters' Tryst, and for his "attendance and advyce in the matter of the waterworks" was given a gratuity of £66, 13s. 4d. by the Town Council in 1673-4. The contractor for the Comiston supply was Peter Bruschi, a Dutchman, who brought the first public gravitation supply to the city from Tod's well, and so pleased were the Town Council with his diligence and care in the matter that they gave him a gratuity of £50 in 1681.

To supply the 3333 families living within the city walls, four Comiston springs were utilised, named respectively— the Tod (fox), Hare, Teuchit (peewit), and Swan, which delivered their water into a stone-built, lead-lined cistern of 1200 gallons capacity, which, although it is now 274 years ago since it was erected, is still as good as ever it was, and is contained in the solid-looking oblong building standing by the side of the field-path north of Comiston Farm, and is 44 feet above the level of the reservoir on Castlehill. Tod's Well is immediately to the east of this building. The Ordnance Survey of 1852 shows eight springs in the immediate neighbourhood. In this main cistern, where the four springs deliver their water, are placed four animals, cast in lead, each answering to one of the four springs. The water is carried to the reservoir in the Castlehill near Ramsay Gardens, and from there distributed to other cisterns lower down, where the old city wells still exist as monuments of historic interest.

By way of annual way-leave or feu for the Comiston Supply the Town Council agreed to " provide for the lady of Comiston the best silk gown it was in the power of the Corporation to bestow, and pay to the proprietor the sum of 7s. 6d. per annum."

The pipes were increased in size from time to time, and in 1761 the Swanston springs were added, the water from which was conducted into the city by wooden pipes, specimens of which may be seen in the Edinburgh Corporation Museum. These were removed in 1790, and replaced by iron pipes. Nine years later the supply was again becoming inadequate, and economy was urged in new regulations which provided " that every person at the public wells should take the water as they came—that is first come, first served, that no person should be allowed to ply with a cask or vessel that would hold more than twenty pints— bakers' tubs excepted—unless before eight o'clock in the morning and after eight o'clock at night: and that each person who had a private pipe should pay a duty of 20s. per annum, for the quantity of water not less than half a hogshead a day."

In view of the extension of the city and consequent building operations in the Braid Burn direction, it may be considered necessary some day to discontinue the use of the Comiston supply,[1] which is not filtered before delivery. This source, though interesting historically, provides in dry weather only about a thousandth part of the supply at the disposal of the Corporation, which is 30 million gallons a day.

The Swanston water is conveyed to tanks in Edinburgh Castle for the use of the Castle itself and the Lawnmarket, after being filtered at Swanston in modern sand filters. In 1912 a six-inch pipe-line was laid to Swanston filters from the Talla Conduit, half a mile away, and the water of the Swanston vicinity is now supplemented by Talla water.

The high buildings in Princes Street are supplied from the reservoir on Castlehill, which is fed with water from Comiston, Swanston, and Alnwickhill.

The Hare Burn from the Pentlands forms part of the Swanston supply, and the area drained by this stream— 160 acres—is now within the city boundary. Some day we may have an extension of the public park at Hillend! Every Pentland-loving citizen would regard a proposal of this nature with enthusiasm. Our successors will probably see the entire eastern end of the Pentlands in the possession of the Corporation.

[1] Comiston supply discontinued 1946.

The other reservoirs constructed in connection with the city water supply are those at Portmore, Gladhouse, and Alnwickhill (1879), and Edgelaw and Rosebery (1880), the last two supplying compensation water to the South Esk.

PARTICULARS OF THE PENTLAND RESERVOIRS

For supplying the City and Compensation Water to Streams

	Surface area when full.	Depth when full.	Capacity, million gallons.	Height of top water above sea-level.
	acres.	feet.		feet.
Glencorse, built in 1822				
enlarged . 1851	52	72	367	738
Loganlee . . 1851	18½	51	117	875
Clubbiedean . 1850	12¾	46	59	771
Torduff . . 1851	11¾	72	110	653
Bonaly . . 1853	14½	25	48	1120

Reserved solely for supplying Compensation Water to Streams

Threipmuir . . 1847				
enlarged . 1890	216½	17	519	835
Harelaw . . 1848	30½	50	160	810
Harper-rig . . 1859				
enlarged . 1890	237	44	900	900
Crosswood . 1868	62	40	175	1012
Lyne (at Baddingsgill) for Bathgate District. Authorised 1924, presently in course of construction . .	60[1]	78	450	1090[1]

[1] Approximate figures.

The scheme for the Talla supply, which comes from the reservoir on the Talla Water, a tributary of the Tweed, was authorised by an Act of 1895 and the work was completed ten years later. The water is conveyed through a built aqueduct which terminates at Mauricewood, near Glencorse, from whence by cast-iron pipes it is taken to the filters at Fairmilehead and Alnwickhill. Pipes also convey the water across the intersecting valleys. The built portion of the aqueduct is about 22 miles long, and includes 21 tunnels, varying from 133 yards to a mile and a third in length.

Over ten million gallons per day can be delivered to the city from the Talla Aqueduct throughout the year, and as the city expands and its need increases even this large supply will no doubt in time require to be augmented; but as the Talla area is small compared with the ample reserve in the area draining to the Tweed at Peebles, this may be the source from which the future supply will be obtained.

The mechanical filters at Fairmilehead have recently been augmented by additional filter-beds, the filtering sand for which is from Loch Etive in Argyllshire.

In addition to the above there is another reservoir picturesquely situated among the hills above Carlops—the North Esk Reservoir—the property of a private company —which was constructed in 1850 to supply power and water used in the process of papermaking, for the mills on the River Esk. It also supplies power for the electric lighting of several of the houses in Carlops village and the Carlops poultry-farm. Sand, whinstone, and sandstone used in its construction were found in the vicinity, and the cart track from the sandstone quarry near the Boar Stane can still be traced along the hills on the Peeblesshire side of the march dyke. The island in this loch is a favourite resting-place of wild duck, teal, gulls, herons, etc., and a description of the mediæval graves found upon it, similar to those at Spitalhagh, West Linton, is contained in Vol. xl. (1905-6) of the *Proceedings of the Society of Antiquaries*.

CHAPTER XIII

A STARLIGHT CROSSING

PENTLAND HILL walkers have few opportunities for indulging in their favourite recreation in the short days of winter, but there are times when the desire for the hills and the open air and nature's silent friendship comes with irresistible force.

It may be just a letter from a friend telling of a winter day on the hills, a note in a newspaper speaking of that fragrant smell of a wood fire, or it may be the arrival of a fresh volume of the Mountaineering Club *Journal*, or a picture of a snow-clad peak, and lo! memory flashes old scenes before our eyes, in fancy we inhale the mountain air, imagination stirs us into action, and we leave all else behind.

And so it came about that at sunset we were leaving Balerno for the high places among the solitudes to answer the call that come to us we knew not exactly how. It was the same mysterious voice that Henley knew—

> " What is the voice of strange command
> Calling you still as friend calls friend;
> With love that cannot brook delay,
> To rise and follow the ways that wend
> Over the hills and far away?"

Many a Pentland walker of long ago remembers the sage advice of the motherly Mrs Veitch of Carlops as she bade adieu to us at the Inn door—" It's a guid thing to let the darkness grow on ye." So we started before the darkness actually fell. The city was fog-bound, but here the stars were shining, so that the crossing by Listonshiels and the Boar Stane was made easy by the clear shining of the lamps of night in the deep blue vault above. There was no moon. The track seemed to shine out before us, covered with a fine sprinkling of snow or hoar-frost, and was easily dis-

GLENCORSE—QUEEN OF THE RESERVOIRS

tinguishable in the surrounding bracken and rank grass. We had no sooner got upon the old right-of-way track than we sniffed up that tang of the Pentland moorland, that nectar of the gods to the hill enthusiast, which quickens the mind and the imagination as well as the blood, and scatters brain-fog as well as brain-fag.

What though stones were kicked and sparks flew from tackety boots, and at times one stumbled over the uneven ground; what of that when one's spirit leapt up and rejoiced in this ocean of freedom and great space, bounded only by the "silent hills and the more than silent sky." Here was air to breathe; had we not been suffocated with fog for three days on end!

In the far distance a train whistled. Now and then a lonely moor bird would send up his good-night cry, then all was silent again. The silence that is among the lonely hills seemed deeper still in the enrobing night, and at times one could almost hear the heart beat.

The chain clanked against the gate in a march dyke as we opened it and passed through to the heathery moors and the winding track leading up to and over the far horizon. The broad base and rock-strewn slopes of the East Cairn were enshrouded in darkness, while hillocks, boulders, and ravines assumed unaccustomed and fantastic shapes. The tall fir-trees under the King's Hill were as the pillars of an ancient temple of the heathen gods, and the strange mysterious moorland landscape shot through with the gleaming waters of Threipmuir seemed "an unsubstantial faery place."

A clump of trees surrounds the farm of Listonshiels on the edge of the moor, and to-night they recall to mind the lines of Keats—

> "Tall oaks, branch charmed by the earnest stars,
> Dream, and so dream all night without a stir,
> Save from one gradual solitary gust
> Which comes upon the silence, and dies off,
> As if the ebbing air had but one wave."

And through the fretwork of branches the farm-house lights were shining.

The glamourie of our hills of home haunted us at every step. Often did these hills resound in far-off days to the horn of the huntsmen as they chased the deer over Deerhoperig, or hunted the boar from his den at the Boar Stane Pass. Knights Templars and the monks of old were familiar figures about this moorland around Listonshiels. In the eighteenth century, that learned physician, Dr John Clerk, grandson of Baron Clerk of Penicuik, lived here, and the famous Ambassador, Sir Robert Liston, and his successors the Foulises, sought quiet and retirement in the old house where once stood the " shiels " that sheltered the beeves belonging to the patrimony of the Kirk at Liston.

But what claimed our attention most was the wonder and the magic of the stars. One recalled the last words of Shackleton in the far South Seas—" In the darkening twilight, I saw a lone star hover gem-like above the bay," and Matthew Arnold's " Still, let me as I gaze on you, feel my Soul becoming vast like you," and in the drama of the Patriarch Job, " the morning stars sang together, and all the sons of God shouted for joy." On such a night one understood how that from times immemorial, poets, philosophers, and wise men have linked their highest aspirations and loftiest sense of mind and spirit with the stars that shine for ever. They are Carlyle's " Street lamps of the City of God," Longfellow's " Forget-me-nots of the angels," Byron's " Poetry of Heaven," but Shakespeare's imagery is the most beautiful of all—

> " Look how the floor of heaven
> Is thick inlaid with patines of bright gold;
> There's not the smallest orb which thou behold'st,
> But in his motion like an angel sings."

And yet it seems as an afterthought that the author of Genesis adds: " He made the stars also." Here in the soltiude of the hills one could look up and feel their strange beauty; and look down, and behold! each blade of grass by the burn side is decked with liquid pearls. " Ye are a beauty and a mystery " we read in *Childe Harold's Pilgrim-age*, " and create in us such love and reverence from afar, that fortune, fame, power, life, have named themselves a star."

Especially still and wild and lonely did we find it in the valley between the Cock-rig and Deerhope-rig. The voice of a hill burn is more emphatic in the starlight than in the broad light of the sun, and at such a time the sense of intimacy and mystery is heightened. The Henshaw Burn was in a merry mood, it babbled and glucked and chuckled, and then for a moment was quiet as if listening to the stars or the fairy harpers on the rig. It seemed a place for fairy voices, a haunt of spirits, like the neighbouring hills of Arthur's Seat and Salisbury Crags, to which the Ettrick Shepherd alludes in the " Queen's Wake "—

> " By mountain sheer, and column tall,
> How solemn was that evening fall!
> The air was calm, the stars were bright,
> The hoar-frost flightered down the night!
> But oft the listening groups stood still,
> For spirits talked along the hill.
>
> .   .   .   .
>
> Came voices floating down the air
> From viewless shades that lingered there:
> The woods were fraught with mystery;
> Voices of men they could not be."

Had we not been well acquainted with the windings of the Esk in the ravine where it enters the loch, we might have experienced difficulty in fording its swollen waters, but " Cockburn's land " was well known to us, and we crossed dry-shod. So still and calm was it that there was not a ripple on the surface of the loch, in which the great stars were wondrously reflected, while all the surrounding hills seemed asleep in their still white shroud. Passing the farm-steading of Fairliehope we kept to the road, instead of scrambling along the rocky path that runs along the hill-side above the stream. We had tasted to the full the joy

of the music of running water as an accompaniment to the
" glorious voice" of the radiant orbs, " ever singing, as
they shine," and so swung merrily along the old farm road
that drops one down at the south end of the village. But
as we approach, it is good to catch—through the trees—
the welcome lights at cottage windows, and perhaps still
more so, the lamp above the Inn door. Carlops as ever
seemed to embody the twin spirit of Peace and Humanity.
It had been a glorious crossing. Another addition to one's
memories of the wonderful Hills of Home.

"Hoolets Hoose" and Loganlee

CHAPTER XIV

SOME HILL NAMES

THE hill-walker and the mountain-climber is usually among the most patriotic of men. He loves his native land, and native hills, and claims them as his own. And his claim is born of intimate knowledge of the hills: he knows them individually, he knows them by their names, and in their varied moods he understands them every one. This knowledge has not been lightly won. There has been extreme patience in the gaining of it, and against all the forces of nature that have played upon and around the hills he has matched his energy and skill, and been successful. Moreover, no one can take from him his experiences of enraptured feeling and ecstatic vision, and as he stands upon the hill-top he is, if not master of all he surveys, master of himself and of his situation. It is with the pride and the humility of the true hill-lover that he takes to his heart the lines of the poet, and often to himself repeats them:—

> " And we who feelingly have been
> Partakers of this wondrous scene,
> Been wrapt in its sublime delight,
> Touched with its pathos infinite :
> How oft from heartless worldly din
> In thought we'll wander back and win
> Refreshment, strength and calm of tone
> From the great vision we have known."

He is also jealous of the names of the hills and the peaks he has climbed. With these names he has linked associations and memories of pleasure and delight, and thrills of exaltation, so that he comes to speak of them as intimate friends: their very names live in his heart for evermore.

Pentland Hill lovers may, at first, experience a sense of disappointment to find that the peaks which they have for long known as the " East Cairn " and the " Kips " were

197

originally termed the " Harper-rig Hill " and the " Scald Hill." This knowledge, however, brings with it a deep satisfaction, when we realise that the old names are much more historically significant and romantically interesting than those now appearing on our maps, and for this reason it would seem desirable that the old names should not be lost.

The Pentland Hills may quite reasonably be named the Pictland Hills, for this part of the country was at one time inhabited chiefly by the Picts. Panthoria, daughter of Asterius, the supposed founder of Roslin, was a Pictish lady who married Donald I. (A.D. 203); and there is a tradition that the daughters of the Pictish kings were wont to be kept in the Castle of Edinburgh—Castrum Puellarum—as a place of safety.

To get to the origin of the names—the Scald, or Bard's or Poet's Hill, now known as the Kips, and Harper-rig Hill or East Cairn Hill, between which, as we shall see, there is a close connection, we have to go back to the times of the Picts and the Druids. We know that many modern antiquarians dismiss the Druidical Order as never having existed, but for our purpose we shall assume that it did exist. The names of such other hills as Dundreich or the Druid's Hill near Eddleston, Tinto Hill from Teinne, fire, and tom, a hill, in Lanarkshire, and Melden or Meltein, the hill of fire in Peeblesshire, so named by the Britons and Picts, also bear witness to the uses to which these hills were put before the Christian era.

It was on the highest hills, commanding far tracts of country and frequently within sight of each other, that the Druids had their places of worship and held their religious festivals. Here the cairns were erected. Every worshipper carried a stone with him to the top and added it to the cairn, and the dimensions of it therefore depended upon the size of the neighbouring population. Upon these high hills at a later date beacon fires were kindled to signal the alarm and call to arms:—

SOME HILL NAMES.

The hill now known as the East Cairn Hill gets its
present name from the druidical Cairn on the summit, said
by some to be a Bronze Age Cairn, probably some 4000
years old, and its ancient name, Harper Hill, from the
Bards who used the harp as an accompaniment to their
songs.   Hence there is the double significance in the two
names, in all that the Cairn stands for, and in connection
with the ancient harper.   The Bards were of the Order of
the Druids, and the Druids were often likewise Bards.   This
is referred to by Ossian (Temora)—

" Beneath the moss-covered rock of Lona, near his own loud
    stream,
  Grey in his locks of age, dwells Clonmall, king of harps "—

and the translator adds: " Cloan-mal, crooked eyebrow.
From the retired life of this person it is insinuated that he
was of the Order of the Druids, which supposition is not
at all invalidated by the appellation king of harps here
bestowed on him; for all agree that the Bards were of the
Order of the Druids originally."

Many eminent writers of antiquity, including Julius
Cæsar, have contributed to our knowledge of the mysterious
Order of the Druids.   Their doctrines, contained in
innumerable verses, were not committed to writing, and
when the Druids became extinct no record remained of the
principles of their creed.   But we know that learning and
every species of knowledge, close guarded behind a veil of
mystery, was theirs.   The sole object of their worship was
Be'il or Be'al, meaning " the Source of all things," and the
sun or fire represented their conception of the Supreme
Being.   The two chief festivals were the Be'iltin or Fire
of Be'il, at Whitsunday (of which we have a survival in the
name of the Beltane Fair at Peebles), when on the hill-tops
fires were kindled and sacrifice offered in honour of the

sun, whose genial spring warmth was felt and welcomed by all living things; and Samh'im or Fire of Peace, on Hallow-eve, in which thanks were returned for the fruits of the harvest, and when the yearly contribution of the people was paid to the Druids. The festivals with their sacrifices were celebrated on heaps of stones which the natives called CARNS, and from these Carns or Cairns on the Pentland Hills and elsewhere, the places where the festivals were held are clearly ascertained.

" The Druids were the prophets, priests, philosophers, poets, physicians, judges, teachers, and oracles of the Gauls. The Bards, like the German Scalds, were, more especially their poets, historians and musicians." Their instrument was the harp, which was also used by the Bards of the Britons, Caledonian Picts, and Scots.

And so we have seen that the Cairns were identified with the religious observances of the Druids, that the Harper Hill and the Scald Hill or Bard or Poet's Hill had a connection with these Orders of Bards who accompanied themselves in their poems and songs with the harp; but the question as to the time when these Pentland peaks were given these names it would be difficult to answer. Pentland names are derived from various sources. There are many evidences of Roman occupation round the Pentland Hills, and the Caiy Stone of Kelstane or Battlestone near Fairmilehead marks the place of a legendary battle between the Romans and the Picts. In the fifth century the Saxons from beyond the mouth of the Elbe overran Lothian, and in the ninth and eleventh centuries came the Danes and the Norwegians, the heroes of the Scalds, and introduced their language. Evidence of the Danish occupation was seen in the Camus Stone, from which Comiston gets its name. This stone has disappeared, as well as the ancient circular encampment on the south side of the road from the toll-house at Fairmilehead to the Hunters' Tryst, and in the same manner as the Stone Circle at Flotterstane, the Cross on the Monks Rig, and the Cross on the South

Black Hill have been broken up nefariously and used in the building of dykes. The Camus Stone was probably erected by or for a Danish commander named Camus.

As the harp came originally to this country from the land of the Saxons, perhaps it was they who gave the name of Harper's Hill. The ancient druidical observances there, and the Cairn with its religious significance, and its warning beacon, must also be included, and so we come to the double name of the Cairn, or Harper's, or Harper-rig Hill. The Danes were the heroes of the Scalds, and so we get the Scald Hill, a much more significant and interesting name than the Kips, by which it is now known.

In the maps of a hundred years ago the old names are given, while what is now known as Scald Law to the eastward appears as the Black Hill.

It would therefore appear that from the earliest times the Pentland Hills and their surroundings have been the scene of many religious and military movements and activities, besides witnessing the lives and works of men devoted to literature and the Muses. And the close association of such points as the Cairn Hill, Harper Hill, and Scald Hill with the Druids and the Bards; the Knights Templars, the Cistercian monks at Newhall, 'Spital, and the Monks Rig, with the romantic Esk in their midst; and all the literary associations of Pennecuik, Ramsay, Gay, Thomson, Brown of Newhall, and many another, makes the district one of more than ordinary interest, as well as being the pleasant haunt of many who, like the Druids and the Bards of old, love the hill-tops, where sacrifice is offered in many a mood of quietness and exaltation.

Torphin is the name given to the hill immediately to the north of Torduff Reservoir, overlooking Juniper Green. Torduff rises on the opposite side of the water supply, and both hills attain to a height of about 900 feet. What, we may ask, do these names signify? If we take the Gaelic derivation it would seem that they are simply the WHITE HILL (Torphin—torr fionn) and the BLACK HILL (Torduff

—torr dubh), in which case there would be a Black Hill with a White Hill on each side, the hill above Bonaly being also the White Hill.

The name Torphin is not confined to this hill. In Corstorphine, we have the Cross of Torphin; and part of the neighbouring county in the West Calder district is named Torphin, with villages of the same name; and there is also Torphins in Aboyne, Aberdeenshire.

There was a Torphin, Earl of Caithness, who came into conflict with the Scottish Crown for refusing to pay tribute when Duncan (grandson of Malcolm II.) was king, 1034. There is also the legendary Torphin, Archdeacon of Lothian. But if we may assume that the Saxons gave the name to the Harper or Harper-rig Hill, we may also presume that they were likely to give the names of Torphin and Torduff after the name of their god Thor, which still survives in our Thursday. Nor is the suggestion unlikely that there were Saxon generals named Torphin and Torduff, after whom the hills were named.

Thor is the strong god, the Thunderer, son of Odin, wielding the hammer. He is the friend of man, incessantly harrying the intractable frost giants, fit guardian, surely, of a water supply.

The picturesque peak of Carnethy, beloved by all Pentland enthusiasts, which, despite the fact that Rhys says the derivation is from " Carneddi," meaning " cairns "—and the cairn on the top of Carnethy is a real cairn—may have been named by the picts. The name is derived possibly from " caer Nechtan," King Nechtan's fort or rock, for Nechtan in Bede is Naiton and Naiton was a King of the Picts about the year 700.

It cannot be said that there has been shown any great aptitude, resource, or ingenuity in naming some of our Pentland peaks. Several are named simply Black Hill and White Hill, the only distinction in such names being that the Black Hills are coloured black or brown with heather or stone covering, while the white hills are covered with

202

grass of the kind which, when it grows long, becomes white and bleached looking, but even this distinction does not always obtain.

But the Pentland Hills, like the romantic city of which they form the southern bulwark, are linked up in story and tradition that we would not willingly forget or forgo; and whatever their individual names may be, we love them still, because of the joy and happiness they bring to every Pentland walker.

CHAPTER XV

PRINCE CHARLIE'S HIGHLANDERS

ON THE LINTON ROAD

THE Pentland Hills make their appeal to all lovers of " Mine own Romantic Town," both at home and abroad, and it would seem that they also appealed to Prince Charlie's Highlanders when they came to Edinburgh in 1745. At least the surroundings did, Swanston and the old road to Linton, more particularly that portion of the road that runs by Mortonhall and Buckstane over the hill to Fairmilehead, down into the hollow at Bowbridge, Lothian burn, and Hillend, and round the back of the hills to Boghall, Woodhouselee, Castlelaw, and Glencorse.

In the Woodhouselee MS. we have a narrative of what happened during the Jacobite occupation of Edinburgh and district in September-November 1745, and among other things the doings of the Highlanders on this Linton Road.

The writer was probably one Patrick Crichton, a saddler and ironmonger in the Canongate of Edinburgh, a man of means and some position, a burgess of the city, and about fifty-five years of age in 1745. He was a keen Whig and pious Presbyterian, and entirely opposed to Prince Charlie and his cause, naming him " a Popish, Italian Prince," and referring to Allan Ramsay as " the mungerall burlesque poet." Keeping in view this standpoint, we have an interesting picture, by an eye-witness, of the doings of the Highlanders, and the intense nervousness and agitation which they caused among the lairds and country folk of this Pentland countryside.

He was in Glencorse Kirk when the news arrived that the Prince and his army were at Corstorphine. During

The Logan Burn and Castlelaw

the sermon one of the elders went out to drive his horses to the Pentland Hills, while the writer, "considering the enemies was at the gaits," climbed one of the hills and "with his prospect" viewed the defending dragoons at Corstorphine. Later he sees "the cavillcade and all the Highland wifes with the heavy baggage," and a guard of 300 or 400 men crossing the Linton Road on the south side of the "Breads Craiges," in "tope spirits with the prospect of a warme qwarters and plenty upon the kind Lord Provost's invitation." (He suspected the provost, perhaps rightly, of Jacobite sympathy.)

Dr Blaikie holds that Provost Stewart did everything that was possible in a position of extraordinary difficulty. His known Jacobite sentiments, which he shared with a large number of the citizens, rather forced him, as falling under certain suspicion, to do more than he might otherwise have done. At the end of the Rising, Stewart went to London to perform his duties as M.P. for the city. There he was committed to the Tower and kept prisoner for fourteen months, and afterwards tried at Edinburgh for "permitting the City to fall under the power of the rebels." He was unanimously acquitted by the Jury.

The Collington Mains farmer, whom the laird meets, is in great distress, and tells him that his horses and carriages have been pressed, his furniture broken, and six silver spoons taken away. The example made of several of the "rebells" at Linlithgow, when they were hanged for pilfering, evidently did not extend to Colinton. The writer states that they approached with good discipline, "for to give them their due never did 6000 thieving naked ruffians with uncowth wappons, rusty rapiers, matchlocks and fyer-locks, rag-tag and bob-tail, make so harmless a march in a civilised plentifull country."

Taking a by-road to Brade he goes down to Canaan Muir, and gets a rear view of the Prince, his retinue and guards. A tenant tells him the Prince was "in Highland dress, a velvet bonnet, both gold lace ringed about both at the head ring and the seeming about." At Grange the Prince stopped, he narrates, " and drunk some bottles of wine," then marched on the King's Park to Holyrood.

It was from Corstorphine that the Prince, on 16th September, sent a summons to the Lord Provost of Edinburgh to surrender the town, and then marched by Saughton to Slateford, where the army encamped on the banks of the Water of Leith. Prince Charlie himself lodged in the Gray's Mill Farmhouse, near Inglis Green.

Half his army under Lochiel marched by Merchiston and Hope Park to the Netherbow Port, where the city was entered, the Judges and great officials having left the town the previous day. On the same day as the city was entered, the Prince and the rest of his army marched by the Braid Hills and Prestonfield, as narrated by the Woodhouselee laird, to the King's Park, the Prince stopping at Grange House to drink a glass of wine.

The army encamped in the Park, and Prince Charlie rode forward by St Anthony's Well and the Duke's Walk to Holyrood, where he was received with great enthusiasm by a crowd, it is said, of 20,000 people, and entered the Palace.

Various accounts are given as to his appearence. A Whig contemporary says the figure and presence of Charles Stuart was not ill suited to his lofty pretensions. He was in the prime of youth, tall and handsome, of a fair complexion; he had a light-coloured periwig, with his own hair combed over the front. He wore the Highland dress, that is, a tartan short coat without the plaid, crimson velvet breeches, and military boots; a blue bonnet was on his head, and on his breast the Star of the Order of St Andrew. The Whigs acknowledged he was a goodly person, but they observed that even in that triumphant hour, when he was about to enter the Palace of his fathers, the air of his countenance was languid and melancholy: that he looked like a gentleman and a man of fashion, but not like a hero or a conqueror.

The Jacobites, on the other hand, were much delighted; they likened him to Robert the Bruce, whom he resembled, they said, in his figure as in his fortune.

At the reading of the Proclamation at the Cross, the laird writes, " I observed there armes, they were guns of different syses, and some of innormowous lengh, some with butts tured up like a heren, some tyed with puck threed to the stock, some without locks, and some matchlocks, some had swords over ther shoulder instead of guns, one or two had pitch-forks and some bits of sythes upon poles with a cleek, some old Lochaber Axes. The pipes plaid pibowghs when they were making ther circle, thus they stood five or six men deep." The Proclamation which was made at the old Market Cross by the Heralds in their Robes of State was that of King James VIII., and Charles, Prince Regent.

After the fight at Prestonpans the whole neighbourhood is overrun by Highlanders on the pretext of searching for arms, which meant the lifting of anything they considered useful. Some of the Prince's men went off in search of stragglers, and at Bow Bridge, near Lothianburn, they found one such and tied him neck to heel, and were going to carry him off, but he redeemed himself by paying 20s. Others went to Straiton Mill, took free quarters and some money, and adds the diarist: " If all the clans come up as is talked they will eat up this poor place if they continue long here."

One day the tenants at Swanston had a visit from the spoilers. " It was braw brose " they had at Swanston, one of the Highlanders is reported to have said, it was made with a churn-ful of cream! But the Swanston folk were not to be outdone, they went to the Prince and complained, and the Prince gave them the answer, not without its humorous touch, that he " would cawse heng them had done the injury if they would poynt them out." And they determined to point them out, for some time later a number of the Swanston men got hold of three Highlanders and took them to the Castle. When they were met by the writer at Buckstane, the Swanston men were carrying them, and using them "not tenderly." And no wonder—they were laden with booty, "like camels!"—so writes R. L. S.

All the countryside was in a state of nervous tension and excitement. A neighbour of the laird of Woodhouselee was riding home on the Linton Road one dark night, on his "mear and his demeepicke sadle," when he gets a fright by, as he thought, some strolling Highlanders, but it turned out they were only two country men who hal "jocked" him, and bade him dismount. The laird goes on to say that although the inhabitants of the city were taxed 2s. 6d. per £ sterling of their real rent to provide the tents, military stores, and arms of the army encamped at Duddingston, he thought the Highland host were "unwilling to lye incamped in tents but preferred to ly in 100s in barns and waste houses so that they could make excursions in the night for plunder and robbery." It is on record that some of the Highlanders objected to tents as being too luxurious. Some butchers on the Linton Road had to stand and deliver, and Braid House also furnished plunder. From Corsehouse at the ford at Glencorse Water they took "cloath and all." They knocked at the Minister's "but got not in"; later they took the poor man's horse. Twenty of them proceeded to the Howgate and took free quarters at Charles Straton's, "hade all his bapes and ale, put on a large fyer, and drunk a bottle of whiscke, went in to the weedow woman Brown's and spoyled her howse. This marrading by such worse than hussars strikes a terror all round."

Whisky was little drunk at this time, although Duncan Forbes of Culloden, President of the Court of Session, encouraged its use as a patriotic antidote to foreign spirits and tea. Tea cost 9s. per pound; ale was in general use, brewing being a flourishing Edinburgh industry, and cost 1d. for a modern quart bottle, while claret, which was largely used by the gentles, cost 1s. 6d. for a similar quantity. Large quantities of claret were consumed. In 1745, when the population numbered about 40,000, the Edinburgh magistrates fixed the price of the 4-lb. loaf of wheaten bread, the staple for gentles and commons, at 5d. for the finest, and 2¾d. for the cheapest household bread, so that the loss to poor Straton of his " bapes " would not be a serious one.

The laird congratulated himself that his own " poor hyred sheeld of Woodhouselee " had not been visited; then he hears that some are nigh at hand, and so everything is hurried out of the way into " holls and boors, beds dismantled and what not adoe," and a couple of days later he learns that sixty of them have arrived at Bow Bridge (near Lothianburn), and " gulravished in the publick hows." Pentland and Straiton and Fulford are next visited, then they come to Woodhouselee. He meets twenty-four of them outside the entrie, and asking what they want, he is informed they are in search of arms. He makes a bargain with them, that if this is their orders, two or three of them might go in, and the rest have meat and drink. But arms were the least they minded, he says; they asked money, and I gave them 5s., although they wanted a guinea. " Ah," he says, " they are artfull thieves for they had their spyes on the hills and rysing ground, and saw the mercier carry home linings [linens] and put under the hay, and when I was in the house they run abowt and took the linings, 2 tablecloths, 9 sheets [?] and aprons and other small linings, and put them under their plaids, they run threw all the planting and found owt Hew Ballentin and took 5s. 6d. off him." " I was lucky to get off for 5s.," he muses, and continues, " he that was ther leader had the impudence to ask me if I had a protection, tho' he showed no warrant for what he did in seeking armes."

After this they " randevouzed " at the back of Fulford House on the hillside, and divided the spoil. Out of this a squabble arises, and they draw swords about it, then march to the next house, get what they can, and so on to the Linton Road again. They meet a coach at Boghall with a Mr Mowbray and his family, and he satisfies them with some money; but Mr Mowbray has to repeat the performance when he meets a second squad at Lothianburn. After all, it was an easy way of satisfying the conquering invaders.

Like the Swanston folk who remonstrated, Mr Lockhart, Advocate, from Craighouse, lawyer-like, goes to the Abbey and insists that the spoilers be apprehended. On the way he is met by some of them, who " spunge him of 2s., all he had." But he succeeds in getting a party of 200 to go and apprehend the robbers, and apprehended they were and things taken from them. " The less vallowable were left at Mortonhall, but the vallowable carried forward to the Abbey. I sent, but our linings were not at Mortonhall."

Some of those who stole the laird's linings paid him another visit. They came over Castlelaw—near Woodhouselee—firing at the sheep, wounding some, but getting none, and as they march up the avenue at Woodhouselee, they are followed by Lockhart of Carnwath's brother, who speaks to them " cavelierly," but all they get this time is bread and milk. A fellow at Castlelaw who was caught, had on a fur hat and shirt with cambric ruffles down the breast, " very clean and white where not bloody." " He called him name Cameron when I asked him, but no doubt he had robbed the shirt."

Sir John Clerk of Penicuik tells us that when the Highland parties came they were civilly used and so committed no disorders about the house, " except that they eated and drank all they could find, and called for everything as they thought fit, for they look't on themselves to be masters of all the country." The impositions on his estate were 6000 stone of hay and 76 bolls of oats, his share being about £200 stg., and all his horses of any value were carried off to England. The Inch at Liberton was requisitioned by both sides, and although Sir Charles Gilmour was a member of the Government and in London at the time on duty, the more onerous demands came from the Government authorities.

No doubt the Pentland lairds and country folks were glad when they marched off that Sunday morning with pipes playing, by Auchendinny and Howgate, to Peebles, with their waggons and carts with provisions, ammunition, and baggage, including " all Gen. Cope's waggons taken at the field of Preston," and after they had commandeered all the horses in the neighbourhood.

The Prince with the other column of the army went by Dalkeith and Soutra to Lauder.

Deserters from the army were picked up here and there among the hills; three made resistance at Castlelaw, but were caught and brought to Woodhouselee: " one was wounded in the head with a stone and all bloodie." They carried them forward, and at Boghall took five guineas and a crown off them. In due course they were lodged in the Castle.

When we have drawn for ourselves a reliable picture of life in Scotland in these rude times, and when we remember that, as Sir John Clerk in his *Memoirs* states, the Highlanders looked upon themselves as masters of the country, as indeed they were, it cannot be said that their demands were excessive—money and food and drink, and horses and " linings," and silver spoons, with here and there a few cases of real oppression. Nor can we overlook that our Whig author of the MS. tells us that the two Appin Stewarts who escorted Mrs Philp of Greenlaw, were found to be " civil " and came and dined with us and told stories, including the humorous story of how they traced that an East Lothian miser had hidden riches in his house, by the fact that when they found him " shilling peas and would give them nothing they saw how careful he was to pick up a peas or two [which] had fallen," so they searched and found his hoard, which the Prince promised to repay, without annual rent, " when he was possessed of his Kingdom."

These two jovial fellows were both brewers, the one from Appin and the other from Lismore Isle, both sergeants in the "Rebel Army," and their host must have concluded they were not such bad fellows after all.

Other considerations must of course be observed. The levies which were made on the towns, such as that on Glasgow for £5500 (which, by the way, was collected by John Hay of Restalrig, an Edinburgh W.S. and Deputy Keeper of the Signet), and the supplies which had to be got together, such as horses, carts, arms, corn, hay, etc., for which receipts were given, payment to be made when success was attained, were the inevitable accompaniment of war. No doubt the receipt which the above-mentioned miser obtained was one of such granted by the Prince's authority. The Highland Chief in charge of this department was Maclachlan of Maclachlan. And the fact that the men who demanded admittance to the unfortunate laird of Woodhouselee could show no authority, goes to prove that they were of the number of those who had either deserted from the Prince's army, and after Prestonpans these numbered over 1000, or were merely strolling Highlanders, who wanted money and demanded entry on the plea that they were in search of arms. That warrants of authority were issued is proved from the fact that one such had been preserved in the Dick Lauder Charter Chest, part of which runs:—

"Charles, Prince of Wales, etc., Regent of Scotland, England, France, Ireland and the Dominions thereto belonging, to George Gordon, Gentleman.

"These are empowering you to search for all horses, arms, and ammunition, that you can find in the custody of, or belonging to, any person or persons disaffected to our interest, and seize the same for our use—for the doing of which this shall be your warrant. Given at Holyrood House, the 18th day of October 1745, by His Highness' Command."

"J. MURRAY."

After this follows the detailed instructions given to George Gordon of Beldowy.

In the lecture by Dr W. B. Blaikie on " Edinburgh at the time of the occupation of Prince Charles," delivered to the Old Edinburgh Club, March 1909, which is of the highest value and authority on the subject, we are told that there was nothing which surprised the good folks of Edinburgh so much as the wonderful behaviour of the dreaded Highlanders, whose appearance was so wild and tatterdemalion. The Chiefs were most courteous gentlemen, well educated, many of them fond of letters, " and I like to think of them wandering through the High Street, dropping into the Book shop and into Allan Ramsay's library in the Lawnmarket to see the latest books and magazines." Alexander Robertson of Struan, an aged chief, and a poet in Gaelic and English, and William Hamilton of Bangour, another poet, were among the number.

The discipline of the Highland clansmen was wonderful. Dr Blaikie gives two instances. When marching to Edinburgh, the Jacobite army had to pass the mansion near Kirkliston which had been the residence of the Earl of Stair, who had ordered the massacre of Glencoe. The mansion was now the property of his son, the Commander-in-Chief of King George's army, who was even then collecting troops to fight Prince Charles. Fear was expressed in the Prince's army that the Macdonalds might take the opportunity for revenge. Not only did they indignantly repel the suggestion, but they insisted on furnishing a party from among themselves to guard Lord Stair's house until the army had passed.

When Lochiel, on the morning of the surrender, burst into Edinburgh, and had quartered his Camerons in the Lawnmarket, though the inhabitants plied them with hospitality, offering them meat and drink in abundance, not a man of them would taste spirits, because their Chief had forbidden them to do so before they marched.

Throughout the occupation of Edinburgh there was little excess or oppression by the Highland soldiers: it is on record that there were no riots in the streets, and not so much as a drunk man to be seen. There were, however, minor troubles for which the occupation was responsible.

As was natural, some evil disposed persons who did not belong to the army assumed the white cockade and masqueraded in tartan clothes, plundering where they could, and bringing obloquy on the Highland army. Among these was the notorious Jem Ratcliffe, whom Sir Walter Scott has immortalised in *The Heart of Midlothian.*

CHAPTER XVI

R. L. STEVENSON AND THE SWANSTON
SHEPHERD

"The sights and thoughts of my youth pursue me."
—Dedication of "Catriona."

WE were tramping over the Pentland Hills to Carlops by the Cauldstaneslap, when we met a son of John Tod, the "Roarin' Shepherd" of Swanston. On the hill side we saw a solitary figure climbing up in that zigzag, tactical way peculiar to the shepherd and the keeper. And soon we met. He was an elderly man, burly, broad-shouldered, and bearded, with a shepherd's plaid flung over his shoulder. In the course of our chat I happened to remark casually that he did well to tramp the hills so vigorously at his age, to which he replied: "Ou aye, an' a dinna cairy little weicht, ye see a was born and bred on the Pentlands, a've been on them a' my days, a went as a shepherd frae Spital tae Swanston." Swanston —Stevenson! and he, as if anticipating my thoughts, continued: "Aye, a left Swanston just before R. L. Stevenson came there." "You would know the 'Roarin' Shepherd' then?" With a smile on his face, and a laugh in his voice, he replied, "'Deed, weel, an' sure a should, he was ma faither; nae doubt he had a guid pair o' lungs on him, but it was that budy Patrick, the photographer, that ca'd him the 'Roarin' Shepherd.'" It was the Swanston bee-keeper that "gied Patrick the only richt photo' o' John Tod to copy," and it duly appeared in the photographer's show-case, but not for long: native modesty forbade such ostentatious display, and the photographer had perforce to remove it.

Willie Tod and his younger brother David well knew the lanky lad with the velveteen jacket and the long hair, for they often visited their father's cottage at Swanston when he was there.

Stevenson has paid free tribute to the Swanston shepherd in his *Memories and Portraits,* but does not there, nor indeed anywhere in his writings, name him " the roarin' shepherd." The photographer of the series of picture post-cards of Swanston village coined the phrase, and put it on his post-cards, which continue to circulate widely, and this no doubt accounts in part for the universal accept-ation and repetition of the phrase to-day, but locally—and this is the real test—Tod was known as " Honest John." In all likelihood Stevenson knew of Patrick's photographs of Swanston and " the roarin' shepherd's cottage "; and it is interesting to note that in a letter written by him to W. E. Henley from Bournemouth, in December, 1884, he signs himself " The roaring R. L. S." !

Now this shepherd had a great influence on the life of young Stevenson, who later confessed that " he owed his taste for all that hillside business to the art and interest of John Tod. He it was that made it live for me as the artist can make all things live." In ordinary talk, the shepherd's voice, Stevenson tells us, " fell pleasantly upon the ear . . . he spoke in the richest dialect of Scots I ever heard, the words in themselves were a pleasure, so that I often came back from our patrols with new acquisitions. . . . I might count him with the best of talkers; only that talking Scots and talking English seem incomparable acts."

" Tod was a quiet sort o' chiel," said one of his neigh-bours, " he never went roarin' aboot the place at a'."

But how different when Tod was herding his sheep upon the hillsides: then, like the expert shepherd he was, he rolled out his voice like a blast of thunder, striking terror into the heart of young Stevenson, to whom it was probably a new experience, and at first he was afraid of him, especially when he had wandered up the hillside among the sheep and lambs, with Coolin, his dog, and Tod had been angry with him, and had called him to " c'wa' oot amang the sheep "; and sometimes when he saw the shepherd coming he would slink away out of his track. A local farmer, to whom Tod was well known, told me recently that " the older he got, the stronger and louder became his voice. He was a strong-minded man, aye, a strong-minded man, he was that—jealous o' his sheep and his ain hillsides, as trespassers found out. I ay think o' him wearin' that wee roond ministerial-looking hat." And he was a faithful steward, as the silver snuff-box presented to him in 1875, " as a token of his long service on the farm," by Mr Macara Finnie of Swanston, testifies. As time went on young Stevenson came to be on speaking terms with this big, strong, hardy man of the hillsides, then they grew friendly, and Tod became a giant and a hero to the boy, who looked up to him and liked him, for he came to teach him, in the most impressionable years, everything he knew about " that hillside business."

What was it the Swanston shepherd came to teach Stevenson? Remember the kind of lad Stevenson was— thoughtful and quiet, ever on the lookout for the adventurous, the tragic, the romantic, with a mind and imagination that ever wondered and dreamed, and read deep in a quest for truth and life—yet with all his dreaming, he was a realist, " a most fanatical lover of plain physical sensations plainly and expressly rendered," as he wrote later to Sidney Colvin, hence we have him on the Pentlands, a lover of natural history, a keen observer, in quest of uncommon wild flowers, birds' eggs, etc., and while he was being taught by the shepherd, he had a pencil in his hand noting it all down in a book, for he was ever " learning to write." He had already written *The Pentland Rising*.

By the village folks " he wasna' thocht vera muckle o'," " he had a want," they said, " it wasna jaloosed that he wad ever come to muckle," " he lay aboot the dyke backs wi' a buik," some adventure story no doubt, and Adam

Ritchie, the Swanston ploughman, speaks of him as " the lang-haired idle-set laddie," and tells how " mony a time he wad gang up the rig wi' me when I was ploughin', but he didna gang vera far without takin' oot his notebook and bit pencil, and there he was writin' doon, Guidness kens what. He was never what ye could ca' communicative, but he was a devil ta think, and he wasna sweir ta speir what he didna ken." He was learning to write, and in his friendship with Tod there lay a whole world of romance and adventure. Tod was a man who took his business very seriously, and to young Stevenson he would appear much of a mystery. Here was something for his romantic nature to feast upon. Here was a man who spent days and nights upon the hillsides, with his dogs and sheep, a man accustomed to the far spaces, and the great silences of the hills—friendly, philosophic, physically strong and robust. He spoke to his dogs, and lo! the hillside became alive with bark and baa, pattering feet, heaving humps of wool, wildly beating hearts, and questioning eyes. Not only could he command a far hillside of sheep, with the aid of his dogs, but he would defy all weathers and brave the wildest winter blasts when his hirsel required his care. We can well imagine the Swanston shepherd as the shadows of night began to darken the hills, and the first portents of a snowstorm began to appear, winding up the hillsides over Torgeith Knowe and Ann's Leas—named after his wife— with his eagle eye upon all sides, breaking ever and again into a spasm of bellowing that seemed to shake the hills, while his earnest, attendant, shaggy aides-de-camp performed the operation of massing the scattered sheep and driving them to shelter.

Then Tod knew the drove roads over the hills to the trysts at House o' Muir, Linton, and Moffat, and those that went south into England. He knew all about the dangers and adventures of the wild life of the drovers: often had he journeyed there, and slept upon the hillsides. And if there were few dangers and adventures around the hills at Swanston, there were plenty on the drove roads. Tod knew all about it, and many tales of that kind he told the boy, and the boy never forgot. We remember the drovers Sim and Candlish with their cattle at the Howden Glen in *St Ives*. Now all this would appeal to the young Stevenson, and so it was that the Swanston folks said " he was ay rinnin' aboot wi' lang Tod among the hills, getting him to tell him a' the stories he kent."

When Tod went off on his evening patrol he " gave him a cry " over the garden wall, and Stevenson would overtake and accompany him. Everything the shepherd did was a source of wonder to Stevenson. Full of work is the life of the shepherd, especially at the lambing season: night and day he's at it, fair weather and foul, when neither rest nor peace is his except by snatches; and often Stevenson must have followed him then, when he would ask all about it. " He's an awfu' laddie for speirin' questions aboot a' thing," Tod used to say, " an' whenever ye turn your back, awa' he gangs an' writes it a' doon." This " hillside business " was a great delight to the boy, and Tod was an ideal teacher, a kindly, experienced man who made a deep and lasting impression upon the minds of those with whom he came in contact; and often as they sat there " ayont the Shearie and the Toddle Knowes " with " Swag " and " Cheviot," two of Tod's dogs, at their feet, the boy with wide open eyes would be thinking deeply, for we are told that when Tod spoke of " his own antique business," the thing took on a " colour of romance and curiority that was surprising," such were the shepherd's powers of description.

We do not have a description of the hillside by the shepherd himself, but Willie Tod, the shepherd's son, has often recited to me his own poem describing how his father went to work between Swanston and the Howden Glen:—

" Methinks I see auld ' Swag ' and ' Cheviot ' at his heel,
  As up the ' Green Craig ' he wad spiel,
  Ayon the Shearie and the Toddle Knowes,
  Where aft we buchted a' the yowes.

Noo frae the Green Craig's rocky broo,
'Twas his delight his flocks to view;
Here he'd gie the signal tae auld ' Swag,'
The doug wi' knowin' look his tail wad wag,
Then doon the brae, and through the Whinny Hedge,
Up ower the Routin' Hill by Covers Edge,
Ower a' the leas wi' lanky stride,
He'd turn the sheep aff Birkie side.
Noo John is aff along the Tailor's road,
For two an' thirty years by him 'twas trod,
There he takes oot his guid field-gless,
Views a' the yowes and lambs up Howden Hass;
Across the brae he takes the sklent,
Lampin' ower the wavin' bent,
On tapmaist heicht of Allermair
Breathes in great draughts o' caller air."

Many a wonderful talk they must have had together,
and many a time at night after Stevenson had returned
from the evening patrol with the shepherd, and settled
down before the cosy fire in the lamplit cottage, engaged,
as he tells us, with the *Vicomte de Bragelonne*, he would
rise from his book, and pull aside the window blinds and
look out on the hills, " under the muckle siller mune," or
when the wind was howling and the hills were lashed with
winter's blast, or white with snow, and wonder if his friend
the shepherd was out in it all after his sheep.

Stevenson came to know all the Pentland hillsides and
valleys; the stillness and the peace of the lonely hills
entered his soul.

The dogs, too, were a source of wonder to him, and it
filled him with amazement how they could remember the
" long itinerary " of directions the shepherd bellowed out
to them with " the sharp thunder of his voice." Wonderful dogs, yet Tod often referred to them—in the way most
shepherds and farmers do—with much contempt: " they
were nothing compared with the dogs he used to have!"
yet for one of his present dogs, " Cheviot," he was offered
£40, which he refused. One day Tod had been to the
market in Edinburgh; he had bought sheep from different

dealers, and with different markings, and when bringing them home over the Burghmuir he discovered that two were amissing. Later he learned that a farmer at the Braid Hills had discovered two stray sheep among his flock. Tod applied to him. " Can you tell me their markings?" asked the farmer. " No," said Tod, " but if my doug can seek them out, wull ye let me have them?" " Yes," replied the farmer. The dog got to work, and singled out the two sheep; and shepherd and dog, with the sheep in front of them, kept smiling to each other, as they went on their way by Fairmilehead to Swanston Hollow. That was the day Tod was offered £40 for " Cheviot."

And not only was he gaining experience through his friendship with the shepherd, but it would often be while in his company that he learned to know what made up the hillside atmosphere, that which is seen and heard, and never forgotten, because it is seen and heard in the hillside silence—the bleat of a sheep here and there upon the hillsid, the cry of the whaup or the gull, the pipe of a snipe, or the lonely call of the pee-wees or some other moor bird, the " go-back, go-back " of a startled grouse, the faint undertone of ". . . streamlets, gurgling rills, in joy among the Pentland Hills."

Or perhaps as he sat alone upon the hillside in early summer there were other sights and sounds that were fixed in his memory—the voices of children at play on the village green, the cackling of fowls in the farmyard, a dog barking in the steading, the creaking of a farm cart rocking and jolting upon a hill-track or farm road. And there was Ritchie, honest man, returning with his miry beasts after a long day at the plough, and Young, the gardener, who " crooks his weary back a' day in the pitaty-track, or mebbe stops a while to crack wi' Jane the Cook, or at some buss, worm-eaten black, to gie a look." He was ever asking Tod the names of all the interesting whinny knowes that lie around the foothills behind the village, and often he followed the shepherd's track from the " tapmost heichts

221

o' Allermair, doon Windy Doors and Byreside Nick, where roon the knowes the rabbits jick," to Moolypouches, Broomie Knowe, and the burn side, and here as he sits awhile looking out over the leafy hamlet "fancy traivels far afield." To his youthful imagination impressions were sealed at that moment, never to be effaced by the passing of time. How he loved the place! Here is how he writes about it in " Ille Terrarum "—

" Frae nirly, nippin', Eas'lan' breeze,
Frae Norlan' snaw, an' haar o' seas,
Weel happit in your gairden trees,
    A bonny bit.
Atween the muckle Pentland's knees,
    Secure ye sit.

Frae the high hills the curlew ca's;
The sheep gang baaing by the wa's;
Or whiles a clan o' roosty craws
    Cangle thegether;
The wild bees seek the gairden raws,
    Weariet wi' heather.

Here aft hae I, wi' sober heart,
For meditation sat apairt,
When orra loves or kittle art
    Perplexed my mind;
Here socht a balm for ilka smart
    O' humankind."

Stevenson could never forget this hillside atmosphere, and the memory of his " kintry hame " and " bonny bield," and the Swanston hillside—Halkerside, where he " loved to sit and make bad verses," and where, four months before he left England for good, he told Cummy some day to climb, and sprinkle for him some of the well water from the tiny pool upon the turf

" By the hills and streams of childhood, 'twas his weird to roam."

The Pentland Hills were graven on his heart, and John Tod, the Swanston shepherd, helped to keep them there, and that's why Stevenson wrote to Sidney Colvin from the

South Seas that he wished " he could only be buried in the hills, under the heather and a table tombstone, like the martyrs, where the whaups and plovers are crying!" " It is a singular thing," he writes, " that I should live here in the South Seas under conditions so new and so striking, and yet my imagination so continually inhabit the cold, old huddle of grey hills from which we come."

Many a story about the " hillside business " the Swanston shepherd's son can tell, for he too knows all about it. He began the shepherd's life as a herd boy at Swanston nigh five and sixty years ago, assisting " Jamie " Johnston, his father's right-hand man, and often he delights to tell of Swanston life in his early days. " There was nae sma' commotion, a can tell ye, at Dippin' Time," he narrated the other day, " for Swanston had the first Dippin' Pond in a' the district; aye, that wad be i' the fifties, it was the centre, ye see, for a' the neeghbourin' ferms—Bogha', Hillend, and Morton Mains—an' a' the sheep were brocht tae Swanston tae be dipped." His affection for Swanston's whinny knowes and the Pentland hill-tops is strong and tender, and his father's description of the " antique business " could be no more graphic than that which his son often delights to depict as he recalls the hills around Swanston, " where grazed the flo'er o' Cheviot yowes," and the early summer air resounded to the bleating of the lambs, as he made the afternoon patrol, about which he recites so enthusiastically in his poem, " Swanston's Whinny Knowes." Often he would tell you all about the Swanston shepherd who taught Stevenson all he knew about the shepherd's life on the hills, which made him hope that at least he would " behold again the Hills of Home, and hear again the call of the peewits crying, and hear no more at all." " Aye, he was my faither."

Often in the course of our " cracks " upon the Pentland moors, I urged him to write down his poetry descriptive of the pastoral life upon the hills, his tale of " sheep-shearing on the Pentlands," a realistically descriptive piece of the day's work at a "clippin'," and "Swanston's Whinny Knowes," which contained so many of the local place-names in danger of becoming lost, until at last he was persuaded, with his daughter as amanuensis, to transcribe the above-mentioned piece. He would watch for me coming over the hills on the Saturdays in winter, and one wintry day as the darkening clouds were closing in at evening and he was conveying me down the hillside, he brought himself to speak of it, " and would I look over it for him, and see if it was a' richt?" This was readily agreed to, and later it appeared in print. He recited the poem to a gathering of the Edinburgh Stevenson Club at Swanston. But the sheep-shearing pastoral was lost.

The golden wedding of Mr and Mrs Tod, who lived in the cottage by the North Esk in the heart of the hills, two miles from Carlops, where they were married fifty years before, took place on Christmas Day, 1924, and to mark their appreciation of the sterling and kindly qualities of the worthy couple, over fifty Pentland Hill walkers joined in the presentation of a gift appropriate to the isolated position of their home, of a wireless set in an oak cabinet suitably inscribed. During the thirty-three years that Mr Tod was in charge of the reservoir, his cottage was a place of shelter and rest and gracious hospitality to many a Pentland walker, and a well-known Pentland personality passed away when Willie Tod died on 22nd May 1925, at the age of seventy-three. Mrs Tod, who died 14th August, 1936, and was buried like her husband at West Linton, was a daughter of the previous keeper of the reservoir, Mr Garnock, whose predecessor and the first occupant of the cottage was Mr Alexander, the father of the late Mrs Veitch of the Allan Ramsay Hotel, Carlops.

The cottage and the reservoir were built in the year that R. L. S. was born (1850), and the name of his father, whose firm were the engineers of the undertaking, appears frequently in the Register of Visitors kept at the cottage.

CHAPTER XVII

THE BRAID HILLS

IN the view citywards from the heights of Caerketton or Allermuir, the hills of Braid, Blackford, and Craiglockhart add to the beauty and the variety of the landscape.

In the journey from the city, we pass through the district of Burghmuir, which in the time of David I. formed part of the great forest of Drumselch, where roamed the white bull, the Caledonian boar, the elk, and red deer. Timber cut from this forest was used in building the projecting fronts of the houses in the High Street of Edinburgh. No fewer than six Scottish armies have mustered on the Burghmuir for the invasion of England, the earliest known to history being that in 1384, when the Earls of Fife and Douglas assembled an army of 30,000 men, mounted on small horses, and raided the North of England. But the great event in Scottish history with which the Muir is associated is the Flodden campaign, when in the summer of 1513, James IV. set out with an army of probably about 50,000 men, although ancient chroniclers mention as many as 100,000 men, and marched to the disastrous field of Flodden (where many of the flower of Scotland's manhood fell around their king). And ere they left the muster ground, tradition asserts the Royal Standard was planted on a borestone, which has been preserved, and set upon the wall in front of Morningside Parish Church.

However interesting the story of the muster, the tradition of the Royal Standard, and the Bore Stone, Mr H. M. Paton, Curator of Historical Records, H.M. Register House, in an article in " The Book of the Old Edinburgh Club," Vol. XXIV (1943), propounds that no historical evidence exists to prove the muster on Borough-muir.

Probably Pitscottie's "Croniclis" (pub. 1728) was responsible for the story, followed by subsequent writers, including Sir Walter Scott.

Mr Paton finds that the Lord High Treasurer's Accounts (1513) give Ellem, Near Cranshaws in the Lammermuirs, as the gathering place of Royal Scots before marching to Flodden.

The late Dr Moir Bryce found there could have been no Royal Standard, for it was not ready before the King left Edinburgh. The supposed Bore Stone, says Mr Paton, is just an old Stone, without any historical association.

In the writing of Marmion (1808), in which the muster and the flag incident are repeated, Sir Walter refers to it in correspondence not as an historical account of the battle, but as a "romantic poem" containing "romantic lore," in short a "poetical romance." (Letters [ed. Grierson].)

We also pass the historic golfing ground at Bruntsfield Links, with the old Golf Tavern—the Golfhall, as it was anciently called, situated in the midst of what was named Wright's Houses, although the original village of that name was on the west side of the present main thoroughfare. Football was prohibited in 1424, as interfering with the more necessary science of archery, which was practised here. No mention is made of golf in this Act, but in an Act of 1457 it is referred to, and the inference is that the game was introduced about the middle of the fifteenth century, being first played on Leith and Musselburgh Links. About 1508 sandstone quarries were being worked on the Bruntsfield Links, and golf was only possible at that time with the quarry-holes as bunkers. Sunday golf was prohibited by an Act of the Town Council in 1592. In 1599 members of the Kirk Session of St Andrews were punished for playing "goulfe" instead of attending to their duties, the fine being 10s. for the first fault, 20s. for the second, public repentance for the third, and if these failed to correct the delinquents, "deprivation fra their offices" ensued.

Playing for stakes was as common long ago as it is to-day, as is shown in the following entries in a note-book of Sir John Foulis, Bart., of Ravelstoun:—

1672

Jan. 13. Lost at Golfe with Pittaro and Comissar Munro	£0 13	0
Lost at Golfe with Lyon and Harry Hay .	1 4	0
Feb. 14. Spent at Leith at Golfe	2 0	0
March 2. For three Golfe balls	0 15	0
Lost at Golfe at Musselburgh with Gosford, Lyon, etc.	3 5	0
April 13. To the boy who carried my clubs, when my Lord Register and Newbyth was at the Links	0 4	0
Nov. 19. Lost at Golfe with the Chancellour, Duke Master of Saltoun, etc. . . .	5 10	0
Nov. 30. Lost at Golfe with the Chancellour, Duke Hamilton, etc.	4 15	0
Dec. 7. For a Golfe club to Archie (his son) . .	0 6	0

The payments are of course in Scots money, not sterling. Golf balls would then cost about 5d. sterling.

The uniform of the " Thistle Golf Club," instituted in 1815, who played on Leith Links, consisted of " a scarlet single-breasted coat, with a green collar, and plain gilt buttons, a badge on the left breast, with the device of the thistle embroidered with gold upon green cloth; the trowsers white."

Wagers were not uncommon. For a bet, a ball was driven over the Melville Monument in St Andrew Square, Edinburgh; and in 1798 in the Burgess Golfing Society, there was betting that no two members could drive a ball over St Giles' steeple (161 feet), but early one morning this was performed without difficulty, the balls being driven from the south-east corner of Parliament Square, and soaring over the top of the weather-cock, were found near the Advocates' Close.

As we come over the hill—Church Hill (where no fewer than seven churches of six different denominations are grouped together)—we obtain a fine view of the hills, and look down upon the valley in which lie the old farm lands of Egypt and Braid. It is not so long ago since there was an old village of Morningside, lying upon the hillside. As we proceed, we come to where the old smithy stood; but the merry ding-dong is heard no more, for a Public Library now occupies the site. A few yards farther on stood Reid's Dairy Farm, opposite the entrance gates to Falcon Hall, the ornamental pillars of which are surrounded by large stone falcons, now adorning one of the gates at the Zoological Gardens. Morningside Asylum near-by, one of the first institutions of its kind in Scotland, built in 1809, owed its origin to the efforts of Dr Andrew Duncan, inspired through witnessing the sufferings of the poet Fergusson.

Through this little picturesque village passed the carts coming in from the country carrying their load of produce —eggs, butter, and buttermilk. It was a healthy district. It was called the " Montpellier " of the East of Scotland, and visitors came here for change of air, despite the fact that in 1770 there were chemical works at Tipperlinn village, and magnesia works near Canaan Farm in 1797. It seems to have been also an inspiring neighbourhood, for a certain Dean of Edinburgh (a minister of St Paul's, York Place), writing in 1823, speaks of his beautiful summer residence near Braid, where he studied Hebrew in the mornings, and thought of writing his Journal in blank verse. In 1862, however, we learn that Jane Welsh Carlyle wrote: " I am just going in an omnibus from Morningside to ' Duncan & Flockhart's ' for morphia to induce me to sleep." Later we learn the bus failed to pay, as there were so few passengers.

Dark deeds have also taken place in the neighbourhood, and proceeding up the historic Old Braid Road we pass the spot where the last case in Scotland of hanging for highway robbery took place, on 25th January, 1815. In the middle of the road near Cluny Drive are two large flat stones upon which the gibbet was raised.

From the Minutes of the Trial, we learn that David Loch, a carter and residenter in Biggar, being employed to bring a gentleman's horse to Edinburgh, was passing along the highway " betwixt the village of Briggs of Braid and Braid's Burn " about six o'clock on a November night, when he was set upon by two robbers—Kelly and O'Neill. They pulled him from his horse, threw him into a ditch, struck him on the head with the butt-end of a pistol, threatening to take his life if he made any resistance, and robbed him of 4 £1 Bank Notes, 20/- in silver, a twopenny loaf of bread, and a spleuchan or leather tobacco pouch. Among the witnesses were Andrew Black, Smith at Braid's Burn, who came to Loch's rescue on hearing his cries of " Murder," and Grizel Paterson, Change-keeper, Wright's Houses Toll-bar, where the accused visited the same evening. Loch convinced the jury that the spleuchan was his by the fact that his wife had " put three steeks in the corner of it " before he left Biggar; and although the robbers pled " not guilty " to the various counts in the indictment, of which this was the third, the jury found otherwise, and the two men paid the full penalty on this gibbet in the Braid Road, before a great gathering of people.

The Hermitage of Braid, which we pass on the left hand, was once the home of Sir John Skelton the historian, and the entrance lodge is the old Morningside Toll-house, removed from its original position near Braid Church. The road here passes over the Braid Burn which, rising in the Pentland Hills in a spring that flows into Clubbiedean Reservoir, glides through Bonaly and the picturesque ravines at Dreghorn and Braid Hermitage, and winds its way to the sea at Portobello.

Before we enter the Braid Hills by the gate leading to " the ride," another item of interest claims our attention. This is the Buck Stane, now built into the end of the boundary wall of the villa named " Allermuir," facing the high ridge named Buckstane Snab and Mortonhall Golf Course, which tradition has associated with the grant of the ancient barony of Penicuik to the Penicuiks of that Ilk, perhaps as early as the thirteenth century, under the curious reddendo of " rendering three blasts of the horn on the Common Moor of Edinburgh, formerly called the Forest of Drumsselch, at the chief hunting of the King thereon in name of blench farm." This reddendo is repeated in Charters by James IV. in 1508 and by Cromwell in 1654. When, therefore, the King rode past to the hunt, his vassal would stand upon the Buck Stane and wind three blasts of a horn. Hence the Clerks of Penicuik have adopted as their crest a demi-forester proper winding a horn, with the motto, " Free for a blast." The tenure is referred to by Sir Walter Scott in *Ivanhoe* and in " The Gray Brother "—

> " That fair dome where suit is paid
> By blast of bugle free."

It may, however, be stated that Maitland, our first local historian, in his *History of Edinburgh,* p. 507, asserts that the Buck Stane was so called because here the King's buckhounds were unchained and thrown off; and that it was upon the Hare Stane that the laird of Penicuik stood and blew his horn. This Hare Stane[1] may be identical with the Bore Stane previously referred to, and spoken of as the " Standard Stane " in the Town Council Register of 1586; and as the situation of this stone was " on the Common Muir," while the Buck Stane was outside the boundary, Maitland's statement would appear to conform more closely to the terms of the reddendo.

Arrived upon the " furzy hills of Braid," which are public property, having been acquired in 1889, we move from point to point to survey the wondrous scene on every side.

The Elf Pond on the southern boundary of the hills has an ancient association with the fairies, and is noted for

---

[1] No recorded evidence exists to support Maitland's statement with regard to the Hare Stane.

the number and variety of the micro-fauna found in its waters.

We have to go far back to the second half of the twelfth century to find the first trace of the name of Braid. The owner at that time was Sir Henry de Brade, Sheriff of Edinburgh, who may have been a son of a Norman knight of the days of David I., and for nearly two hundred years the estate of Braid remained in his family. He also owned Bavelaw on the Pentlands, Plewlands, and the Blackford Hill. The Braid lands afterwards passed into the family of an Edinburgh merchant—William de Fairley, and among later proprietors were the Dicks of Craighouse, Browns of Gorgie, Gordons of Cluny, and Gordon Cathcart.

There was a mansion-house of Braid, but its site is now unknown. During the latter half of the sixteenth century there was much turmoil around the mansion-houses between the Braid Hills and the town. The old residences of the Scottish lairds or lesser barons were garrisoned with soldiers, and no matter how disposed to peace and quietness their owners might be, they were alternately suspected and annoyed by either the King's party or the Queen's party. The Regent Mar endeavoured to reduce the town by famine, acting under the advice of the English ambassador, Sir Wm. Drury. The Pollock manuscript says: "The regent and the King's favouraris, stuffit [garrisoned] the houssis of Craigmillar, Merchingstoun, Sclatfurd, Reidhall, Corstorphine, and the college thairof, and the abbey, with all the places about the town of Edinburgh. And all inhabtouris within two myles to Edinburgh wer constranit to leave thair houssis and landis, to that effect Edinburgh should have na furneissing; and damnit poor men and women to the deid, for inbringing of victuallis to Edinburgh."

Fairley of Braid did not escape the prevailing storm. Like the Laird of Merchiston he was a friend of the Reformation; and Richard Bannatyne, the Secretary of

John Knox, in his Journal of the period, narrates an incident which shows how the most peacefully disposed families were affected by the unhappy wars of the period. Upon Friday the 25th of May 1571, Fairley of Braid was sitting quietly at supper, his own miller bearing him company, when a dozen soldiers attacked the miller's house. The miller rushed out to the rescue, followed by the laird, but he was overpowered by the soldiers and dragged back to the gate of Braid, where they then turned their attentions upon the laird, whom they insulted with vociferous and contumelious speeches, and bade him come out to Captain Melville, or they would " burn the house about his luggis." The laird being " a quyet man," told them to depart; and that if Captain Melville had wanted him, he would not have sent such messengers. But on seeing his miller being further ill-used, this quiet laird sallied out with a great two-handed sword, followed by a few servants, and laid about him lustily among the soldiers. Their " hagbutteris," some of them loaded with three bullets, were repeatedly discharged at the laird of Braid, who was fortunate to escape unhurt. Meantime he had struck one of the soldiers to the ground with the flat of his two-handed sword, and immediately made him prisoner; the soldiers then fled to the town and alarmed their Captain at arms. " So the alarm struck, and all come furth to the querrell-holes; bot hearing the truth, were staid by the Laird of Merchiston, who shaw Captain Melville that there were uther men cuming from Dalkeyth for the lardis relief, as that they did with speid."

Fairley was not only " a quiet man," he was also a generous man. During the Great Plague in 1585, he gave to the city his houses at " Little Egypt " for the purpose of brewing beer therein for the convalescents who were housed in wooden huts on the lands of Morningside, Canaan, and Greenhill, then part of the Burgh Muir, bounded on the south by " the Strand " or Jordan Burn. The principal hospital was at the foot of Blackford Hill.

Edward I. of England and his army of 100,000 men, of whom 15,000 were cavalry, camped on the Braid Hills from 11th till 15th July 1298, when he invaded Scotland because of the hostile Treaty made by the Scots with France. From the Braids he went by way of the Old Braid Road and Morningside Road to Kirkliston and Linlithgow, and fought the Battle of Falkirk on the 22nd of that month, returning to his former encampment on 19th August.

It was here upon the Braid Hills that he was met by the French Ambassadors, who came to point out to the King with reference to his former proposal for a Treaty of Peace with King Philip, that as Scotland was allied to France, any proposal for peace which Edward desired to make with France must also embrace her ally, Scotland. But Edward would have none of it: he refused to recognise Scotland as allied to France; he was at war with Scotland, and Balliol was his prisoner. And so the Franco-Scottish Alliance, which was first made between John Balliol, King of Scots, and Philip IV., King of France, at Paris, on 23rd October 1295, was confirmed in a practical manner upon the Braid Hills three years afterwards, and continued to play an important part in Scottish affairs for nearly three centuries.

From the Braid Hills, Edward, surnamed " Longshanks," moved to Glencorse[1] (spelt Glencrosk), by Fairmilehead, on 20th August, to West Linton (Lynton Rotheryk) on 21st, and on 26th was at Ayr. The presence of his army at Glencorse no doubt accounts for the large discovery of English coins, chiefly of his reign, made nearby at Penicuik in January 1898.

Among those who took the Oath of Allegiance to Edward at Berwick-upon-Tweed, following upon the defeat of the Scots and the imprisonment of Balliol, was Henry de Brade.

The Galachlaw, where Cromwell's army camped " betwixt Braid's Craigs and the Pentland Hills," is the

[1] *Itinerary of King Edward the First,* Henry Gough, ii. p. 168.

ridge sloping from the Braid Hills and Mortonhall towards Fairmilehead, upon which there was no shelter of any kind. An incident in the story of the encampment is that they erected a gallows for a sergeant who " looted a cloke," because there was " no tree to hang him on." The camp was much disliked by the English soldiers on account of the cold and wet weather, and one of them in a letter referred to the site as " the inhospitable and pestiferous Pentlands."

As we look towards the Blackford Hill we think of Sir Walter, who after referring to the furzy hills of Braid, which he knew so well, tells of his bird-nesting and lying on Blackford Hill, a truant boy, on a fine summer day. The lines from *Marmion* are well known:—

> " Blackford! on whose uncultured breast,
>   Among the broom, the thorn, the whin,
> A truant boy, I sought the nest,
> Or listed as I lay at rest,
>   While rose on breezes thin,
> The murmur of the city crowd,
> And from his steeple jangling loud
>   Saint Giles's mingling din."

A citizen of no mean city, muses the native to himself, as he descends from the hills; a romantic town, beautiful for situation, exclaims the visitor; and the noble prospect fills all alike with a parting thrill—

> " Where the huge Castle holds its state,
>   And all the steep slope down,
> Whose ridgy back heaves to the sky,
> Piled deep and massy, close and high,
>   Mine own romantic town!"

CHAPTER XVIII

WALKING

ALL nationalities, types and classes are included in the Brotherhood of Walkers, and as varied as their background are their views on walking. No definite bond unites the members of this band one to another, as in other pastimes and sports, and there is no school of orthodoxy.

Some prefer to walk in the city, like the celebrated Dr Johnson, who remarked that Boswell was right in saying that walking in the country was not equal to walking in Fleet Street; and Charles Lamb, who preferred " the sweet security of streets," and said that " for the streets, noises and sins of London, the mountains of Keswick might go hang." There are others who, with Hazlitt, enjoy the highway, and the exhilaration that comes with even pace and swing, though their number must now be growing less, since we are told that the open road of the future will be made for wheels alone. And yet there are few walkers who do not wish for a bit of the country highway either at the beginning or the end of a day's tramp. There are also those who, with Carlyle and Dickens, have found a mental tonic in the night walk; but few would care to share the feelings of Coleridge echoed in the lines—

> " Like one who on a lonesome road
>   Doth walk in fear and dread,
> And having once turned round walks on
>   And turns no more his head;
> Because he knows a frightful fiend
>   Doth close behind him tread."

Then there are the giants, who devour the miles like hungry men. Carlyle, for instance, in his day's walk—alone —of fifty-four miles from Muirkirk to Dumfries. John Forbes, a laird of Carlops and Newhall, whose muscular vigour corresponded to the energies of his mind, walked from Edinburgh to Glasgow, and returning the same day, danced at a ball at Newhall in the evening. Archbishop Temple once stated that as a young man he walked six miles an hour, and could do fifty a day easily! Ben Jonson, at the age of forty-five, walked all the way from London to Edinburgh. The freedom of the city was conferred upon him, and he was entertained to a Civic Banquet, and spent three weeks at Hawthornden with the poet William Drummond. "Now that I am in love," he makes Lovel say to the host at the New Inn, " I can outwake the nightingale, outwatch the usurer, and outwalk him too."

But the majority of the real brotherhood are those who love the mountains and the hills, the moors and the valleys, the roads and winding paths, whose hearts are open to all the varied impressions of nature.

Just as there is infinite variety in the Brotherhood of Walkers, so is there variety in the method and style of walking. Hill walking is different from road-slogging or the walk of the city man, and there is much to be learned from those whose daily round takes them over the hills and moors. The method of experienced guides—that slow, swinging stride, and perfect balance, as each foot is carried forward and placed upon the ground in no uncertain fashion, almost in line with the preceding step, enables the walker who has mastered the art of correct breathing to continue walking for long stretches, without fatigue. It has become natural to the hill folk, like the instinct of finding the easiest and least tiring ascent of a hill. Only do not imagine if you have short legs that you must take long strides to keep up with the six-foot keeper, you will soon find that fatiguing: the length of the stride does not matter much. Do not cramp your body or keep it stiff as if on parade, relax and feel at ease, breathe deeply, and cultivate a proper swing and balance, and a natural style of walking, effortless and graceful, will come to you, which will become as mechanical as that of the wise and untiring mountain guide. Pursue an easy pace: to hurry and rest at intervals is more fatiguing than an even pace with as few breaks as possible; let the breaks be occasioned only by some incident of interest, or backward view.

As to food, the expert's advice for climbers is equally applicable to hill trampers, and there is no better authority on the subject than Archibald E. Robertson of the Scottish Mountaineering Club, who has climbed his 300 peaks in Scotland over 3000 feet in height. He says: " Eat little at a time, but eat often, say every two hours or so; take jam or marmalade sandwiches, ginger snaps, crystallised fruit, chocolate, raisins, not meat sandwiches. Meals should be taken before and after the day's work, but not in the middle of active exercise."

For walks in winter on the hills we require a good thick Harris-tweed suit, a pair of strong boots with tackets—in very cold weather boots lined with pieces of newspaper keep one's feet warm, and a newspaper stuffed into them at the end of the day will absorb the moisture; a cromak which cannot be too long—you will find it useful when snow is covering drains and ditches; a haversack to carry fruit and a dry pair of socks or stockings, and your choice of the above sugary foods. Ferguson's black rock broken into small pieces is hard to beat. While if you prefer a ruck-sack to a haversack you will also have room for your gifts to the hill folk, and the gifts from the gamekeeper, if, like the true hill-walker, you count him among the best of your friends. Waterproofs and overcoats come under the heading of *impedimenta,* the term used by the Romans for luggage. Hill Burton recommended the plaid as the least impedimental in weight and inconvenience for the amount of comfort obtained from it. A coat or cape made of Tyrolean camel's-hair loden cloth affords the best protection against both cold and wet weather, the material being light in weight, soft, warm, waterproof, and self-ventilating.

237

There are perhaps three different kinds of walkers, each with varying aims. The first walks to get there—to arrive. If it be twelve miles, he needs must do it in three hours. The fine art of walking becomes to him a mechanical art. He likes exercise, delights in swinging motion, talks and tells stories all the way, and is not concerned with scenery or impressions or any alliance with nature. In fact he is not a real walker at all. The pleasure of a walk is not to be measured by the number of miles we cover, or the time we take to accomplish it.

The second walks in order to experience the joy of what happens on arrival—the dinner—after the three hours' walk, or the " bottle of sherry and cold chicken " of Hazlitt, or some other more prosaic but none the less satisfying meal; and although he may differ in his pursuit from that of the genial Isaak Walton, yet he is one with him in cheerily demanding upon arrival at the Inn—" Come, Hostess, where are you? Is supper ready? Come—first give us refreshment; and be as quick as you can, for I believe we are all very hungry." A certain author has told us he enjoys walking, even though it rains and he gets wet, tired, and hungry, just for what comes after—the real objective, the farm-house tea, home-baked scones, and fresh butter, the hot bath, and the " spiritual lordliness " with which you sit down to dinner.

The third class knows with this author and with R. L. S. all about the joy of arriving, and knows how good it is. Stevenson speaks of lounging before the inn door feeling so strong and clean, and doing everything with " a kingly sort of pleasure," but he believed also in travelling hopefully as being better than arriving.

As we cross the moor and climb the hill and tramp the highway, the body may tingle with the flowing of new life, but there is something else that speaks when coy nature reveals her secret, shows her handiwork on the earth and in the sky, and awakens some responsive chord; when

238

through the filmy winter mist there bursts a light that floods the landscape with a silvery radiance, or when the silent sunset fills the clear sky with a warm ruddy glow, and there falls upon the earth a benediction, and we are still, asking the meaning of it all and seeking to control our emotions and to understand them aright. Impressions have quickened some inner consciousness, and made life rich beyond all dreaming; something has become a real possession, and made life worth while.

It is good to be on the hills when the spring wind blows. Out of the distance it comes, gathering as it flies the scents and odours of awakening woods and breaking buds, ploughed fields and grasslands, hill and woodland moisture, the memory of which creates a hunger in future days, so hard to satisfy. The dancing daffodils with their delicate glory send forth their appeal in every farm and cottage garden, and we love to think of the woods we know carpeted in deepest blue, shimmering through black tree trunks in a violet gauze of fairest beauty.

The wind rises and falls, it blows fitfully, and the spring-tide odour comes in puffs. The genial warmth of the sunshine uplifts our spirit, and we seek the hill-top to fulfil our heart's desire. Nature is rejoicing, and we feel her inspiration. Before us flashes the symbol of buoyant and joyful youth—the lapwing in his gambols with the wind—but for sheer abandon the missel-thrush on the topmost point of a neighbouring wood, calling aloud for very joy of living, is the symbol with the deepest meaning of all. How he sings! just because he loves to sing, what impassioned abandon! here is living poetry, and in the distant days we recall the poem, and fancy we hear the singing of the idyllic days of youth.

And it is when the wind blows, clearing the brain, rejoicing the heart and kindling enthusiasm, that we too spontaneously would shout aloud for joy. "Yes," says Jasper, "there's the wind on the heath; . . . if I could only feel that, I would gladly live for ever."

It has been said of walkers, as of poets, that they are born, not made; that it requires a merry heart, and a direct dispensation from Heaven, to become a walker. Others have claimed that only when you go afoot do you grow in the grace of gentleness and humility; that the shining angels accompany the man who walks, but that the dark spirits are ever looking out for a chance to ride. But such generalities do not always stand the test of individual experience. Man is a complex being, and his relationship to nature is no less difficult to understand; and while the purely physical aspect of walking may appeal to one person, nature's companionship may be the joy of another. Much will depend upon what we are in ourselves—our qualities of heart and mind and soul, our natural temperament and training, our relationship to the all-pervading Spirit, and upon the influences which affect us; but that it is a healthy, purifying, and character-revealing exercise most walkers will agree. The very unrest within us that sends us forth upon our walks is an interesting problem. The adventures and experiences we meet give a zest to life itself, and often reveal its meaning, and it is with the memories of these we fashion our temple of the hills.

As to whether a companion is essential, that will always be a debatable point. There is much to be said in favour of sharing our joys with a companion. You will learn by experience to interpret your own feelings, and to know just when and why you wish to have a companion, or to walk alone. It is not everyone you will take with you on a hill walk, but to have one like-minded, who will not interfere with your exercise of free will and choice in thought and action, is a joy indeed.

It is better that two people should so understand each other that the choice of each may be exercised without offence, and even without too much talking. If Johnnie prefers " The White Swan " he goes there; Jimmy prefers " The Spread Eagle," and so they part—and meet in the morning—a perfect understanding, requiring no talking, no explanations or reasoning. " Can two walk together except they be agreed?" asked Amos, the herdsman of Tekoa, in his prophetic teaching long ago.

One of the finest things I think Burroughs ever wrote deals with the charm of companionship:—

" The roads and paths you have walked along in summer and winter weather, the fields and hills you have looked upon in lightness and gladness of heart, where fresh thoughts have come into your mind or some noble prospect has opened before you, and especially the quiet ways where you have walked in sweet converse with your friend, pausing under trees, drinking at the spring—henceforth they are not the same, a new charm is added; these thoughts spring there perennial, your friend walks there for ever."

Sir Walter Scott, with his inimitable power of description, portrays the right temperament of the walker and his friend, who talk when they feel inclined, but enjoy each other's silence also:—

> " The wild unbounded hills we ranged,
> While oft our talk its topic changed,
> And, desultory as our way,
> Ranged, unconfined, from grave to gay.
> Even when it flagg'd, as oft will chance,
> No effort made to break its trance,
> We could right pleasantly pursue
> Our thoughts in social silence too."

Marmion, Intro. to Canto IV.

Happy is the man who finds a walking companion who knows how to keep silence and when to talk, who is in unison not only with himself but with all the vibrant chords of nature around.

I have stood in woods that held such a hush of sanctity that one was constrained to talk with a companion in whispers, conscious of the countless eyes and ears open on every side.

On the other hand, if you wish to absorb all the stillness and the strength of the hills, if you bare your soul as an Æolean harp to be played upon by every breeze; if you are eager for every fresh impression, and anxious that the unchanging hills will reveal to you your true self, then go alone. Emerson said that you will generally fare better to take your dog than to invite your neighbour. The dog is full of enterprise and adventure and wonder, and every field and wood is a new world to him, and he knows he is sure to find something farther on, every place is good to him.

The experienced walker and nature lover will in most cases and in certain moods prefer to walk alone; he revels in the joy of it, he is self-contained, and all his adventures and experiences combine to make him independent of all company, because he is aware of a voice in the silence, and like Marius the Epicurean, " becomes conscious of a companion." All that he counts of greatest worth comes out of the solitude. To him the voices of the wild are soothing nepenthe, and the wind among the trees and the music of the corrie burn are his inspiration and delight. We shall often find him to be of a serious and philosophical nature, and yet in love with life and the beauty of the world. He loves company, and knows the value of social intercourse; but he also loves his own companionship, and the fruits of solitude, and early learns the truth expressed by Burns in the lines—

> " The Muse, nae Poet ever fand her,
> Till by himsel' he learn'd to wander."

The true walker may not ask much from his pastime; but he is often surprised at the richness of the gifts which he receives. What he desires when he starts upon his walk he seldom contemplates, yet the heart yearns for a renewal of some experience, although he would not think of giving it utterance. It is with the open mind and heart that he sets out to receive whatever phantasies may come his way, hoping at the back of his mind, it may be, that some measure at least of the fuller revelation of the wonderful and mysterious in nature may come within the power of his assimilation, and lured on in the hope that answers may come to his questionings, in the spirit of the wind upon the hill-tops and in the solitude of sequestered vales; and returning with the wealth of a quiet mind and a peaceful heart, and a certain assurance that holds within it sufficient longing to send him forth again when the time arrives.

Hill-walkers are adventurers all, they know not when they set out what the results of the day's walk will be; yet it is a strange experience, is it not, that such bountiful gifts and refreshing fruit may come to him,—that he may attain to this mood of tranquil meditation, out of which arise intermittent musings, half-conscious soliloquies, and a sort of feast of mental orderliness—a frame of mind in which decisions are made without effort, and truth comes without argument? Every such adventure that is contained in this simple and primitive pastime, so near to mother earth, attracts not only the walker who would claim no other qualification than that he loves to tramp the old highways and the hills, but philosophers and poets and men great in simplicity. It becomes a fascinating pursuit, a pastime that is in itself a delight and a joy.

If the level country be a type of the ordinary life of the day, often monotonous because uninteresting and failing of recognition or success, then the oftener we can leave the plain for the hills the better for our comfort and ultimate happiness. There is ever need for the widening of our horizons, the correction of our perspective, and many a fresh start, lest we find ourselves among the pitfalls of the plain, swallowed up in trifles. The benefits of the hill walk and the far view will keep us, body and soul, fit and sound. Nature's physician will provide medicine for the mind, and life become a real and jolly thing again.

Longfellow knew the virtue of this hill medicine:—

" If thou are worn and hard beset
  With sorrows that thou wouldst forget,
  If thou wouldst read a lesson that will keep
  Thy heart from fainting, and thy soul from sleep,
  Go to the hills! . . . ."

Winter is the ideal time for walking, and to the vigorous heart, rejoicing in its youthful exuberance and care-free abandon, there is great attraction in the stormy elements —within reason—among the hills in winter, when we are one with the spirit of the wind. There is real philosophy in the Highlander's remark—" A fine day but coorse." A windy day with all the music of the woods, a stormy, showery day with its flashes of sunshine, even a spell of climbing against rain and snow and hail—these exert their own peculiar feelings of exhilaration. There is an intimacy in the wind and the storm which sings, however exultingly and boisterously, among the trees, laughs in the valleys like a giant, and screams along the rocky hillside, expressions of its liberty and sublime power.

The great numbers who now find pleasure and delight in the Pentland Hills proves that the inhabitants of our enlightened city are not lacking in love and feeling for nature, natural beauty, and grandeur. The picturesque, the beautiful, and the sublime in turn bring their own peculiar enjoyment and delight. And whether it is the picturesque that makes its fleeting appeal, or the sublime that incites to wonder and awe, it is the beautiful to which the walker is perhaps most susceptible. The fascination of the beautiful is as wonderful in its appeal as it is powerful to uplift and recreate, and the hill-walker is ever on the look-out for it, and open to its refining influence. There is a complex intellectual and imaginative activity at the source of it that gives free play to the faculties which it stimulates.

The sympathy and unity of feeling between Man and Nature was responsible for the nature symbolism in Words-worth's poetry. By the power of insight, moved by love and passion, he " saw into the heart of things," and read into nature the expression of intellectual, moral, and spiritual qualities. "Beauty in Nature," said Emerson, "is the herald of inward and internal beauty." Every thoughtful walker knows what this means. He sees the very soul of liberty and joyfulness in the restlessness of the burn that comes tumbling down from the hills, sparkling and foaming through the open heathery moorland and the birken glen. This symbolism in nature is illustrated in poignant fashion in a hundred different ways, at every period of the revolving year.

Why is it, we may ask, that the walker is so often attracted to the hill-top, and what is the reason for the emotion which he experiences in the far view, with its effect upon thought and feeling and imagination? Is it the primitive instinct that still works in us, inherited from our forefathers, who upon the heights found refuge and security from their enemies, and so were elated because the shadow of fear was removed? The hill-walker and the mountain climber will hardly think so. For them the mountain track symbolises the way of the soul's ascension. There is implanted deep within the human heart the desire to ascend. In daily speech and language we talk of lofty aims and high ideals. It is to the heavens above, declaring the Glory of God, that the psalmist first points us, then to the firmament as showing His handiwork, and with the hill-tops are associated many of the world's great events. It is the working in us of a great benevolent Spirit that sends us to the high places, there to experience this feeling of elation with all that it brings of life consciousness, and physical and spiritual enjoyment.

But simply to possess the power like a bird to fly from one peak to another would not bring to us additional or higher experience. No height was ever gained that was worth the gaining without toil and effort, and if the walker were presented by the good fairy with a pair of wings, I think he would, in certain moods, refuse them. He would prefer to walk or climb to the mountain top, to experience all the physical pleasure of well-being, and obtain a true equipoise of mind and spirit to register the varied emotions which through the sense of vision are transmitted to the sense of feeling.

If it be a changing scene—a sunrise or sunset, or the effects of wind and cloud and travelling shadows, the sense of admiration and wonder is quickened, and we gaze with rapt attention on nature's wondrous ways; but if there is no such cinematograph of nature's happenings, but a wild tumble of hills and mountain ranges and peaks, there is awakened in us a great desire to renew the experience of the emotions that were ours on first attaining the summit: following upon the sight of distant hills comes the desire for further activity, the places we see we desire to move towards, to climb, to view from, to enjoy once again this pleasurable emotion of feeling what we see. This may be explained by the fact that at the root of feeling is action; activity creates and produces pleasure, and the activity and the pleasurable feeling act and react. In this we become conscious of life, and the highest life is realised in the highest action. It is one of the purest and most ennobling strains of the sense of feeling, bringing with it an elevation of spirit in which all that is a weight upon us drops off and we leap to a new freedom and consciousness of self-realisation. Strange things have happened upon hill-tops since the beginning of time: there men have beheld a land that was very far off; and such times of clear vision, often revealing the meaning of life itself, are cherished by every walker and every climber.

But this feeling of exaltation is not limited to those who climb to the hill-tops. There are others whose walking and dwelling is upon the plains and among the valleys, and for them the surroundings account for a further variety of experience. Let us take the hill folk, whose habitation it may be is in the far distant glens and outlying places. How lonely, we say, how quiet and monotonous life there must be, but this is not always so. There is no monotony in the hills to them, on the contrary the hills they knew in the days of youth remain to them an exaltation, although they do not now climb to the tops. All through life, on to the days beyond the span, and even when linked by old age and infirmity to the cottage fireside, their action or energy consists in picturing to themselves the sunset close of day descending on the sheep upon the hill, and the gradual fading of the hills into the night, and then the silence; and with it all falls a great happiness, for they are all at one in unity with Mother Nature, the nature in each of them working with perfect harmony and concord with the nature around. Is this then the solution of the riddle? Does the spirit that is on the hills, and in the blowing winds, in the smell of earth and tang of moor, and in every vibrating call of the wild, awaken within us sympathy and response? If so, then all our walking and our climbing will enable us to attain the freedom and the happiness we desire. And the measure to which these are attained will depend upon the nature of our experiences, and the extent to which we have laid hold upon the revelations which have come to us.

The hours when we company with nature among the hills and in her bounteous domains will for ever be our great possession. "Christopher North" summed it up thus:—

> " This is a holy faith, and full of cheer
> To all who worship Nature, that the hours
> Passed tranquilly with her fade not away
> For ever, like the clouds; but in the soul
> Possess a sacred, silent dwelling-place,
> Where, with a smiling visage, memory sits,
> And startles oft the virtuous with a show
> Of unsuspected treasures."

CHAPTER XIX

PENTLAND COVENANTERS

THE frost had gone, the morning sky was breaking, and fresh light came streaming over the hills. The air was cool and exhilarating, and it was pleasant to leave the hard highway and take to the soft springy turf by Linton Golf Course and the right-of-way track. Here was wide space of sky, rolling hills and moorlands, and in this freedom we rejoiced as we started for our day upon the Pentlands with memories of the Scottish Covenanters. At North Slipperfield we took our way westwards through the glen that has Mendick hill on one side, Catstone on the other, and in the middle distance Dunsyre hill. Crossing the West Water or Pollentarf we come to a fork in the track at the pine trees, left hand for Fernieheugh and Dunsyre, right hand for Medwinhead, and Auchengray. We followed the latter, a green track of subtle allurement, up and down it goes, into valleys, over knolls, crossing watercouses, revealing fresh aspects of the rolling landscape. Soon the pine woods around Medwinhead appear. The valley opens out and the view expands, comprising a semi-circle of hills with Dunsyre in the centre. A few mountain hares, fast becoming white lolloped on ahead, grouse whirred soft and croaked angrily, and a gentle sough of the south wind ran through the waving bent now in pearly flower.

The solitary trees amidst the ruins of the Blackhill shepherd's dwelling, well known to walkers, seem doomed to disappear, two of them are already lifeless, like their predecessors and companion, for only one now remains. Trees, bushes and plants do not long survive after a place has become ruinous, they flourish only with human companionship. Hill and moorland walkers are indebted to The Scottish Rights-of-way Society for preservation of old Pentland paths, and the addition of white posts leading to

the Covenanter's Grave, is a real benefit, for there is now
no difficulty in finding the place of pilgrimage under
ordinary conditions, marked by the century old stone, com-
memorating an event that took place in 1666. "What
mean ye by these stones?" asked the gallant leader long
ago . . . "these stones shall be a memorial for ever."
Such memorial stones on the moorlands preserve the
Covenanting struggle for all time, and impress the warfarer
in a way that the printed page may fail to do.

Covenanting associations crowd around this part of the
Pentlands (see pp. 31 and 162). Blackhill farm has
memories of the Covenanter Carphin of Lesmahagow, who
fought at Rullion Green and came to the farm for succour,
but died at Oaken Bush on the West Water, and was buried
there. When his remains were removed and buried on the
Black Law, in sight of his Ayrshire hills, in accordance
with his request, two Dutch coins, the size of crown pieces,
dated 1620 were found in the neck of his once red cloak.
One is in the British Museum, and the Covenanter's Bible
is now in possession of descendants of Sanderson of Blackhill, and was used at a memorial service at Rullion Green,
August 1945. Dunsyre had many Covenanters, and
Carphin was not the only fugitive. William Veitch (1640-
1722) in his Memoir narrates how in escaping he was
suddenly recognised—"Ho! this is one of the rogues!" but
Lord Loudon's horse which he rode was too swift for his
pursuers. Nearing his home, Westhills, Dunsyre, a shepherd took charge of his horse, and a message for his wife,
while he remained in hiding. One moonlight night he
ventured to Anston farm dressed as a shepherd, and found
some countrymen holding horses of troopers searching for
Major Learmonth, son-in-law of John Hamilton, the laird.
Speaking to one holding four or five horses he was bid take
two horses and lead them, thus making converse possible.
"What brought you here?" "To speak with the laird."
"That is impossible, for they are taking him away prisoner;
and a party is searching your own house at this moment."

They found neither him, nor his horse, which had been taken out to the moor. Veitch held the stirrups as the troopers mounted, carrying away the laird. Later, Hamilton was again apprehended on a Privy Council Order for hiding Learmonth, for all who sheltered Covenanters, sympathised with them, or refused to abjure their tenets, were victims of relentless persecution, but proof being impossible he was freed on bail of ten thousand merks (Wodrow 1.266). Veitch spent that night in a shepherd's calf-house. Later, he escaped, being forfeited life and fortune, travelling in Scotland, England and Holland, exercising his ministry for over fifty years. Two of the ten children born to him and Marion Fairley (of the Fairley's of Braid) were born " at the Hills of Dunsyre," as entered in his Bible.

Before returning to Linton we rested at the Covenanter's stone and smoked the pipe of peace and remembrance. Curious it was to think that, after all, the ammunition that fired the train was a charge of pieces of broken tobacco pipe, fired in a gun by one of the Dalry Covenanters by which one of Sir James Turner's troopers was wounded— troopers who were threatening a prisoner who refused to pay a fine. Turner was in charge of a force of military police—he and Binns were sent to disarm the South-West counties, or more particularly " to see to the execution of all Acts of Parliament and the Privy Council concerning the Kirk." It was too much to expect that Turner would remain quiescent when one of his men had been shot full of pipeclay. He summoned a meeting at Irongray. Next day the Covenanters went to Dumfries, lifted Turner out of his sick bed and took him off with them, along with his papers and his money, but minus his clothes, so that he travelled in his shirt and his bedsocks. But he must have recovered somewhat for he was with the Covenanters as they marched through soaking rain to Colinton. Turner wrote: " While we were on our way, one Major Learmonth accosted me and used me with many insolencies telling me he had known me before. At that time, he said, you were a gentleman, but now you are not, for you are a persecutor of God's saints, and hath made yourself a slave of Prelacie. I told him though all his language were true, yet he had timed it very ill."

The Covenant army went by Dreghorn, Hunters' Tryst and Hillend, and so by the Linton road past Fulford (Woodhouselee), and crossing Flotterstane Bridge climbed Turnhouse hill on the slopes of which the fight took place. Dalziel and his army climbed the Kirk Brae out of Currie, and arrived on the eastern shoulder of House of Muir hill, having come by Clachmede and crossed the Glencorse Water where now the reservoir lies, by the old Drove road, which can still be discerned on the south side. There are various detailed descriptions of the fight: about fifty were killed and many more taken prisoners, the rest scattered and made off in the darkness—the last encounter being after sunset on 28th November, including the wounded Carphin, Turner and Peden going different ways. Only a fortnight had elapsed since what was known as " The Pentland Rising " began and ended.

A memorial stone, erected Steptember 1738, to the two Irish Ministers, Crookshanks and McCormick, who fell in the first assault, " and about fifty other true Covenanted Presbyterians " stands on Turnhouse hillside at Rullion Green above House of Muir farm. The word " Rullion " by the way has a different significance in various localities. " The Rullion Green " may mean just the noisy Green or meeting-place, as indeed it would be during the battle, but also when the sheep markets were held there. In the West country wild, rough, uncultured bodies are called " Rullions "; in Fife the word applies to a coarse-made masculine woman, and a " rouch rullion " a man who speaks his mind freely and roughly. Galloway folks apply it to a rough ill-made animal, many of which no doubt found their way to the House of Muir Markets at The Rullion Green. A Covenanters' memorial service is held at intervals in the green haugh by the Glencorse burn at Flotterstane nearby conducted under the auspices of the Loanhead branch of the Reformed Presbyterian Church. "The victory," says Crookshank in his history, "was celebrated with almost as many guns from the Castle, as there were men slain in the field, and the prisoners were all crowded together in a place near the Tolbooth called Haddo's Hole, now one of the City churches," on the order of the Provost Sir Andrew Ramsay of Abbotshall "the most notorious of all Edinburgh's Lord Provosts, a reputation due to his tenure of office, the longest on record (1655-58 and 1662-1673) and his career of time-serving and corruption." He was the first to have the title "Lord Provost," was a Privy Councillor, Lord of Session and Member of Parliament ("The Lord Provosts of Edinburgh, 1296-1932"). Haddo's Hole in St Giles' Church was a small chamber over the porch on the North side, receiving its name from the Royalist Sir John Gordon of Haddo, ancestor of the Earls of Aberdeen, confined there in 1644 when he was "headit at the Cross of Edinburgh" as a traitor by the Instrument called "The Maiden." (Proc. Soc. Ant. Scot., vol. iv, p. 289.) Both The Maiden and the Iron Yett of the Hole are in the Antiquarian Museum.

The Covenanters died bravely, and they stirred public sympathy. They were sincere in their belief, and had enthusiastic courage. "Whatever may have been their faults," said Prof. Flint, "their fidelity to conviction has been seldomed equalled in the history of the world."

The Battle of Rullion Green or Pentland took place on 28th November 1666. Much had happened since 28th February 1638 when the National Covenant was signed—"one of the most momentous events in Scottish History" (Lord Tweedsmuir). The result of it all was that the Government lost the peace; and the Covenanters ultimately triumphed. The first signing of the Covenant (embodying the Confession of Faith 1580-1, and not to be confused with the Solemn League and Covenant of 1643 which had the same object but a wider scope) took place in Greyfiars Church (not in the Churchyard), and in The Tailors' Hall, Cowgate, by nobles, barons, ministers and Commissioners of Burghs, and in Trinity Church (foot of Leith Wynd) by the people of Edinburgh, and for over a year thereafter signing went on all over Scotland.

The great day of the Covenant in Edinburgh was 1st April, but for the Pentland Parish of Currie[1] the momentous day was 18th March, a solemn Fast Day specially appointed. The moving scene is described in John of Wariston's Diary 1632-1639 (Scot. Hist. Soc., vol. 61). " The minister John Charteris read the Covenant, and explained it, showed his warrant for seeking and theirs for giving the Oath . . . and as the congregation stood and lifted up their hands and swore to the Eternal God . . . there fell such an extraordinary influence of God's Spirit upon the whole congregation, man and woman, lass and lad, pastor and people, that Mr. John being suffocat almost with his own tears, and astonished at the motion of the whole people, sat down in the pulpit in amazement, but present rose again when he saw all the people fallen down to their knees to mourn and pray; And he and they for a quarter of an hour prayed very sensibly with many sobs, tears, promises and vows to be thankful and fruitful in time coming." " God's great work in Currie Parish "

[1] *Note.*—Formerly Killeith. " Was of old a special rectorie and personage appertaining to the Archdeane of Lothian as a part of his patrimonie and special mansion and dwelling place . . . lately taken from the said benefice and created in favour of the Provost, Bailies, Council and Communitie of Edinburgh, and disponed to them by King James." (" Report on the statistics of various Parishes in Scotland, 1627.") The Church was dedicated to St Mungo. Adam Letham (Lichton, Leighton), 1568. In 1574 Hailes and " St Catherine's of the Hopes " were also under his care. His son Matthew (signs " Mathow Lichtone ") succeeded, 1591-1631 (p. 23); followed by John Charteris (1631-68) presented by The Town Council of Edinburgh) who suffered imprisonment in Tantallan (Wariston's Diary, 1652, p. 177).

being duly reported to the noblemen and barons by Wariston, was followed by memorable scenes in Edinburgh.

Sir Archibald Johnston (Lord Wariston, 1611-1663) tells us he was married in Currie Kirk (1634); and " On Sunday 29th (April 1638) the first day that the Communion in puretie was restored to Currie Parish (after Episcopacy) I attended as an elder." (Diary, p. 346.) He acquired the property of Wariston, Currie (1636), from his brother-in-law, Alexander Hay, Lord Foresterseat's son. His mother was a daughter of Sir Thomas Craig of Riccarton, and his aunt, wife of Sir James Skene of Curriehill, President, Court of Session (1626-1633). The National Covenant owed much of its comprehensiveness, boldness and precision to him, and in the preparation of the Solemn League and Covenant he also had a hand. He was the trusted adviser of the Covenanting leaders, and was perhaps the most remarkable Scotsman of that very troubled period of British History that began with the Service Book Riot, the swearing and subscription of The National Covenant, the abjuration of Episcopacy (1637-8) and ended with the overthrow of the Protectorate and the Restoration of the Monarchy in 1660. He died a martyr, being hanged at the Market Cross (1663) on " a gallows of extraordinary height, surrounded by the King's Life Guards on horseback, with their carbines and naked swords, trumpets and Kettle-drum, and a guard of the town of Edinburgh with their colours displayed " (Nicoll's Diary).

It was in 1592 that the Scottish Parliament abolished Episcopacy and established Presbyterianism; the Act was repealed 1612. The Church of Scotland became Episcopal in 1610 and continued so till 1638—period of The First Episcopacy. The Second Episcopacy lasted from 1661 till 1689; November 1689 saw The Revolution, and in 1690 Acts of Parliament restored Presbyterian Church Government, and settled most of the controversies agitating the Church since the Reformation, 1560, including restoration of ministers expelled since 1661. Episcopacy was finally abolished in 1689.

" With the Revolution Settlement, 1690, the constitutional development of Scottish Presbyterianism reached its maturity; and with the Treaty of Union, 1707, the arrangement then made became part of the British Constitution." " The first official act of a British Sovereign on Accession and before Coronation is the signing of the oath to maintin ' the Government, worship, discipline, rights and privileges of the Church of Scotland,' and on it depends the Sovereign's claim to the allegiance of Scotsmen." (Lord Balfour of Burleigh, " Presbyterianism in Scotland.")

The Christian Faith and Religion, and the precious worth of civil and religious liberty (originally embodied in the Covenant, and now part of the British Constitution) ought to be cherished by all good Scots if they would be worthy of such a heritage, for that heritage of liberty of conscience is enjoyed to-day no less by the detractors than by the most ardent admirers of the Scottish Covenanters.

CHAPTER XX

"OLD PENTLAND" VILLAGE

Its Ancient History and Covenanting Memories

HOW did the Pentland Hills get their name? If the name were Pictland there would be little difficulty, for the Picts were here inhabitants. Sir Henry St Clair, who lived in the reign of William the Conquerer (1066-1087) obtained from King Malcolm III. the "Barony of Pithland" (i.e., Pentland).[1] There was, however, an ancient Parish of Pentland, comprising the manors of Pentland and Fulford, with the north-eastern part of the hills, including Glencorse valley. The name occurs in twelfth century Charters, and the "Moor of Pentland" appears in the 13th and 14th centuries. Authorities differ as to whether the hills took their name from the parish and moor-lands, or vice versa. "Caledonia" holds that the name means "Pent" (Old English) "enclosed" and "land," the enclosed land, enclosure on the moor, which would aptly apply to Glencorse and Logan Valley, but the moor probably extended to the Moor-foot hills. The Parish Church of Pentland was granted to the monks of Holyrood at the founding of the Abbey, confirmed to them in 1240, became an independent Rectory before Alexander III.'s death, and from the 14th to the 16th century was under the Patronage of the Earls of Orkney and Barons of Roslin, the St Clairs. In 1633 the Barony of Pentland passed to the Gibson family. The founder of Roslin Chapel endowed it with the Church and lands of Pentland in 1446, and under James V. Pentland Rectory was taxed at £5 6s 8d. Among pre-Reformation Ministers were Stephen de Kyngorn, 1296; Sir David Hutchesone, who

[1] *Note.*—"Rosslyn, its Chapel, Castle and Scenic Lore," by Will Grant.

suffered for his faith, and in 1540 sentenced for heresy; Sir John Sinclair, who became Dean of Restalrig, Bishop of Brechin, Lord President of the Court of Session, and solemnized the marriage of Queen Mary and Darnley at Holyrood (1565); and Sir John Robesoune, the last incumbent. ("Lasswade Parish and Loanhead in the Olden Times," Christopher Aitchison, 1892.) The Parish ceased to exist after the Reformation, 1560, and was united to Lasswade 1647. Although no trace is visible of the old Church, the foundations are in the graveyard, and were uncovered when improvements were made before 1892. Pentland is reputed to have been a hunting centre. Robert the Bruce and a lordly retinue passed this way bound for the Pentland hills to hunt deer, and later gave to Sir Henry St Clair for his homage and service Crown lands in the Moor of Pentland. (Register of Great Seal, April 12, 1316) ("Pentland Days and Country Ways," ch. XV.). Strange historical transactions may lie behind the entries "Rental of Pentland Moor formerly £26:13:4 per annum, now £6:13:4 from the War 1335-6," and "one-third of the Moor forfeited by Alicia, Widow of Henry St Clair, September 10, 1336 given to Geoffrey Moubray," she going over to the English side, and he having custody of the Baronies of Cousland, Roslin and Pentland (Bain's Calendar, vol. III.). Moubrays held Fulford and Bavelaw in the 16th century. Henry St Clair had a Charter from Robert III. of the Castlewards of Pentland and Roslin, built the dungeons of Roslin and certain walls thereabouts, and laid out parks for fallow and red deer. In the reign of Robert III. St Clair granted to Sir John Nudrie lands forming the east quarter of the Moor of Pentland, with half of Erncraig (p. 94) in the Manor of Pentland, in exchange for the place and yards of King's Cramond; and in 1410 St Clair gave his brother John the lands of Sunellishope and Loganhouse in the Moor of Pentland (Reg. of Great Seal) (the boundaries of the lands of Erncraig and Sunellishope cannot be traced); while Sir Henry de Brade, laird of Braid and Bavelaw, gifted the teinds of Bavelaw to the Monks of Holyrood for the support of the Chapel of St Katherine in Penteland (pp. 190 and 93). This Chapel along with Mount Lothian was added to Penicuik 1635. There was an " Adam of Pentland," a monk at Holyrood, Jan. 7, 1298, and a " John de Pentland," and a " Ralph de Pentland " both employed at Berwick by Edward I., 1304 (loading wool and hides) (Bain's Cal.).

So much for the ancient name of Pentland. What of the old village or hamlet (commonly called " Old Pentland ") to distinguish it from the modern " New Pentland," east of Hillend and Lothianburn and adjoining Clippens shale bings? To-day, the school, presented by Lady Gibsone, occupies a central position. Behind it is the site on which stood a small thatched building, a meeting-place of Cameronians (named after Richard Cameron, the Covenanter, see Smellie's " Men of the Covenant "), where met the oldest congregation of the Reformed Presbyterian Church, dating back to the days when the fires of persecution were at their hottest. A " Society " was formed at Pentland, where in prayer and worship faith was strengthened and encouraged, and out of such meetings grew the Pentland Congregation, somewhere about 1681. This thatched building was the first Dissenting place of worship erected in Scotland after the Revolution. " The Auld Cameronian Meeting-House " in Edinburgh was in Blackfriars Wynd. The Reformed Presbyterian Church thus point to Pentland as a historic place just as The Church of Scotland point to St Andrews or Glasgow Cathedral, and the Free Church to Tanfield Hall, Edinburgh. (U.F. Ch. Record, Oct. 1925.) The youngest and last of Scotland's martyr sons, Rev. James Renwick, M.A., had a Pentland connection, for he often found refuge there, held Conventicles on the Pentland, Moffat and Peebles hills and at Old Woodhouselee on the Esk, his " fair, rapt countenence with spiritual fire transfigured," and at intervals in the period of his ministry (1683-8) he preached to Pentland Society. Upon him devolved the whole care and management of the United Societies popularly called "The Cameronians." These worthy followers of Cameron, Cargill and Renwick disapproved of "The Revolution Settlement" on both its civil and ecclesiastical side and maintained their claim to be "the historical representatives of the Covenanted Church of Scotland." (McCrie's "Scotland and the Revolution, 1688.") After the Revolution the Societies were without a Minister for 16 years. From 1706 Rev. John MacMillan was sole Minister of the Societies, including Pentland. In 1743 The Reformed Presbytery was set up. The first Minister of Pentland as a separate local Congregation Rev. John Thorburn (1767) was a remarkable scholar, thinker, and author of "Vindiciæ Magistratus," an exposition of his Church's principles. The Pentland Congregation removed to Loanhead in 1792, where still the banner of The Cameronians is held aloft ("R. P. Witness," Dec. 1925). The last meeting-place in Pentland is incorporated in the school, and the stone lintel of the manse that stood nearby, with date 1731, is preserved locally.

No reference to Old Pentland would be complete without the story of that heroine of the Scottish Covenanters, so closely associated with James Renwick and other leaders, Helen Alexander of Pentland, spouse first of Charles Umpherston, tenant in Pentland, and thereafter of James Currie, Merchant, there. Renwick, who officiated at the second marriage, Nov. 30, 1687, found shelter in her house "even in the very heat of persecution." When he was in prison she visited him, and receiving his body at the scaffold prepared it for burial. He was 26. "In the mountains, glens and moors of Ayrshire, Galloway and the Pentlands, chap books still tell of her marvellous story of courage and devotion . . . she ministered dauntlessly to the fugitives . . . she stood by the friendless at the bars . . . she spent days and nights in prison with "the suffering remnant." (Dict. Nat. Biog.) She was fined for attending a Conventicle (1681) on the Pentland hills, at " Yearn Craig." (Erncraig was mentioned in 1648 as a possible site for a new St Katherine's, p.94.) James Currie heard Renwick preach at " Brades Craigs " (see p. 212, also Wilson's " Tales of the Border," Renwick at Braid Craigs). " Passages in the lives of Helen Alexander and James Currie " (1869) gives their experience, the " Pentland Children's Covenant " (1683), Genealogie of Umpherston and Aitchison Families and particulars of Martyrs' monument in Greyfriars' Churchyard, first erected in 1706 by James Currie and others, by private subscription and Warrant of the Town Council—the " others " are unknown, the original Petition being amissing. When renewed in 1771 the open Bible with quotations from " Revelations " was retained, and a tall pillared tablet with additional inscription, surmounted by an entablature and pediment, replaced the original slab, now in the City Museum (Huntly House) (see " The Martyr Graves of Scotland," John H. Thomson, 1875). The tombstone of James Currie (1656-1736) and Helen Alexander (1654-1729) is also in Huntly House, having been removed from Pentland, where the old graveyard still interests the inquiring pilgrim. The Pentland Cross Slab, two 14th cent. Grave Slabs and the panel designs: " Musical Cherubs " and " The King of Terrors " are mentioned in the Society of Antiquaries' Proceedings, vol. V., Fourth Series.

What of the Castle of Pentland? Was there such a place? I find that Edward I., who knew the countryside (ch. XVIII.) left Holyrood on August 16, 1304, and marched by Pentland and Eddleston to Peebles. While at Pentland (17th) the King " commanded Richard de Bremesgrave to send to Wm. Bisset two tuns of good wine from Berwick to Cambuskenneth, at the King's cost, as soon as possible, given under the Privy Seal, (Pentlan(d)." Another record says " The King was entertained at Pentland in Maurice of Glasgow's houses (probably cottages), and compensation was paid for damages caused to crops, corn, etc. (no doubt in connection with the camp of his troops). (Bain's Calendar.) But I find no reference to any Castle at Pentland, or to the legendary royal jollification and damage to property calling for compensation at the hands of the Lord of the Castle of Pentland! The original Tower of the Castle of Rosslyn was built about 1304.

CHAPTER XXI

HABBIE'S HOWE

" I've gathered news will kittle your mind with joy."

MANY lovers of the Pentland countryside have asked " Who was Habbie?" and " Where is Habbie's Howe?"

To find the answer we must consult Allan Ramsay's Pastoral Comedy, " The Gentle Shepherd," of which we read in Chap. VI. One of the principal characters is Sir William Worthy, represented as having fought under Montrose against Cromwell, and recovered his estates with the Restoration of Charles II. Ramsay modelled the character and manners of Sir William upon those of the then Laird of Newhall, Carlops, Sir David Forbes, with whom he was on intimate terms, and all the action, thought and colour, the characters and the scenery, the crofter, shepherds, milkmaids and witch were drawn from the natives of the district around the estate, the Esk Valley and the Carlops. Newhall House was the meeting-place of the " literati " of the time, and it is not surprising that amidst such an assemblage of distinction, talent and taste, Ramsay should court invitation by compliment, and be desirous of the opinions, advice and assistance of such company in his pursuit after literary fame. Many of the visitors were members of " The Worthy Club " that met there in summer, and at their meetings Ramsay recited parts of his Comedy. William Tytler (1711-1792) in his edition of King James's Poems states that " While I passed my infancy at Newhall, near Pentland hills, where the scenes of this pastoral poem were laid, I well remember to have heard Ramsay recite, as his own production, different scenes of ' The Gentle Shepherd,' particularly the two first, before it was printed." This was confirmed by

Sir James Clerk of Penicuik, where Ramsay frequently resided. Ramsay in poem, Ode and Elegy made due acknowledgment of the assistance he received from Sir David Forbes, and his distinguished literary friends.

In the Comedy the Laird is represented as returning unknown and unrecognised, but, before his appearance, there is a rumour of his return, and this is discussed by two old shepherd tenants—Symon and Glaud:

> Symon—" Seeing's believing, Glaud; and I have seen
> Hab, that abroad has with our master been;
> Our brave good master, who right wisely fled,
> And left a fair estate to save his head:"

> Glaud —" That makes me blythe indeed !—but dinna flaw;
> Tell o'er your news again, and swear till't a'
> And saw ye Hab! and what did Halbert say?
> They have been e'en a dreary time away."

Hab or Habbie or Halbert is the faithful old servant and retainer of the Laird, sharer in his dangers and exile who announces the Laird's return to his tenants and friends. Hab had a cottage and garden on the estate, in that part of the Esk valley which was known in the Laird's time and is still known as " Habbie's Howe," of which Ramsay gives a description in his Comedy.

David Allan (1744-1796), Scottish artist (p. 123), who painted rural life and character (1783) before David Wilkie, visited Newhall (1786), collected the same scenes and characters as Ramsay, and published a Scenery Edition of The Gentle Shepherd (1788), which surpassed all previous impressions in its aqua-tint plates, one of the first works of its kind in Scotland—a delightful volume.

The costumes, character studies and expressive humour are in the true Scottish spirit of the times, and the genuine spirit of the author. Allan, like Ramsay, was a humorist, and was known as " The Scots Hogarth." The English Hogarth inscribed his " Hudibras " engravings to Ramsay, a not unfitting compliment in view of the Comedy's Cromwellian association. Allan found old people around Newhall who remembered Ramsay reciting his own poems, and the shepherds singing his songs.

At a later date an attempt was made to prove that the scene of the Comedy was in the Pentlands, and that Habbie's Howe was at the head of Logan Valley, but the Statistical Account of Glencorse Parish (1795) by the Rev. Wm. Torrance, Minister, and the Rev. Dr. John Walker, formerly of Glencorse (p. 113), after mentioning with apparent discredit a report that the scene of the Comedy was laid in the parish, and that Sir William Purves of Woodhouselee, His Majesty's Solicitor in the reign of Charles II. was the model of Sir Wm. Worthy, confessed that "this appropriation must be allowed to be entirely conjectural, and to rest more upon fancy, pleasing itself in clothing its own pictures in the garb of reality than upon any basis of evidence." A few years later, however (1880), there was published a London Edition of Ramsay's Works, containing a "Life of Ramsay," and "Remarks on his Writings," by A. Fraser Tytler (1747-1813) (Lord Wood-houselee, 1802), in which the exploded suppositions as to a connection between Glencorse and Sir Wm. Purves and "The Gentle Shepherd" are repeated without any evidence to substantiate the contention. This Edition maintained that the scene was on Woodhouselee estate, various natural characteristics such as the waterfall in Logan Valley, and the ancient Tower at Foulford, being used as arguments to this effect. •Lord Woodhouselee (who was born only eleven years before Ramsay died) erected a summer-house or rustic temple behind his mansion house and called it "Ramsay's Seat" and placed in it a stone with the inscription—

Allano Ramsay
et genio loci
Posuit. A. F. T.

"Here amidst those scenes that taught thy Doric Muse
Her sweetest song; the hills, the woods, and stream,
Where beauteous Peggy stray'd, list'ning the while
Her Gentle Shepherd's tender tale of love."

Leyden, who frequently visited Woodhouselee, slept in "The Shepherd's Room," where Ramsay slept! Many Edinburgh citizens and modern Scottish writers are under the impression that Habbie's Howe is in the Logan Valley, and even the Ordnance Survey map (1908) and the Dictionary of National Biography, are not immune from error!

Ramsay, however, had no connection with Woodhouselee. The Purves family left there before he was born, and in Ramsay's day it belonged to James Deans. Tytler further stated that "the hinds and shepherds of the Pentland hills . . . are eager to point out to the inquiring stranger the waterfall of Habbie's Howe" (in Logan Valley). A few years later "enquiry was made of some country people found cutting grass near the waterfall, whether Habbie's Howe was in that neighbourhood, and it was found that they had never heard of any such place." (Beauties of Scotland; Midlothian, vol. I., 1805.) The Carlops weaver poet James Forrest wrote a poem on his visit (1806) to the place called Habbie's Howe up near the head of Glencorse Water—"bout whilk there's been sae muckle clatter." "How was I cheated! when I saw the elritch place! Preserve us a'! Naught's there t' inspire the poet's lays, or fire his breast wi' Nature's praise." The opinion quoted by Miss Warrender ("Walks near Edinburgh") that the locus was round "Hunters' Tryst" and the Braid Burn is quite erroneous. The 1808 Edition corrects the 1800 Edition, and gives views of the original scenes.

According to the poem "Carlop Green" (errata), the herds of Logan Valley were quite prepared to show enquiring visitors just exactly what they wished to see, receiving in exchange the usual reward for services rendered:

THE CALL OF THE PENTLANDS

" The leean' Loon, frae Logan-house,
That herds about the fa'
Below Carnethie's carned tap
Abuin the Howlet's ha'.

Here tells tae what great gowks he'd shown
Come ferlies there tae see,
For Glaud and Symon's houses, each,
The found o' a sheep-ree.

For birks a wee bit scrunty row'n,
That near't nae witch may win;
For bathing pool, a dub for ducks,
Instead of ' little lin.'

And gar'd them feel sae satisfied
Frae these, 'twas ' Habbie's How '
They'd seen, they filled his luifs wi' cash
For empty thanks and bow."

INDEX

INDEX

INDEX